HANDS-ON ANCIENT PEOPLE VOLUME I

ART ACTIVITIES ABOUT MESOPOTAMIA, EGYPT AND ISLAM

Ancient Egypt has been of interest for hundreds of years. The great civilization began 5000 years ago as a long, thin country running along the length of the Nile River. Due to the hot, dry climate and the religious practice of preserving the royal dead with treasures, we have museums full of Egyptian objects. Thirty of these artifacts have been adapted to paper and clay in an effort to replicate this remarkable culture.

This book is dedicated to Emily Mortensen my youngest daughter.
Her consulting and genuine interest in the details of a small publishing effort and her advice on management have made a difference. Pictured is her delightful family: Spence, Anna, Lily, and Mia.

Book design by Art & International Productions, LLC, Anchorage, Alaska
Laurel Casjens took the photographs.
Mary Simpson illustrated the book and assisted with the development of the crafts.
Nancy Mathews and Madlyn Tanner edited and proofread the text.

Books by the author
from KITS Publishing:

Hands-on Africa
(ISBN 0-9643177-7-X)

Hands-on Alaska
(ISBN 0-9643177-3-7)

Hands-on American Vol. I
(ISBN 0-9643177-6-1)

Hands-on Asia
(ISBN 0-9643177-5-3)

Hands-on Celebrations
(ISBN 0-9643177-4-5)

Hands-on Rocky Mountains
(ISBN 0-9643177-2-9)

Hands-on Latin America
(ISBN 0-9643177-1-0)

Hands-on Pioneers*
(ISBN 1-57345-085-5)
*Published by Deseret Book

KITS PUBLISHING
2359 E. Bryan Avenue Salt Lake City, Utah 84108
(801) 582-2517 fax: (801) 582-2540
e-mail - info@hands-on.com web - www.hands-on.com

First printing November 2002
Printed in China

Library of Congress Control Number: 2002109559
ISBN 0-9643177-8-8

HANDS-ON ANCIENT PEOPLE VOLUME I

ART ACTIVITIES ABOUT MESOPOTAMIA, EGYPT AND ISLAM

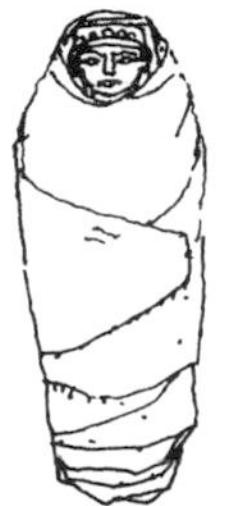
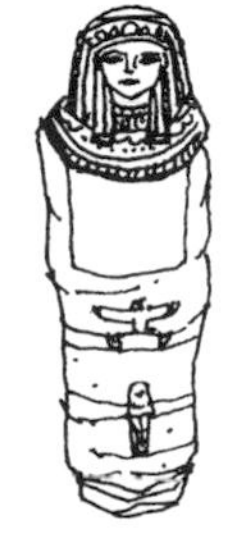

Yvonne Y. Merrill

KITS PUBLISHING

TABLE OF CONTENTS

Three Cultures: A Study in Patterns

Pattern is the combination of shape and color to create designs. Each of the cultures presented had sophisticated and different pattern styles. The two ancient civilizations of Mesopotamia and Egypt consistently engraved, wove, painted and wrote patterns. The Islamic and Arabic people have surpassed most with their architectural and decorative patterns, continuing today. As the activities are explored refer to the authentic pattern ideas on this page.

The Mesopotamians

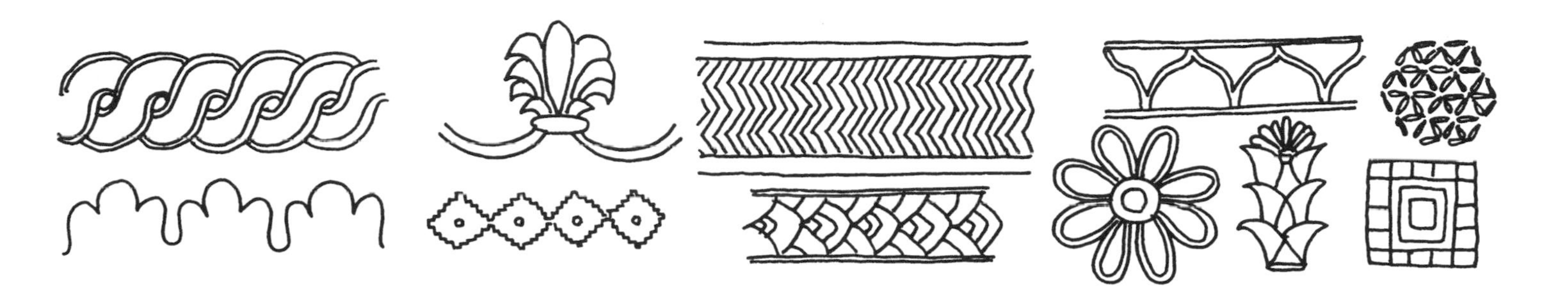

The Egyptians

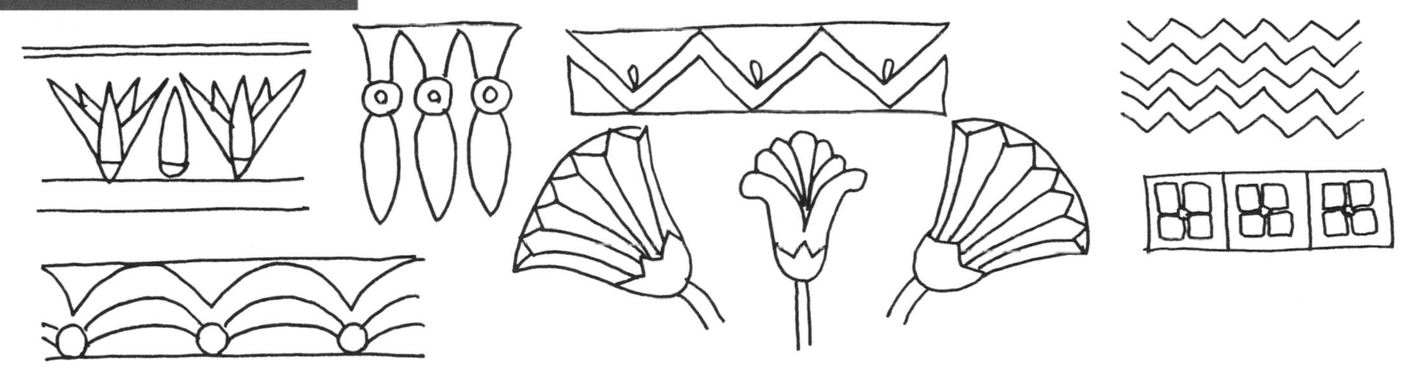

The Islamic Culture

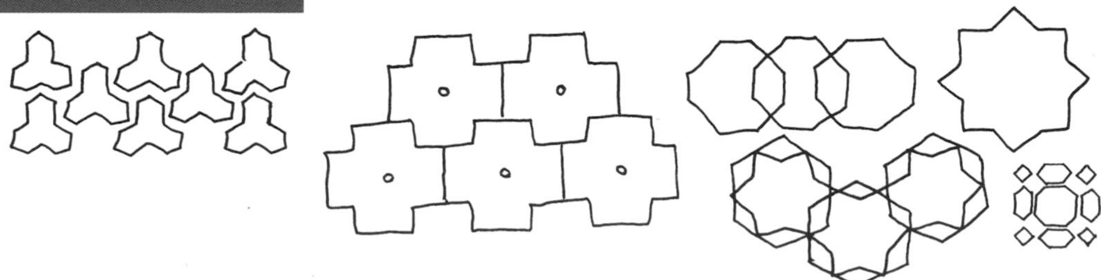

Stone-Looking Magic

Many artifacts in these arid areas are made of stone. To make stone-like projects we recommend commercial air-drying clay or this oven-baked salt clay: 2 c. flour, 1 c. salt, 1 c. water. Bake at 200-250 degrees until hard (2-4 hours).

20 FEATURED SITES ON THE MAP

6. Mt. Sinai

7. Adu Simbel

8. Sphinx at Giza

9. Aumn at Siwa

10. Luxor

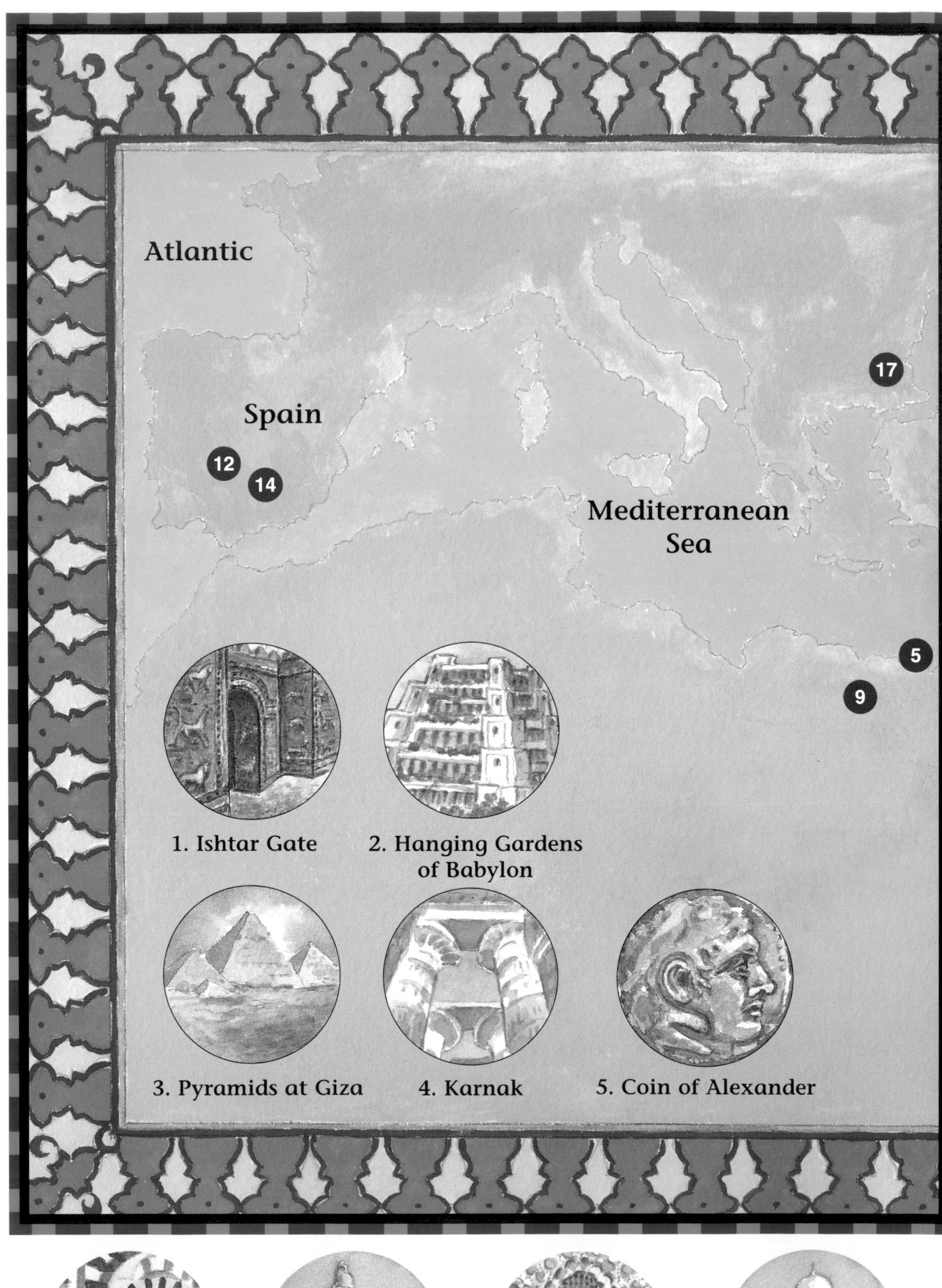

1. Ishtar Gate

2. Hanging Gardens of Babylon

3. Pyramids at Giza

4. Karnak

5. Coin of Alexander

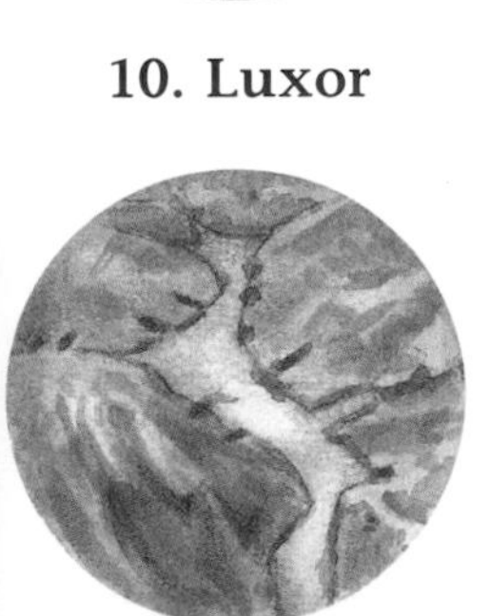

11. Valley of Kings

12. Mosque of Cordoba

13. Adu Dulaf

14. Alhambra

15. Taj Mahal

OF NEAR AND MIDDLE EAST

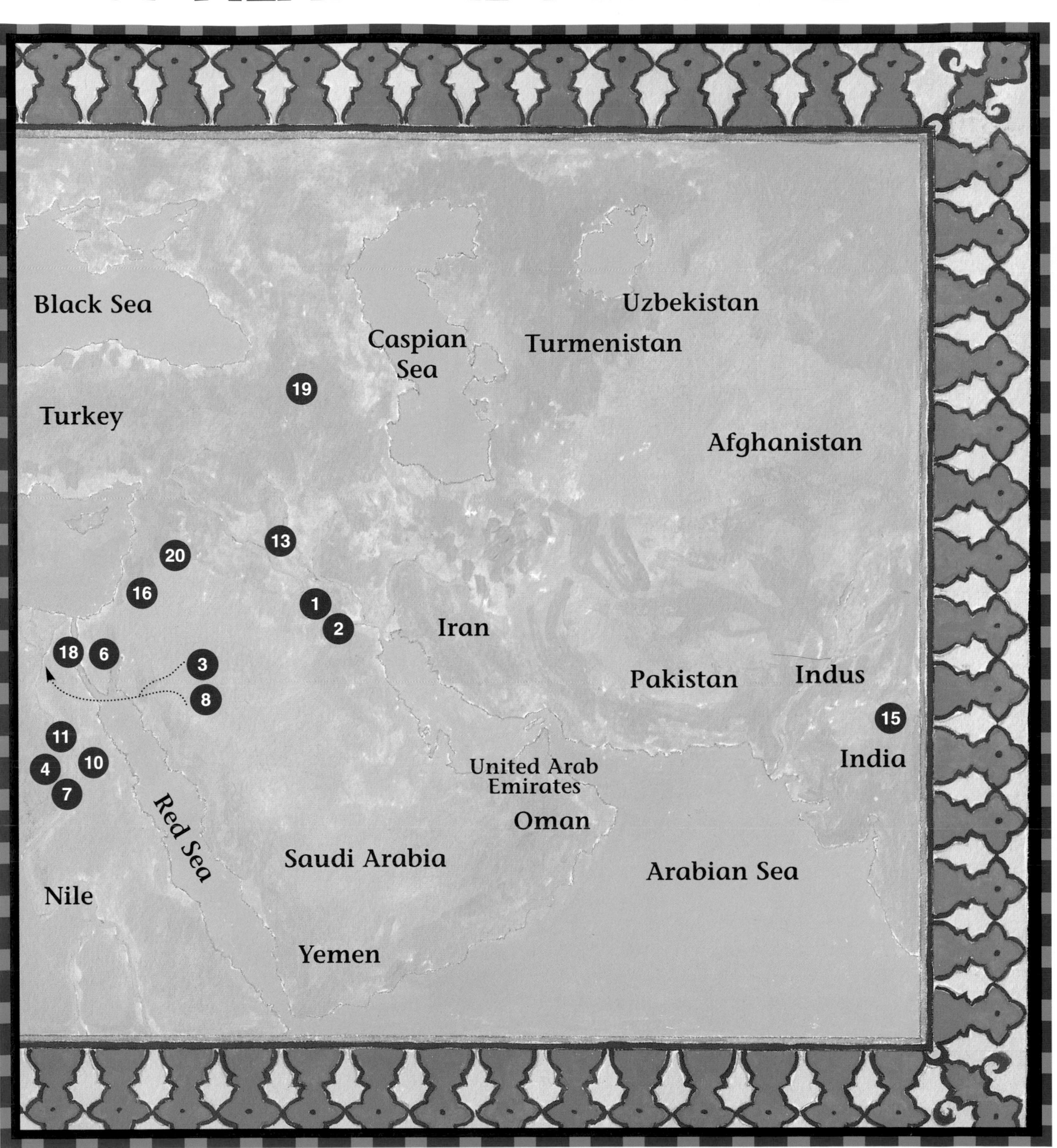

16. Dome of the Rock

17. Blue Mosque

18. Ibn Talun

19. Mt. Ararat

20. Umayyad/ Damascus

THE AMAZING MESOPOTAMIANS

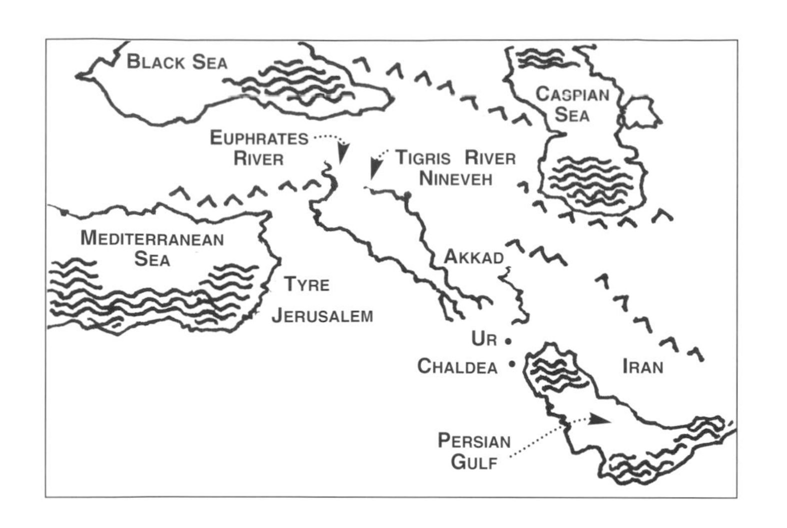

Map of ancient Mesopotamia

Map of area today

Western civilization traces its beginnings to Mesopotamia, the "cradle of civilization." Through its complex and rich history, we find evidence of the world's first experiments with agriculture and irrigation, medicine, astronomy, and architecture. Mesopotamians invented writing, used the first wheel, built the world's first cities, and developed the basic elements of modern mathematics.

A TIME LINE

10,000-3700 B.C. People lived along the Tigris/Euphrates rivers.

3700 to 2900 B.C. The oldest cuneiform tablets were found when the city of Ur was uncovered. This Sumerian city of 20,000 people was a great walled, oval-shaped site dominated by a massive temple complex called a ziggurat. In 1920 Leonard Wooley found the Royal Cemetery where several Sumerian rulers were buried in deep tombs packed with amazing goods. By 2700 B.C. the city of Ur was at its peak, and loose city-states surrounded this southern area.

2400-1750 B.C. The Akkadians invaded Sumeria and built Akkad.

1750 B.C. The date of Hammurabi's legal code, the first written laws.

1792-1595 B.C. Babylonia replaced the Akkad region and the great city of Babylon was built. The Kassites invaded and lived in Babylon. Then the Assyrians invaded northern Mesopotamia and built the cities of Nineveh and Nimrud. The Assyrians borrowed cultural strengths from others.

1400 B.C. The first Assyrian Empire. The Queen of Sheba and King of Tyre are part of this era.

820 B.C. Damascus was destroyed and the Chaldeans invaded southern Mesopotamia and restored Babylon.

586 B.C. The seige of Jerusalem when the Jews were brought by the thousands to Babylon to provide slave labor for the great buildings Sargon II wanted to build. This is known as the "exile" period.

612 B.C. The Assyrian Empire fell, and by 539 B.C. Cyrus and the Persians conquered the area.

1921 A.D. The country of Iraq was established.

CONTRIBUTIONS

WRITING can be traced to the Sumerians, the world's earliest literate and urban culture. Cuneiform tablets dating from 3300 B.C. have been found in Ur graves. (Cuneiform is a technique of pressing wedge-shaped symbols into wet clay.) Cuneiform was the writing method used by all Mesopotamians.

THE WHEEL was first invented by the Sumerians for making pottery, and archeologists speculate this wheel was eventually turned on its side and attached to a cart. Sumerian wheels did not have spokes. A famous work of art called the Standard of Ur shows the four-wheeled chariot used in war.

MEDICINE was surprisingly advanced, including drugs made from plants, animals, and minerals. Cuneiform prescriptions were used. A thorough understanding of human anatomy is evident. The skeletal remains found in Ur graves indicate surgery was practiced. Drawings categorizing plants and animals have given modern scientists clues as to what the environment was like in Mesopotamia.

CHEMISTRY of practical use interested the Mesopotamians. Colorful dyes were mixed. Fig and date wines were produced. Archeologists have discovered the world's oldest written recipe, a tablet dated 3750 B.C. recording the process for making beer.

MATHEMATICS can be traced to Sumerians in 1800 B.C. when many elements of modern mathematics were first used, including the decimal system, Arabic numbers, and the base of 60 used frequently today in 60 minutes, 360 degrees, and so on. Sumerians first used the concept of zero. Babylonians are credited with the idea of place value as well as with concepts used 1,000 years later in the Greek Pythagorean theorem.

cuneiform tablet

weights for measuring

the sun god and Ishtar

ASTRONOMY shows careful and precise record keeping which has provided valuable information about the planets, stars, and rotation of the earth. The Babylonians invented a time system based on the stars.

ARCHITECTURE shows the mastery of engineering skills, including multi-storied buildings. The varied use of stone and sand is evidence of creative construction. Glass used as glaze on pottery was invented from studying soil and sand. Bronze made from tin and copper dates back 4000 years.

Gilgamesh

a ziggurat

pottery

MYTHS from Mesopotamia have familiar themes like Gilgamesh and the Great Flood, Pyramus and Thisbe, similar to Shakespeare's ***Midsummer Night's Dream,*** Verdi's ***Nabucco*** about the exiled Jews, and the basket of reeds and the rescuing of Moses in the Old Testament.

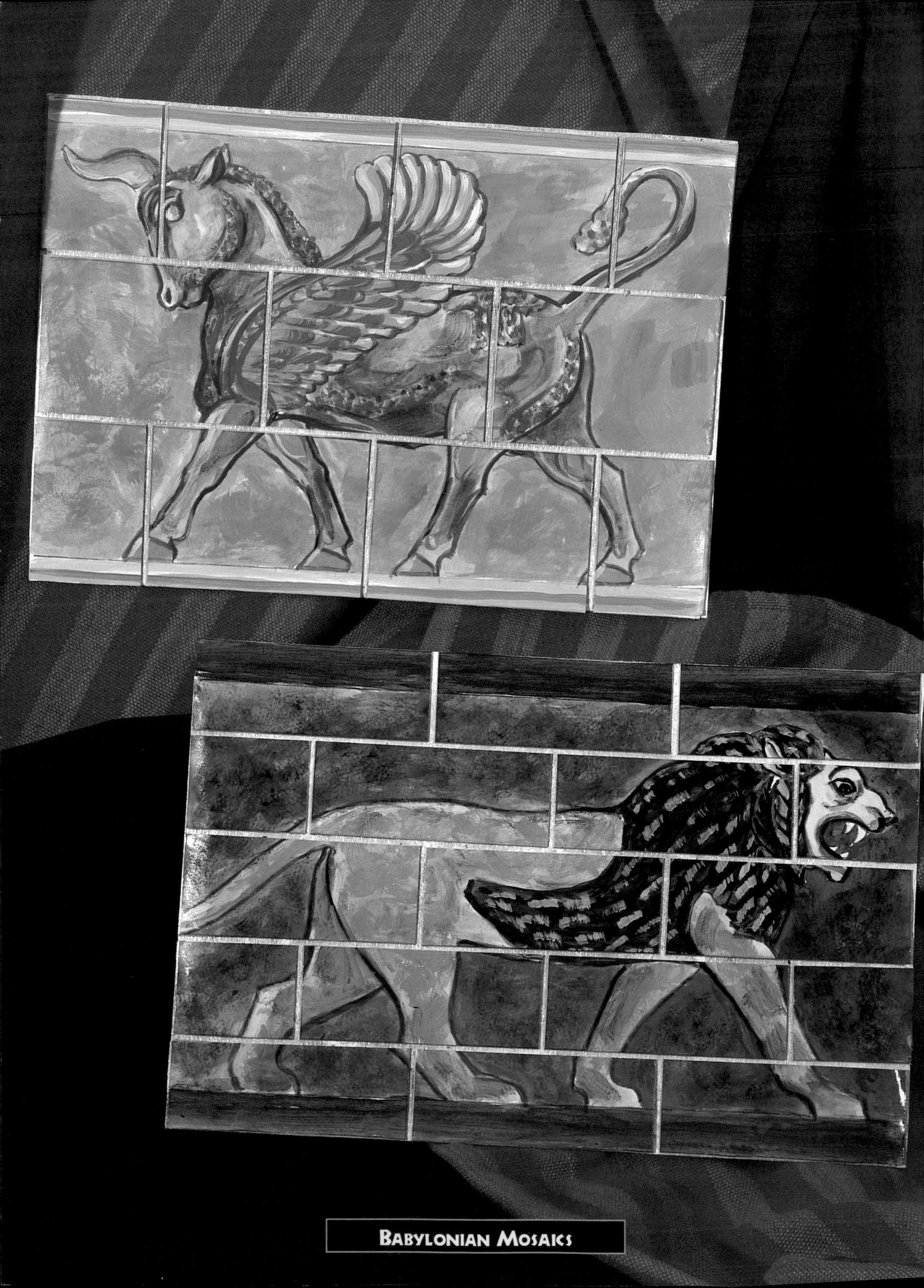

Babylonian Mosaics

Babylonian Mosaics from the Gate of Ishtar

Materials: For each animal panel: 2 posterboard panels with one a few inches larger than 8 1/2" x 11", acrylic paints, brushes, sponge, glue, scissors or paper cutter, clear acrylic spray (for a shiny ceramic effect), patterns on page 80.

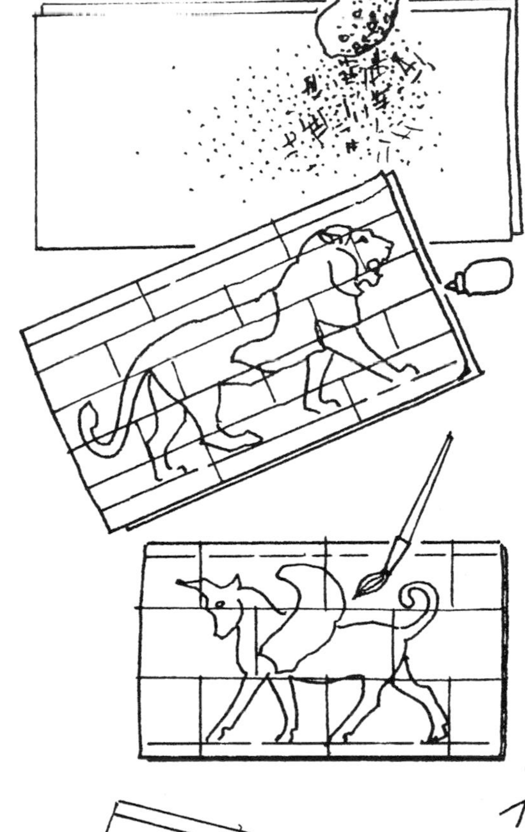

1. Produce a mortar-like background surface for the tiled bricks: using light grey paint, sponge-texture a large posterboard.
2. Enlarge lion or bull patterns as desired. The sample in the photograph is twice the pattern size. Glue pattern evenly onto smaller posterboard making sure all parts are securely attached.
3. Paint with acrylic paints; thin paint with water so brick patterns show through for later cutting. Let the paint dry.
4. Spray animal with clear acrylic finish. Let dry.
5. Cut painted animal along vertical and horizontal brick lines to make "tile-looking" bricks.
6. Reassemble bull or lion bricks onto faux-mortared background leaving space between the bricks for the grey mortar to show through. Glue in place.

The magnificent Ishtar Gate in Babylonia was covered with these magnificent animal mosaics. It was at the head of the Processional Way, a ceremonial street in Babylonia. It is speculated that 150,000 people of many nationalities lived in the walled city of Babylon. The ruins of Babylon were excavated in 1902 and archeologists found a building with gardens at each level. Were these the famous Hanging Gardens? The Ishtar Gate was in fine shape when it was uncovered and the animal mosaics were astonishing. The Lion, representing the goddess of Ishtar, was most often repeated. Nebuchadnezzar II built the great city in 604-502 B.C. Thousands of Israelites were brought to Babylon after the destruction of Jerusalem in 586 B.C. This story is recorded in the Bible's Old Testament.

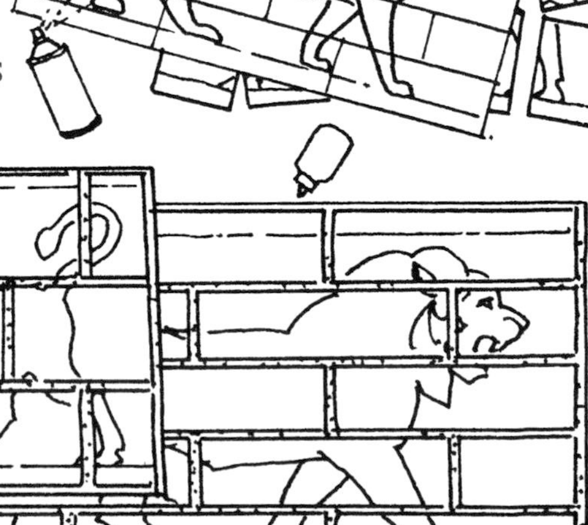

Three Sumerian Chariots

Three Sumerian Chariots

Materials: A piece of white or cream-colored railroad board or a manila folder 12" x 18", air-hardening clay or the salt dough recipe on page 7, a 1/8" doweling piece 20" long, fine-tipped black marker, orange and brown paint, brushes, glue, straws, 1/4" wooden dowel.

One-Person Chariot

The small one-seater chariot was probably pulled by a small animal like a dog or a goat. The museum model claims it might be 8000 years old!

1. Roll out your dough or clay and cut out two, 2" wheels. Round them with water. Cook them in a very low oven or–if clay-let them air dry overnight.
2. Cut two pieces of wooden dowel 3" and 4" long. Make axle holes with a straw. Push the short wooden piece through the holes in each wheel. You now have one of the six simple machines: the wheel and axle.
3. Mold the clay around the 2" dowel in the middle to make a seat. Insert the longer dowel at a right angle in front. Wrap extra clay around each axle dowel on the outside to keep the dowel in place. Paint the dough a wooden color when it has hardened.

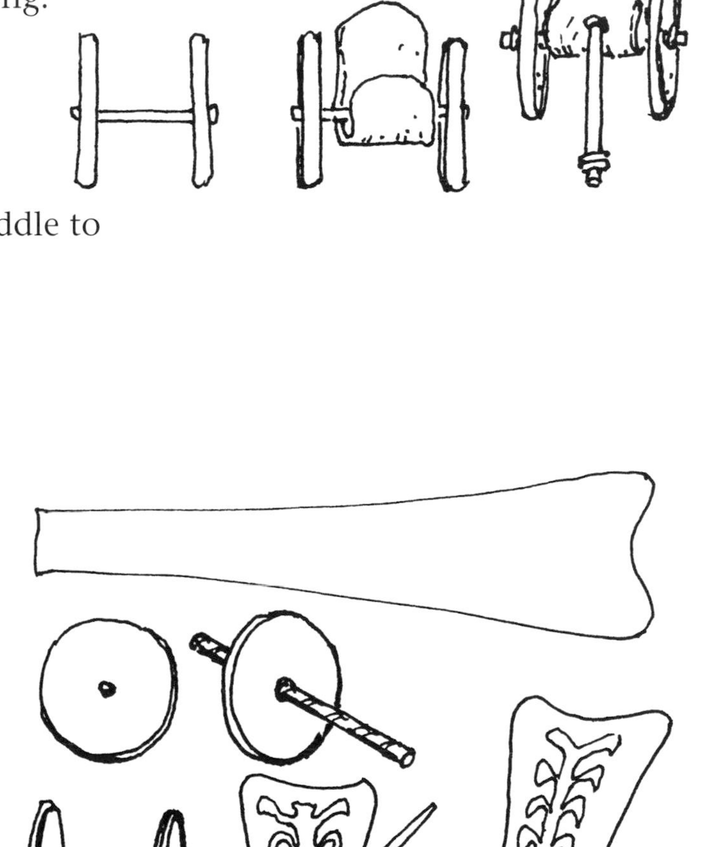

Tall Back Chariot

Tall, carved, wooden-backed chariots were used by warriors and important people.

1. Cut a piece of cardboard 2" x 12" in this shape.
2. Roll out the clay or dough and cut out 2 wheels 2 1/2" wide. Make axle holes with a straw.
3. Insert a cut dowel 3" long into the prepared hardened wheels and add clay hubs. Make a glue design on the chariot cardboard. When the glue has dried, paint it brown so it resembles wood with a carved design. Lay axle over the chariot about 3" from the end. Glue.
4. Cut a 6" dowel, paint it brown, and stick it through the holes punched in the flap and the chariot back.

(continued on page 70)

Sumerian Board Game

MATH ART SOCIAL STUDIES

A Board Game from Sumerian Ur

Materials: A cardboard top or bottom of a box between 9" x 14" or larger (much smaller will not work). Twelve round discs 1 1/4" in diameter. Thick and thin black marker, a ruler, white paint, brown and orange paint, brushes and a pencil.

1. With a ruler and pencil make three long rows of eight rectangles, each one the same size. Our rectangles are 2 1/2" x 2 3/4". The rectangles will be measured according to the box size. Erase the two outside lines that make box #3 and #4. They are solid colors and NOT part of the board game (see the photograph). Draw with a strong black marker on the grid lines.
2. Paint the squares white and rub a mix of brown and orange paint on the 22 important game rectangles. (The board game was carved of ivory which becomes brownish when very old.)
3. Here are the **five** boxed patterns. Enlarge or reduce these boxes and copy them onto your game board in thick and thin black marker. Add touches of red, brown, and orange color on some squares.

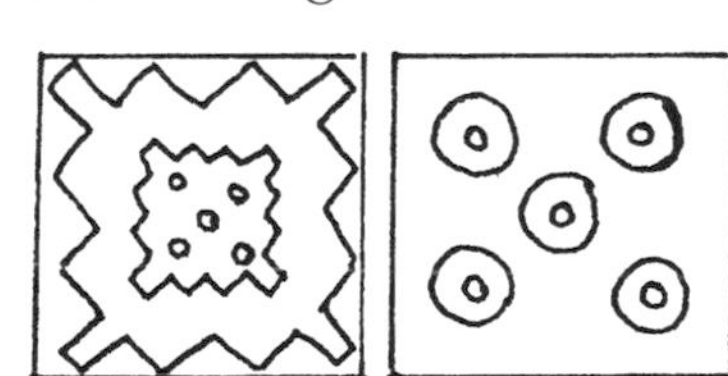

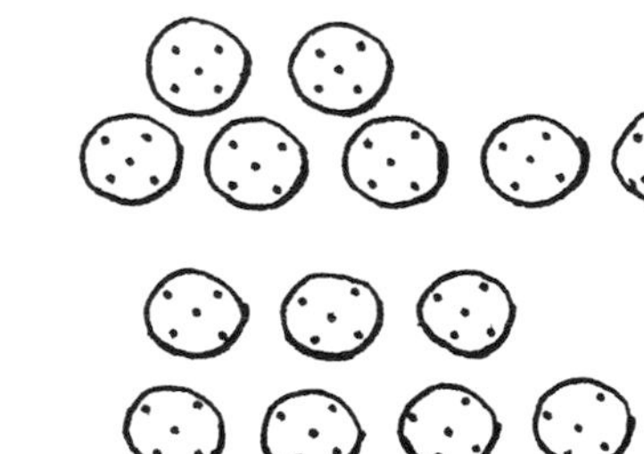

4. Notice the sides of the box which are the all-seeing eye divided by various numbers of stripes.
5. Your replicated game board should be handsome and ready for the two sets of discs that are the players. Cut circles from cardboard or paper or buy wood circles. Paint 6 of one color and 6 a second color and paint five dots of black or white on each disc.

This handsome board game was excavated in the Sumerian city of Ur. It was found in a royal grave. No one has any idea of its rules or how to play it, but someone could design a fun game using their imagination from the discs and the board.

Two Ziggurats

Two Ziggurats

Materials: Any Styrofoam cone at least 10" tall and 3 1/2" at the base, a sheet of Styrofoam 2" thick by 12" x 36" long, a ruler, marker, good knife for smooth cutting, flour and paste, newspaper strips, glue, sponges for paint dabbing, brushes and paint for patterns, string, a small box.

The Cone Ziggurat

1. Wrap a piece of string around the cone and mark its spirals. These are the ramps that will be built to get to the top of the structure.
2. Mix 1 c. flour with 1/2 c. water. Mix until the paste is smooth. Add more water until it is the consistency of thick soup. The ramps are a papier-mache' process.
3. Tear newspaper strips 1"-2" wide. Make a thick base of about 15 newspaper layers and slowly build up the ramps. Make fat ramps at the bottom and thinner ramps as they approach the top.
4. Place a square on the top that could have been a temple.
5. Let the papier-mache' dry overnight. Sponge or brush paint with a clay-colored mix of orange, brown, and white.

The Stepped Ziggurat

1. Cut these Styrofoam forms:
   a. 10" x 10" x 2" thick
   b. 7" x 7" x 2" thick
   c. 5" x 5" x 1 1/2" thick
   d. 4" x 4" x 1 1/2" thick
   e. 2" x 2" x 1" thick
2. Stack the cut pieces so they have even edges and glue them together. Let them dry for several hours with a two pound weight on top (like a book).
3. Paint any earthen-like clay color and add authentic patterns.

The best known architectural forms of Mesopotamia are the religious monuments called ziggurats or "staged towers" which dominated the important cities. Ziggurat means "the house that is the foundation between heaven and earth". The temple on the top was where the gods descended from heaven to receive offerings. Scholars suggest the form reflects mountains from a country of origin, or perhaps a giant sacrificial altar. High places have often been regarded as holy places. Ziggurats were made of clay bricks covered with limestone. They were painted with brilliant colors and patterns.

Mesopotamian Patterns

MESOPOTAMIAN PATTERNS

Materials: Jiffy® foam is recommended, rolls of white school art paper (24″ to 36″ square per person), big brushes and sponges, recycled pie tins for paint, clean-up cloths, and cardboard supports for patterns, small brushes, yardstick and pencils, scissors, white paint, paint of preferred colors, water for brushes and clean-up, pattern ideas on page 7.

1. The background paper must be prepared before you print your handsome patterns. Cut the paper the size you need (probably around a square yard or smaller). In the pie tin mix white paint, water and your background colors. **Do not stir together.** With your big sponge or brush cover the paper with uneven but blended colors. It should look old and rich in natural dye colors such as tans, yellows, soft greens, or blues.

Here are 10 sample patterns:

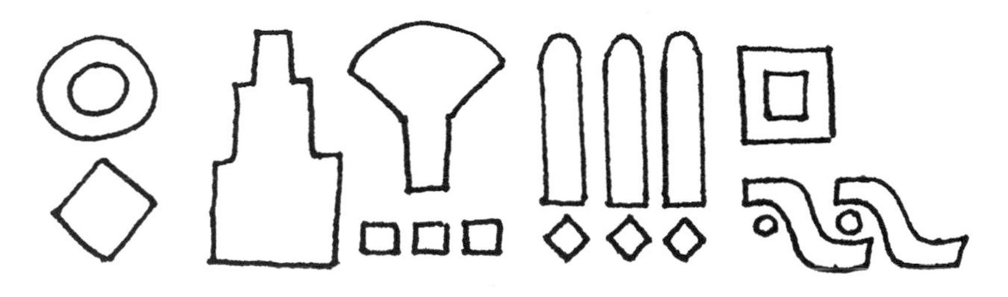

2. Sketch the design on Jiffy foam and cut it out. Mount it on a cardboard support.

3. With a pencil and yardstick lightly measure lines for the design you hope to print.

4. Put the paints for the pattern colors in individual containers. Have a small brush available for applying the paint onto the mounted design or push the design into the paint. Experiment with a scratch paper. Clean the brush with water when a new color is being used.

When the remains of Sargon II's Assyrian palace (now in Iraq) were uncovered by the Frenchman Botta in 1843, the world was astonished by the rich and superb painted patterns and mosaic work. Sir Austen Henry Layard from Britain worked in Nineveh and Nimrud writing a best-seller on his archeological finds..."especially impressive were the massive winged bulls with human heads, now in the Louvre in Paris and in New York's Metropolitan Museum of Art." Ludmilla Zemen has illustrated and retold ***Gilgamesh, the King,*** (1993), ***The Revenge of Ishtar,*** (1992), and ***The Last Quest of Gilgamesh*** (1995), William Heinemann Ltd., London.

Marduk and Ishtar

Marduk and Ishtar: Babylonian Gods and Goddesses

Materials: Salt dough recipe on page 7, rolling pin, dull knife for cutting, a cutting surface, cereal, buttons, red hots, etc. for sticking into the dough and decorating the figure: buttons, colored cereal, candy, tools for texturing such as a nail, straw, hole of the straw, straight edge, watercolor paints, small and big brushes, foil and waxed paper, an oven, cardboard for mounting, and string or ribbon for hanging figures, patterns on pages 79 and 84.

1. For all of the figures roll a golf-ball-size dough piece out on foil with a protective piece of waxed paper. Using the pattern on page 79 cut out the dough figure. Lightly draw the body and face sections with a pencil or nail. Either texture the figure sections or decorate. When you add the decorations, brush a paste of dough and water onto the surface first; this acts as a glue.
2. Look at striding Marduk. He is textured and painted. Look at standing-tall Marduk. He is decorated, textured, and painted. Remember that the Mesopotamians loved pattern. Make a hole in the head top if you are going to hang the figure.
3. After your figure is decorated, bake it on foil for 4-6 hours in a warm oven (200 + degrees). Let the figure cool. Now it can be painted.
4. Lay the figure on a piece of cardboard and trace around it. Cut out the shape about 1/4" smaller than the tracing. Punch a hole through the cardboard that lines up with the figure hole. Generously glue the dough figure to the cardboard. Put a weight like a newspaper pile on the top. Let it dry for several hours.
5. String a ribbon or twine through the hole.

Marduk was the ruler of all Babylon's gods and the city patron deity. In the Babylonian Epic of Creation, Marduk killed troublesome monsters and also Tiamet whom he cut in half and made the sky from her top half and the earth from the bottom half. Then Marduk created humans to serve the gods. The goddess Ishtar is considered to be young, beautiful, and impulsive. She was the first goddess of fertility and love. The Greeks called her Aphrodite; the Romans named her Venus. She was the force that gave life to all: people, plants, and animals. She was the patroness of food and controlled the weather. She is often depicted with a lion whose roar represented thunder.

Christopher Moore and Christina Balit have written ***Ishtar and Tammuz, a Babylonian Myth of the Seasons,*** Kingfisher, NY, 1996.

CUNEIFORM

LITERACY ART SOCIAL STUDIES

Cuneiform: Ancient Clay Messages

Materials: Air hardening clay or salt dough recipe on page 7, warm water, rolling pin, waxed paper 12" square per project, foil if baking, straws, scissors, ruler, brown, orange, yellow paint and brush or sponge, marker.

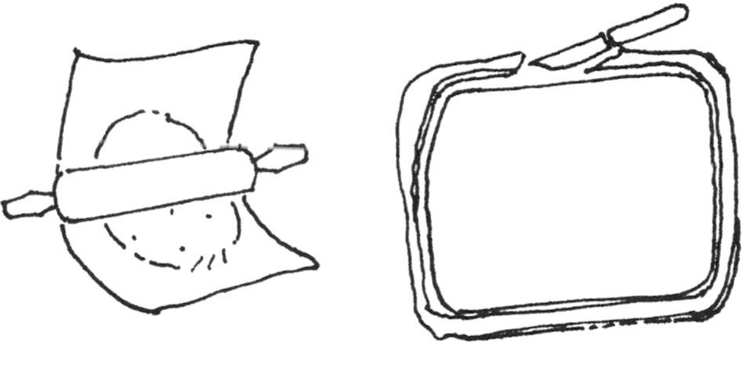

Baked Dough Message

1. Roll the dough out on foil paper with a piece of protective waxed paper on top of the dough ball. When it is 1/8" to 1/4" thick cut out a piece roughly 4" wide and 5" long. Peel away the waxed paper and the foil. Carefully place the rolled dough back on the foil for future baking.
2. Study the cuneiform wedge and curved shapes that create the Sumerian alphabet. Write down your message, translating it into cuneiform.
3. Cut a plastic straw into a "v" on one end and a curve on the other. A knife point will help to give you a clean mark.
4. Look at the clay and dough samples in the photograph. Make your message in the soft dough.
5. Oven-bake your cuneiform message on the lowest possible heat for at least 4-5 hours. Give it an ancient-looking wash with brushed-paint or a paint-dipped sponge. If the marks are hard to see, go over them with a brown small-tipped marker.

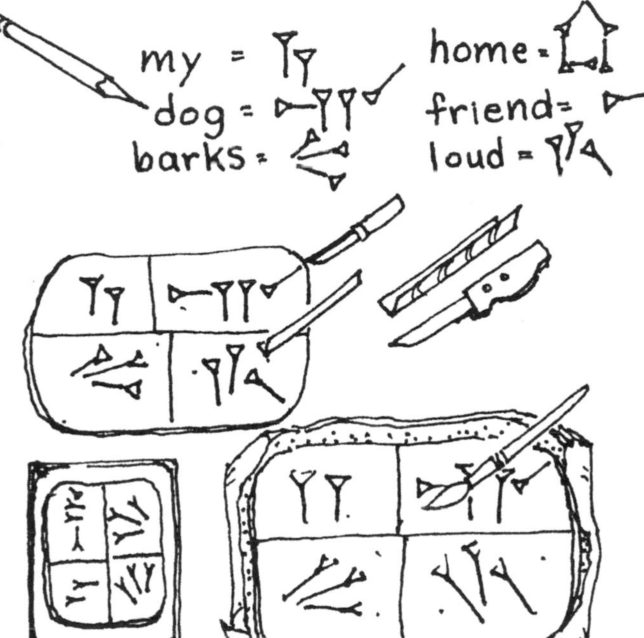

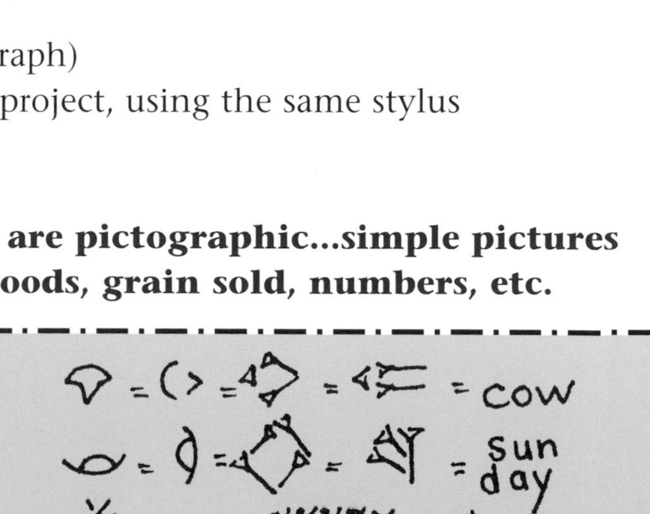

Clay Message and Envelope (like the photograph)
The clay can air dry. Proceed as with the dough project, using the same stylus (plastic straws) and knife points for the wedges.

The earliest surviving samples of writing are pictographic...simple pictures which were used to represent livestock, goods, grain sold, numbers, etc.

= bird

= fish

= mountains

= cow

= sun day

= grain

(continued on page 70)

EGYPTIAN ART AND CULTURE

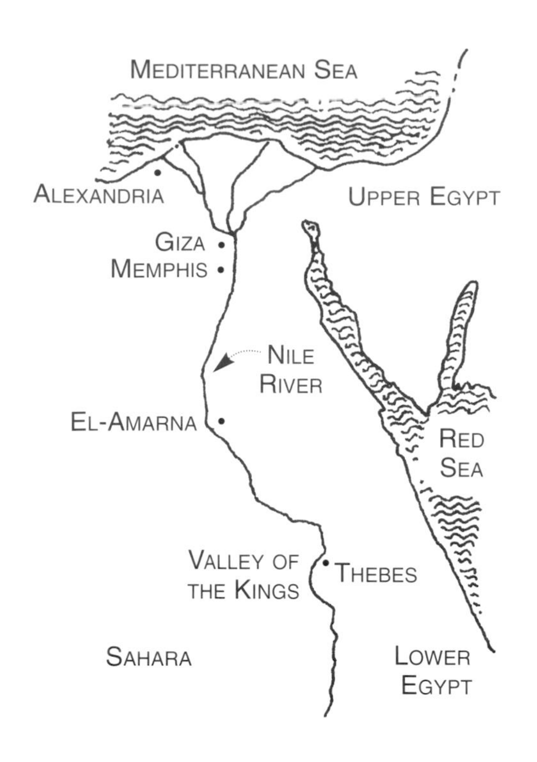

Egypt lies on the northeastern coast of Africa, bordered by the Mediterranean Sea to the east and the Sahara Desert to the south and west. Today, Egypt's neighbors are Libya, Israel, and Sudan. In ancient times political frontiers were always changing as rival peoples like the Hittites, Assyrians, and Persians gained and lost land. Herodotus, writing in the 5th century B.C., called Egypt "the gift of the river," as without the Nile people would never have been able to survive there. They called their land "Kemet", the Black Land, because of the rich black soil in the Nile floodplain. In the south the Nile created a valley of steep cliffs and was called Lower Egypt. In the north it slowed down, spread out, and created a huge triangular area called the delta, or Upper Egypt.

GODS AND GODDESSES

Gods and goddesses hieroglyphic symbol was a flagpole sign. Flagpoles were erected at temples to remind ancient Egyptians of the invisible powers that ruled their universe. Temples were built for specific gods and employed priests. It was believed that deities used animals as temporary bodies on earth. Deities often had a male or female body and an animal's face or headpiece. Some of the most important deities as the Egyptians depicted them.

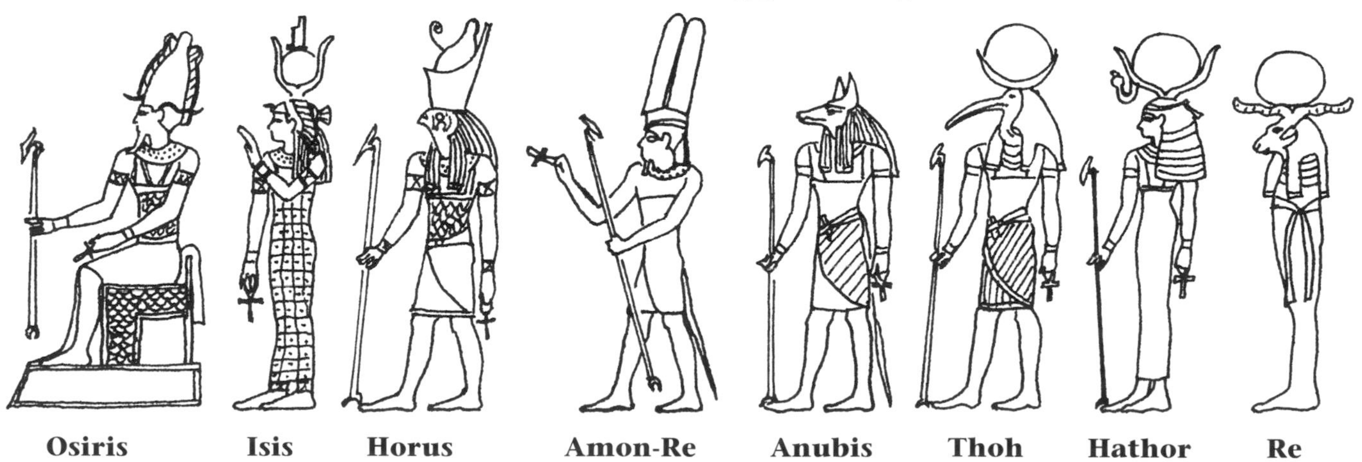

Osiris **Isis** **Horus** **Amon-Re** **Anubis** **Thoh** **Hathor** **Re**

Egyptian artworks were early drawings by prehistoric hunters. Art was associated with magic. Artistic effort flourished in tombs in the form of carvings, paintings, murals, and statuary to provide the needs of the dead in the next life. Reliefs were carved on temple walls to ensure the gods could always overcome evil.

Egyptian artists were traditional and tended to copy the work of previous generations, probably because they thought there was some special power in the ancient way of showing things. Egyptians believed that pictures had great power, so they represented a scene carefully and accurately. Dangerous things were painted as harmless: for example, scorpions did not have stingers.

EGYPTIAN PERSPECTIVE

Egyptian painters had to follow strict rules about what they painted and the colors they used. They were very good at observing and portraying nature and drawing birds, animals, plants, and people.

People were shown with their head, arms hands, hips, legs, and feet as seen from the side.

Eyes, chests, and shoulders were shown from the front.

a god a king
Gods and kings were the largest in size.

a husband
Husbands were larger than wives.

a wife and the children
Children were very small.

HISTORICAL BACKGROUND

Recorded history in Egypt began around 4000 B.C. when nomadic hunters settled in the Nile Valley. But it was in 3100 B.C. that Egypt crowned her first Pharoah, Menes, who later unified the country's two regions, Lower Egypt (The Delta) and Upper Egypt(from Giza to Aswan in the South). Egypt's history can be summarized as follows:

Predynastic Egypt: 5000 to 3200 B.C.

Dynastic Egypt: 3200 to 2700 B.C. Development of society, law and religion

The Old Kingdom: 2700 B.C.- 2600 B.C. Great achievements especially in the fields of administration, astronomy and architecture.

The Middle Kingdom: 2260 to 1780 B.C. An era of prosperity and expansion of political strength and economic horizons. Thebes became the capital. Later, Egypt was invaded by the Hyksos, coming from Caucasia, who remained for 150 years until finally driven back.

The New Kingdom: 1580 to 1085 B.C.Four centuries of splendor, prosperity, and spiritual and artistic achievements. Architecture reaches great heights.

(continued on page 75)

Shabti Figures

Shabti Figures: Workers in the Afterlife

Materials: Salt dough clay recipe on page 7, rolling pin, knife, foil, white, red, blue, green, black, brown, gold paint. A 10" x 10" x 3" deep box, white paper, glue, all colors of markers, an oven for baking. Note: the box is not necessary for the shabti project but they were enclosed in this type of wooden box when found in tombs, pattern ideas on page 7.

Shabti Dolls With Hieroglyphics

1. Most shabti figures were 8" long and generally the same shape. Most were painted with black hair, a whitish gown decorated with hieroglyphics and folded arms. Whichever shabti figure you make, you can paint it natural or brown, or the Egyptian blue-green of the less shapely shabti.

2. Make the salt dough. This recipe will make 6-8 figures. Roll out the dough on foil. Use a template that has been cut from a folded newspaper so it is symmetrical. Lay the template on the salt dough and cut out the doll. Carefully remove it from the foil and replace it on the foil again. Roll dough pieces to create the relief of arms, face, hair and feet. Apply to the dough by brushing on a mix of dough and water. Give the hair texture with scissors. Bake the figure in a warm oven 250 degrees for 3-4 hours.

3. Paint the figure. The hieroglyphics might be your name and a message you have made after studying this writing. (See hieroglyphics on page 47.)

Shabti Box: *Materials are any rectangular box like a small cereal box, white paper to cover the box, heavy cardboard piece for base, markers, paints, glue.*

1. Prepare your box. Measure around the box to determine the "mini mural" size. Cut the paper to fit with a piece for the top.
2. Plan the mural and border designs. The box mural shows the jackal god Anubis welcoming a shabti to the underworld. Draw and paint the mural. Glue mural to the box. Glue box flaps to the base. ***(continued on page 70)***

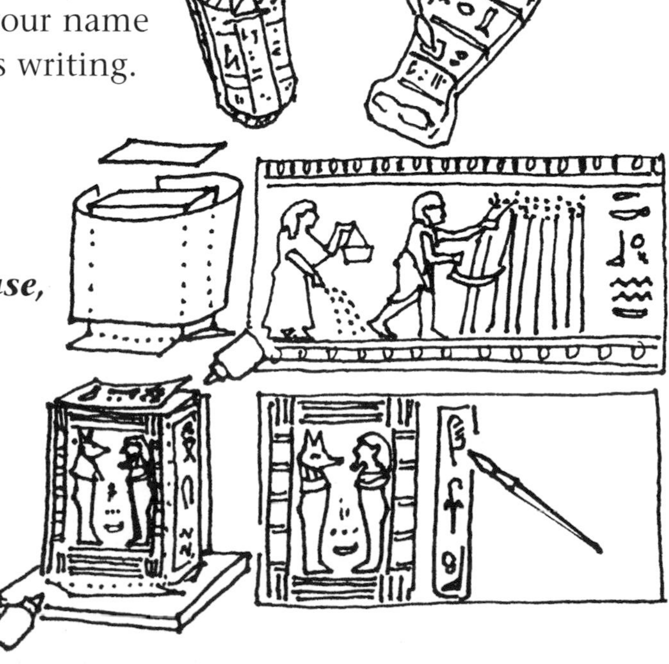

TOYS FROM THE TOMBS

Toys from the Tombs

Materials: Cardboard that can be cut 18" x 18", manila folder, Styrofoam balls 6" and 8" in diameter, ocher, red, black, green, brown paint, fine-tip brush, 3" square of black fabric, cotton, string and needle, red, black, beige, yellow, green markers, glue, plain paper, rubber bands, light and dark brown and orange paper, scissors, 8" of 1/4" doweling cut in half.

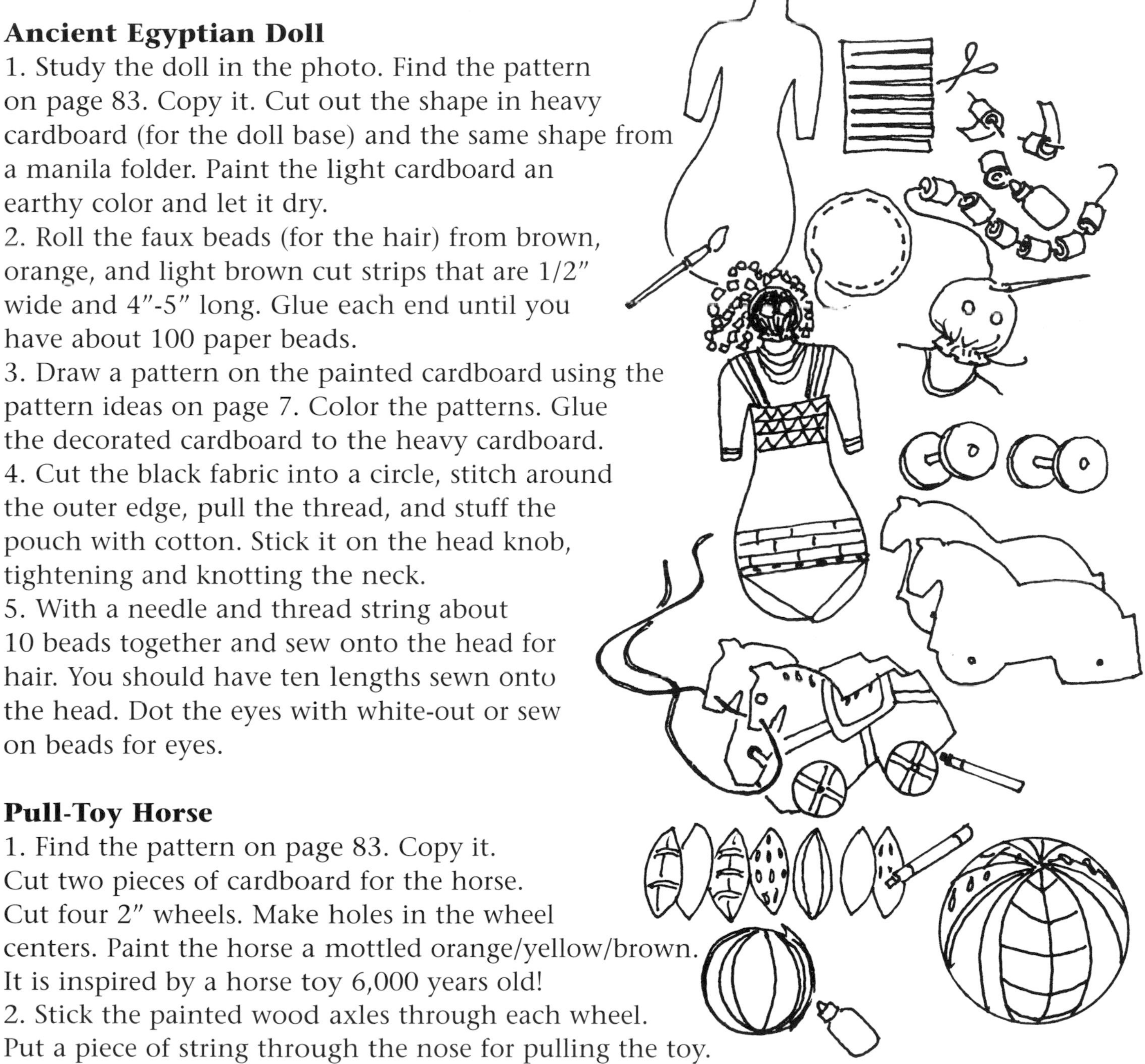

Ancient Egyptian Doll

1. Study the doll in the photo. Find the pattern on page 83. Copy it. Cut out the shape in heavy cardboard (for the doll base) and the same shape from a manila folder. Paint the light cardboard an earthy color and let it dry.
2. Roll the faux beads (for the hair) from brown, orange, and light brown cut strips that are 1/2" wide and 4"-5" long. Glue each end until you have about 100 paper beads.
3. Draw a pattern on the painted cardboard using the pattern ideas on page 7. Color the patterns. Glue the decorated cardboard to the heavy cardboard.
4. Cut the black fabric into a circle, stitch around the outer edge, pull the thread, and stuff the pouch with cotton. Stick it on the head knob, tightening and knotting the neck.
5. With a needle and thread string about 10 beads together and sew onto the head for hair. You should have ten lengths sewn onto the head. Dot the eyes with white-out or sew on beads for eyes.

Pull-Toy Horse

1. Find the pattern on page 83. Copy it. Cut two pieces of cardboard for the horse. Cut four 2" wheels. Make holes in the wheel centers. Paint the horse a mottled orange/yellow/brown. It is inspired by a horse toy 6,000 years old!
2. Stick the painted wood axles through each wheel. Put a piece of string through the nose for pulling the toy.

Colorful Balls

1. Cut 7-8 sections for the small ball. Color the sections with stripes, checks, and plain colors. Glue the sections onto the ball with rubber bands securing the sections while they dry.
2. Paint the larger ball sections with a stripe of gold dividing the sections.

(continued on page 71)

The Scarab

The Scarab: An Egyptian Good-Luck Charm

The Turquoise Winged Scarab: ***Materials are salt dough clay (recipe on page 7) or air drying white clay, rolling pin, foil, pattern on page 74.thread, needle, black paint, black, blue and gold markers, glue, toothpicks, paper punch, dull knife, scissors, and paper for templates.***

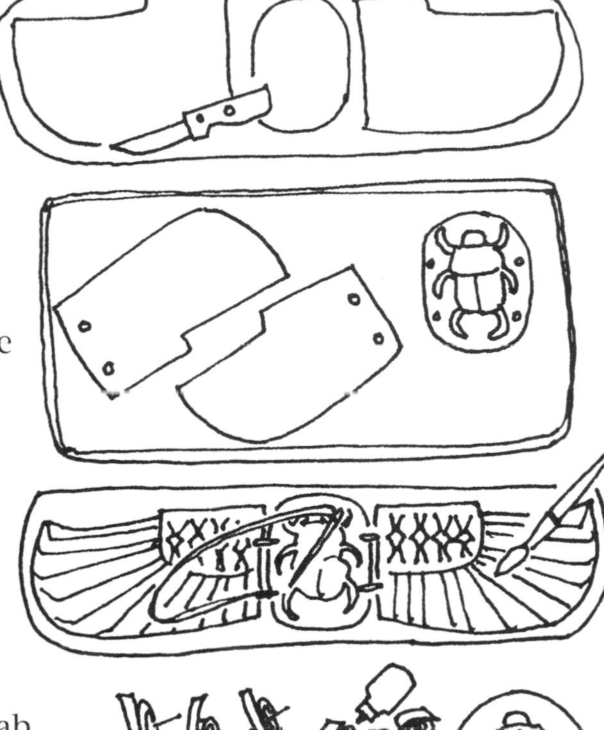

1. Roll out your dough/clay material to 1/4" thickness. Cut a template for the wings and beetle body on the paper fold. Place them on top of the clay piece and cut around it with the knife. Gently pick them up and place on foil or a cookie sheet. You have three pieces to dry: the middle shape for the scarab, and the dough circle as a base for the scarab, and the two wings. These can be any size as long as they are to scale. Mold the scarab onto the base with two front legs and two back legs. Make 8 holes: 2 on each wing, and 4 on the disc, and 2 on each side.
2. Bake the dough for 3-4 hours in a warm oven 200–250 degrees. Let the clay dry overnight.
3. Paint the entire piece in turquoise except the scarab. Add the black marker designs and black paint on the scarab.
4. Using black thread and a needle, sew the wings to the scarab. The piece can be mounted on gold cardboard for easier handling.

The Scarab Bracelet: ***Materials are gold cardboard, salt dough, 150 rolled paper beads, cardboard closures, needle, thread, glue, paint, scissors, toothpick, gold marker.***

1. The paper beads are most effective if you paint your own paper with mottled carnelian red, lapis dark blue, and turquoise. Use gold marker on paper for the gold beads. Roll your beads. They are 1/4" thick and 3-4" long. Roll on a toothpick and glue the end.
2. Make the beetle and dry. Paint it blue. Color the 2" round cardboard disc with marker and make three holes on each side. Make the closures punching three holes in each.
3. Assemble the bracelet by stringing the beads with the needle and thread through the closures and attach to the disc holes.

(continued on page 71)

Four King's Crowns

Four King's Crowns

The Atef, the White Crown of Osiris: ***Materials are a piece of white railroad board, all colors of paint including gold and gold marker, scissors, pattern on page 79, glue, rubber bands that are 5", stapler, paper clips.***

1. Enlarge the pattern to be 24" for back and 18" for front. Cut out the front and back. Paint the bottom edge design. **The crown head size should be 21" to 22" for an average head.** Score the crown edges 1/2" and cut notches every 2" up to the knob. Fold the notches outside the crown. Staple and glue the inside and the notches down and stand up on a tall support such as a bleach bottle or a tall vase. Carefully put big rubber bands around the crown to keep the shape as the glue dries (three or four 5" bands).
2. Cut out four pieces that are side serpents and the front cobra. Paint them. The cobra's tail is painted on the opposite side so it can go up the crown with the snake head in front.
3. Score and notch the painted side serpents. Glue them together except for the edges that will attach to the crown. Glue to the crown. Glue the cobra to the crown front. Try it on.

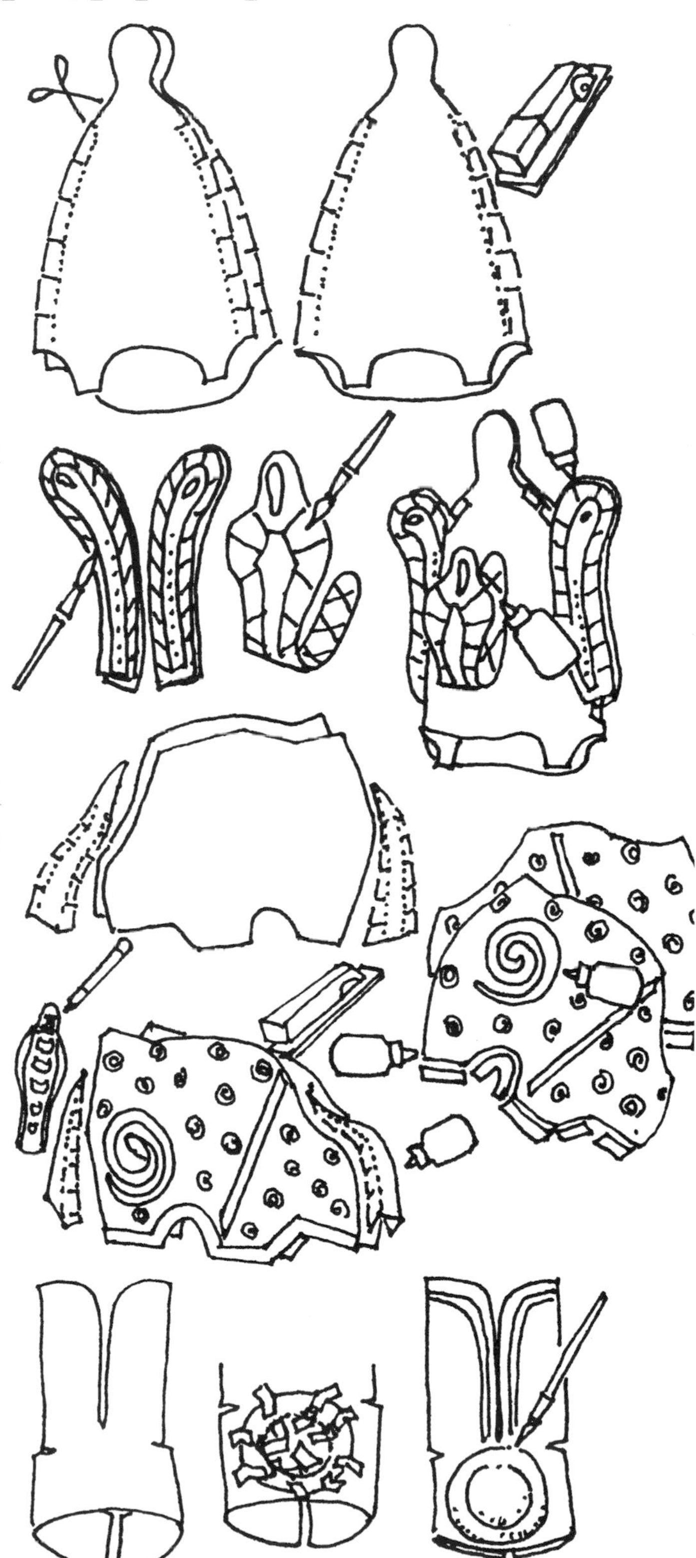

The Nemes, the blue "war helmet" crown: ***Materials are blue railroad board, pattern on page 80 and 84, 15" x 15", gold marker, scissors, glue, stapler, paper clips, plain railroad board, patterns on pages 81,84.***

1. Cut out the five pattern pieces: two helmet sides, front and back insets, and cobra for the front.
2. Decorate the blue helmet pieces with any type of gold disc-looking design. Glue a gold spiral snake coiling on one side. Score and notch the front and back insets. Glue and staple in place. Cut 60" of 1/2" bands from the plain railroad board. Color the bands gold with a marker. Glue the two gold side seams, and cut and glue pieces that line the helmet edge.
3. Make designs on the cobra shape with gold marker and sponge-paint white to create a contrasting color. Your helmet should be 22" around to fit an average head.

(continued on page 72)

Spectacular Collars

Spectacular Collars

Materials: White school paper 36" x 36", ruler, pencil, scissors, glue, gold, red, green, blue markers, shiny origami paper, paper plate, 1 yard gold ribbon.

Paper Plate Collar

1. Cut out a 5" hole from the plate center. Cut a 2" gap for fitting on neck. Try the plate on the wearer and adjust the fit.
2. Pencil the design on the plate. Color the designs with fine-tipped markers.
3. Make pretty closures for the ends. Glue them on, securing the gold ties between the plate and the decorative closures.

Large Gold Collar

1. The collar is 7" wide in front and narrows to 5" wide at the back. The neck hole is 6" wide. Cut out the collar from school paper and try it on the wearer. Glue the collar onto a second paper collar for strength. It has a 1" gold edge. This step is optional.
2. Mark 1" and 2" rows with a ruler and pencil. Design each row using the four colors of Egyptian jewels: red for carnelian, blue for lapis lazuli, gold, and emerald. The actual stones in most collars were colored glass.
3. Decorate the collar with markers. Make an interesting closure to hold the gold ribbon at the back. We used a blue scarab, but many designs would be appropriate.

Shiny Gold Collar

1. This collar is 5" wide from center to the back. The neck is 7" wide. Try it on before decorating.
2. Mark 1" and 1 1/2" rows with a ruler and pencil. Go over the lines with a thick gold marker line.
3. One square of shiny origami paper for each color allows for 35 trapezoids, 70 stripes, 20 rectangles, and 20 circles. Glue pieces on with edges touching. Fix gaps with gold marker repairs. Make an interesting closure with gold such as Horus, the hawk god, and attach the gold ribbon.

The Egyptians loved to wear jewelry! Both men and women wore necklaces, bracelets, anklets, hair ornaments, earrings, pendants, and wide collars decorated with colored glass. Much of the jewelry includes images of gods and goddesses. Even pets wore jewelry. Tomb cats were painted and have been found wearing earrings and fancy collars.

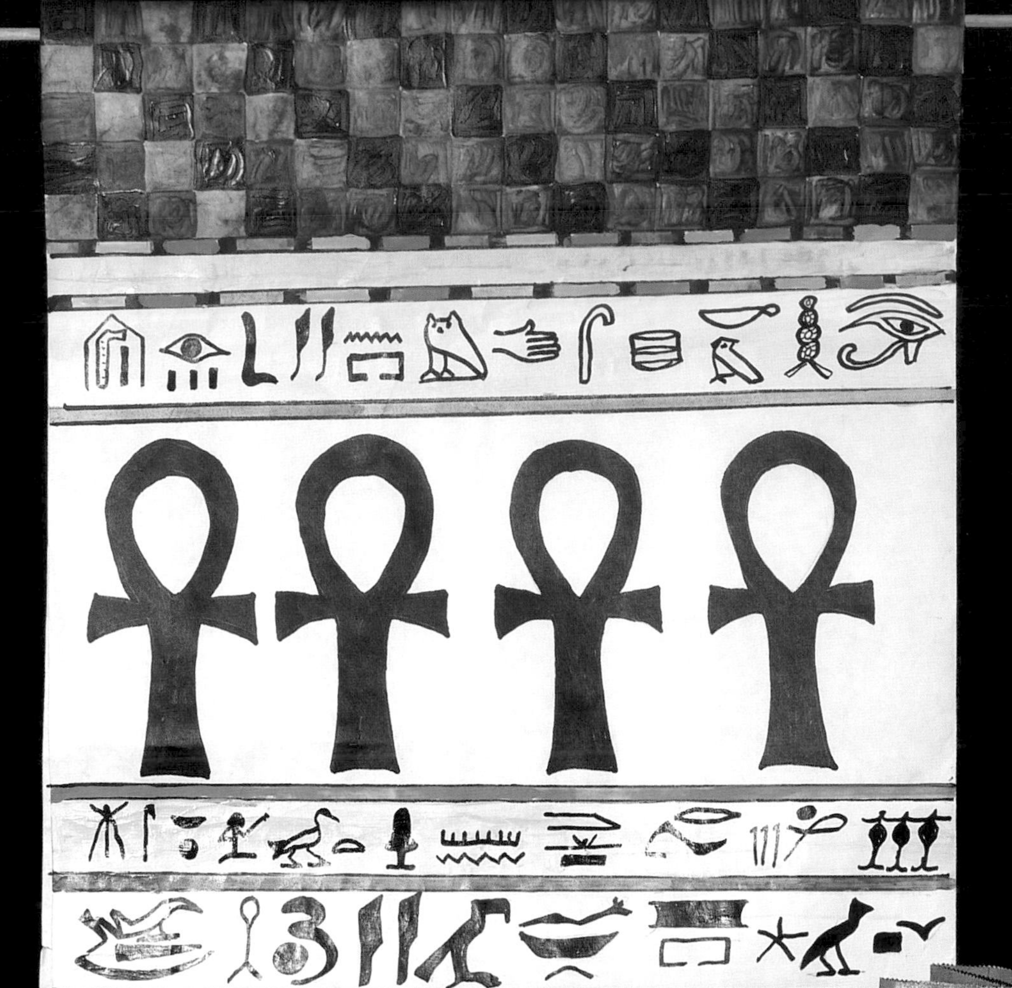

Egyptian Designs

Egyptian Designs

Banner: *Materials are school paper 48″ x 18″, ruler, pencil, paper for templates, acrylic paints, any paint colors, brushes, black marker, 24″ dowel, glue.*
See pattern page 7.

1. Think about the purpose of the banner. Mark off areas that give the banner purpose. Mark all designs that are to be squares or dividers.
2. Paint the banner to look old by mixing cream paint with brown, yellow with brown, etc. Dilute the paint and apply with sponges or wide brush strokes. When it has dried, mark the design with a pencil and ruler. Paint the designs. Use a marker for hieroglyphics. If you do the symbols of ankh or a scarab, cut a template on a paper fold for symmetry. Trace around the template.
3. Fold down the paper's top edge and glue. When the glue is dry insert the dowel for display.

Frame of Matte Board: *Materials are matte board frame, ruler, pencil, black marker, paints, brush.*

1. Prepared matte frames are available at framing shops and art stores for a reasonable cost or free for educational use.
2. The same designs have been used on the frame as on the banner with a different order. After ruling and marking with a pencil, use the black marker where needed and paint the sections. Use your imagination in designing the repeated patterns.

The Terra Cotta Flower Pot: *Materials are a pot, cloth, ruler, pencil, marker, paint and brush, gold marker.*
Proceed with the pot as you did with the previous projects. Plain paper gift bags can be decorated too.

The ankh is the hieroglyphic symbol for "life". The scarab was the most important of all amulets. Thousands of scarabs of all sizes and materials have been found tucked into the linen wrappings of mummies and hung around the necks of mummies. The eye of Horus appears often in Egyptian art. The god Horus had his eye ripped out, then slit into pieces and thrown into the sea. The god Thoth found the pieces and put the eye together again. The eye form, common in art, is known as the *wedjat*. It became known as a symbol of power and healing. *Wedjats* are often found wrapped in mummy linen and placed on the mummies. Richard Balkwill has written ***Clothes and Crafts in Ancient Egypt,*** Gareth Stevens Publications, Milwaukee, WI, 1998.

Animals, Fish and Birds

Animals, Fish, and Birds

Glass Fish: ***Materials are white school paper, scissors, pencil, 3-4 colored markets, staples or glue, stuffing, markers, brass beads,patterns on pages 82, 83.***

1. The glass fish has the same glaze pattern that the Egyptians applied to many glass containers: a wavy pattern with varying colors.
2. Cut two fish patterns on page 83 after enlarging them to the desired size. After cutting out the fish, pencil in your own wavy designs. After covering the designs with colorful markers, glue the two sides of fish together and stuff with wadding. The fish could be a hanging mobile.

The Fish Cosmetic Container: ***Materials are paper, cardboard, markers, terra-cotta and green paint, brushes, scissors, a brad.***

1. Use the pattern piece on page 82, enlarging or reducing it. Cut out the bottom part by making notched lines in the cardboard and then cut with scissors. Cut out the oval center and glue on a piece of cardboard under the oval. This is a replica of a museum cosmetic container. This little bowl is where the cosmetics were placed. The vessel was carved out of wood.
2. Design the bottom section and color in with green and terra-cotta markers or paint. Cut out the top fish, paint it, and attach with a brass brad so it swings back and forth.

Canopic Jars: ***Materials are a cardboard tube for each jar 4"-8" tall, glue, scissors, masking tape, blue, brown and white paint, black markers.***

1. Paint each tube a range of colors from whitish to brownish. Notch the tops about 1" and tape together into a peak. Using the patterns on page 83, cut out two paper pieces for each one. Paint them on both sides. Use your imagination. History shows us there were styles of canopic jars in every color, but the four figures never changed.
2. Glue the beaks, snouts, back, and tops of heads together. Glue the bodies onto the cardboard tubes. Paint the lines on each side with marker.

(continued on page 78)

Women's Headwear

Women's Headwear

Making a Paper Wig: ***Materials are 36″ x 36″ of black school paper cut into 24″ x 1″ strips (for the curly wig) or 1/4″ strips (for the straight hair wig) attached to a paper cap, scissors, glue, stapler, a support structure for the wig (like a blender).***

1. For the **straight–hair wig** cut a paper cap with 12″ on each side allowed for cut hair. The cap is 10″ from ear to ear and 15″ from front to back (allowing 2″ for cut bangs).
2. After you have cut the cap, put it on the head of the wearer and make adjustments with stapling. It should fit snugly and will take some pleating and tucking.
3. Cut the 1/4″ hair strips on a paper cutter: front, back, and side. Cut the bangs with a scissors.
4. Follow the same instructions for the curly headed hair. After cutting the 1″ strips, roll them around a pencil. Glue on more curly haired strips to thicken the wig.

The Gold Crowns: ***Materials are gold railroad board, black marker, scissors, glue, 10′ of ribbon, blue, red, green and yellow paint, brushes, stapler.***

The gold crown with decorative overband

1. Cut each band of gold 24″ x 1 1/2″ for overband crown. The overband is 15″ long. Cut 6 gold discs that are 1 1/2″ wide. Cut four gold eagles (or vultures) with flanges for attachment (see pattern on this page); cut a 1 1/2″ rectangle for crown front.
2. Paint the decorative discs, 1 bird and front rectangle. Glue them in place.
3. Attach the overband and glue the backs together. Try on the handsome crown with one of the wigs.

The gold crown with ribbon and cobra

1. The crown band is 2″ x 24″. The four upright forms are 12″ x 2″. They are one piece and split down the middle. The cobra is 10″ long. Attach the upright forms 2″ apart, the middle upright piece, the 5 ribbons on the bottom edge. Staple and glue these pieces. Paint the cobra and attach tail, bending the swollen body up and head bent down.

Queens often ruled jointly with their husband kings and were called "The Great Royal Wife". One of the most powerful of queens was Nefertari. She was buried in the Valley of the Queens. Nefertiti, the chief wife of Akhenaten, had great influence over her husband. They had six daughters. The wall paintings at Amarna show the children playing with their parents. Having family intimacy portrayed was an unusual thing. Women in Egypt are painted with lighter skin because they stayed indoors. Women could own their own businesses and farms.

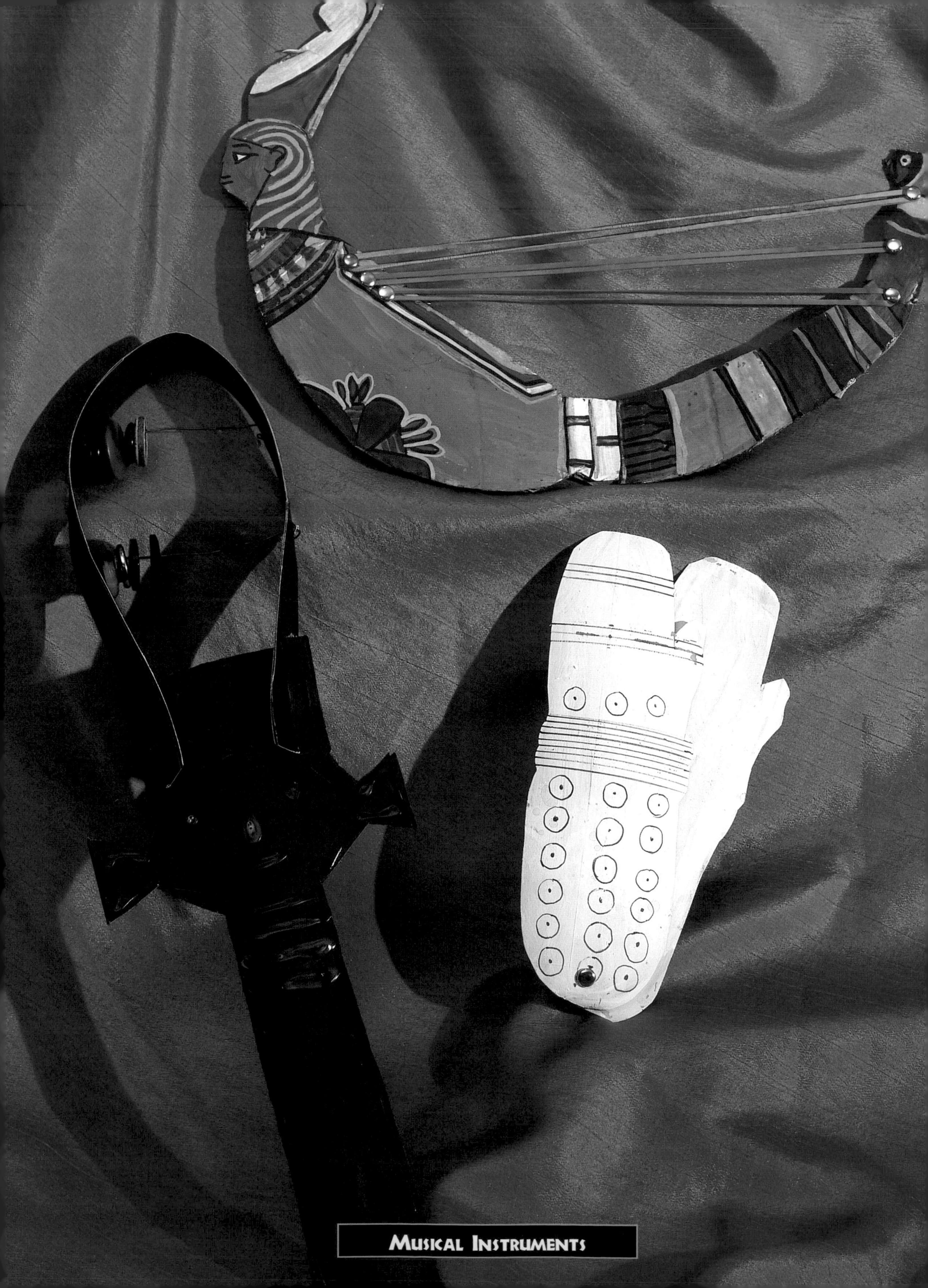

Musical Instruments

MUSICAL INSTRUMENTS

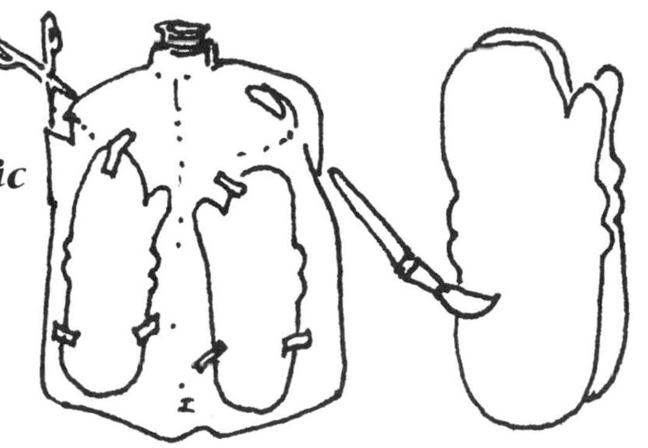

Hand Clappers: ***Materials are plastic milk bottles or bleach bottles, strong scissors, white, yellow and brown acrylic paint, brush, a brass brad, fine-tipped black or brown marker, hand pattern page 83.***

1. Look at the plastic bottle. Find the two flattest surfaces. You must have a flat surface. Trace the hand on two flat surfaces. The hands are joined where the thumbs meet.
2. Cut out the hands at the wrist using a strong scissors or knife.
3. Paint all sides of the hands with a mix of paint. The hands were made of ivory. They are whitish to brownish. Add a second coat if needed. Let dry a few hours.
4. Pencil the decorative circles onto the top hand. Trace with a fine-tipped marker. Punch a hole at the base of each hand and push the brad parts through. Practice clapping them against your hand. How do they sound?

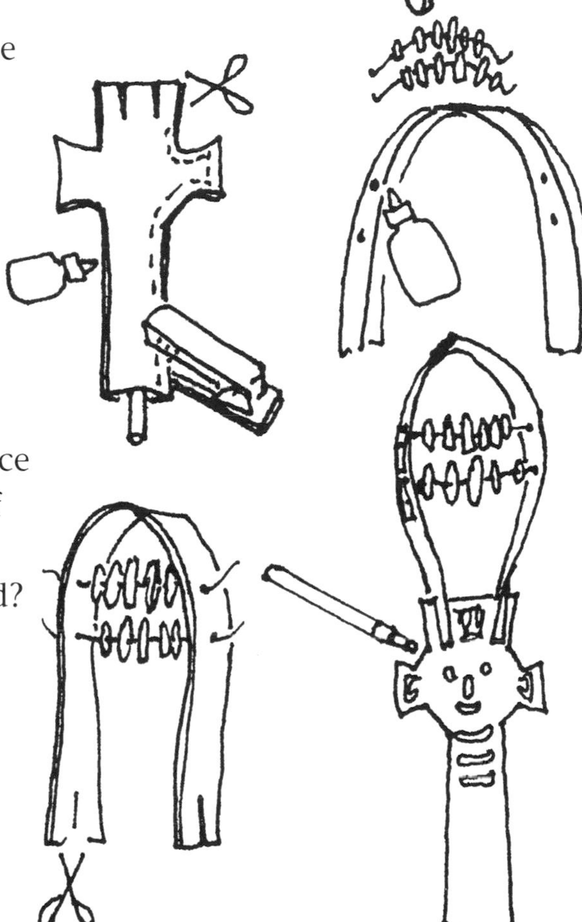

Sistrum Rattle: ***Materials are black railroad board 12" x 12" and two strips 22" x 2", glue, scissors, strong wire, 12-15 buttons, stapler, 10" x 1/4" pencil or dowel. Pattern on page 82.***

1. Cut out the handles. The figure can look like the sample or just be a simple handle. The top must be 4"–5" wide. Glue any decorative design on the front piece and let dry. Staple the edges together. Cover up the staples with black marker. Insert a pencil or dowel piece into the handle.
2. Glue the two long bands together. Make holes with a scissor point 5" and 3" down if you want two rows of rattles. String wire with buttons through the holes. Cover wires with black tape or a paper patch.
3. Cut 1 1/2" notches 3/8" in from each side of the handle and at the end of the band. Put the slits together. Reinforce with more paper patches. Rattle your sistrum. How does it sound?

(continued on page 73)

Hieroglyphics

ART LITERATURE SOCIAL STUDIES

Hieroglyphics: Pictures as Letters

Materials: A manila folder that has been aged with tea, coffee or dabbed brownish paint. Scissors, fine-tipped and broad-tipped black markers, pencil, eraser, a skewer, and glue, cartouche pattern on page 73.

1. Study a hieroglyphic alphabet. Here are some of the common ones. Egyptian scribes wrote a person's name in a cartouche. You are looking at two cartouches in the photograph.

2. Age the light cardboard. Make a 1/2" border on the edge with a black marker or paint. Think about the message you wish to put on the cartouche: your name, instructions, etc.

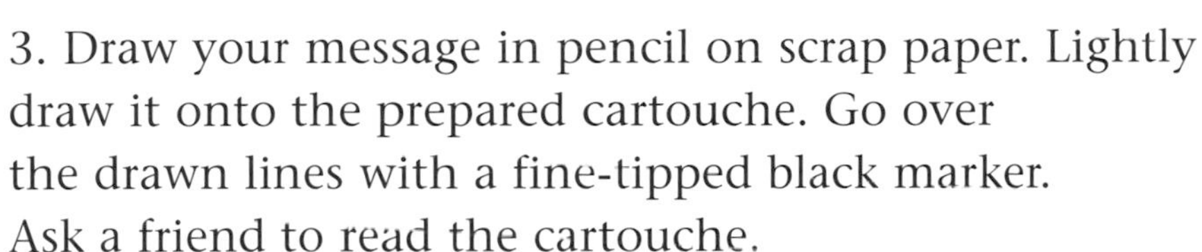

3. Draw your message in pencil on scrap paper. Lightly draw it onto the prepared cartouche. Go over the drawn lines with a fine-tipped black marker. Ask a friend to read the cartouche.

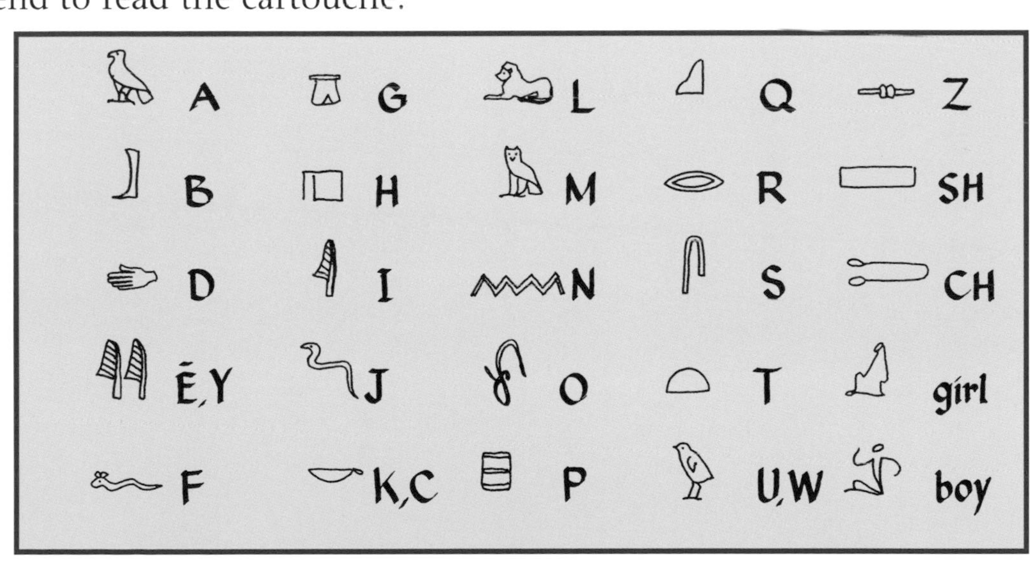

Cuneiform, on page 74, appears to be austere, geometric, and abstract in contrast with Egyptian hieroglyphics which are poetic and fascinating... almost alive in the stylized drawings of feathers, birds, animals, and plants. According to ancient Egyptians it was the God Thoth who created writing and bestowed it as a gift on humankind. It remained little changed for 3500 years, though the signs increased from 700 to 5,000. In contrast to the Sumerians, the Egyptian's writing system expressed everything they wished to record. Jean-Francois Champollion penetrated the secrets of the writing in 1822 by deciphering the Rosetta Stone found in 1799. The history of Egypt might have remained largely unknown had we not been able to decipher tomb writings.

Tamara Bower has used hieroglyphics in the story ***The Shipwrecked Tailor,*** Atheneum, NY, 2000.

The Egyptian Pyramid

The Egyptian Pyramid

Materials: White or buff railroad board, ruler, scissors, pencil, paint that makes a sandy color: white, yellow, brown mix, sponges, rectangle printing material, glue, paper clips, masking tape.

The pyramid is a geometric form: the equilateral triangle with four triangular sides.

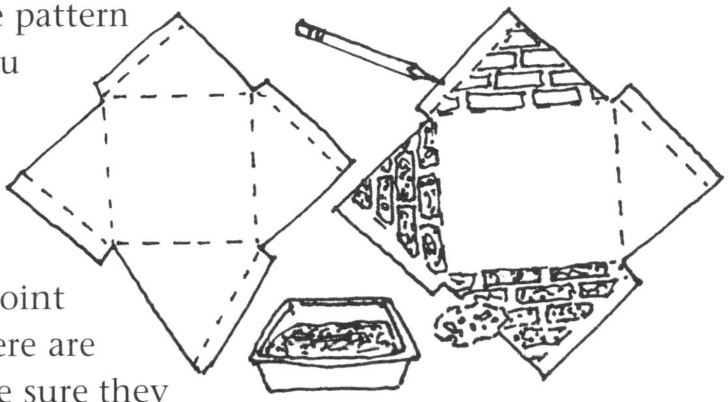

1. Decide on the size of the pyramid. Find the pattern on page 81. Double or triple the size when you copy it.
2. After copying the pyramid pattern, trace around it on the railroad board. Cut out the equilateral triangle.
3. Score along all triangle lines with a sharp point such as your scissor's point. Fold wherever there are scores. Put the pyramid sides together to make sure they are going to connect. Mark the horizontal line of each triangle with a pencil so the finishing textures are horizontal. 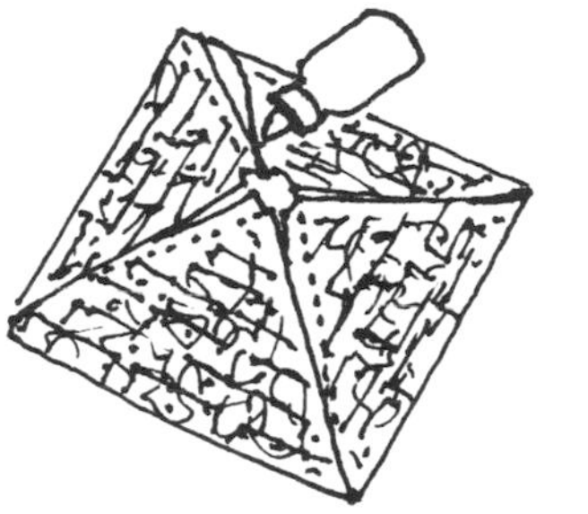
4. Mix the sandy colors a little, but not too much as you want the pyramid to have several color textures. You should have something rectangular that is to scale with the pyramid. In order to print the stones, a 10" pyramid would have a rectangle 1/2" x 1". It might be a sponge piece, a foam piece, or a cardboard piece. It should be easily gripped.
5. Dip the rectangle piece into the shallow paint dish and stamp "stones"onto the pyramid surface or brush the paint onto the rectangle. Do this on all pyramid surfaces but leave the bottom plain. Let the paint dry. 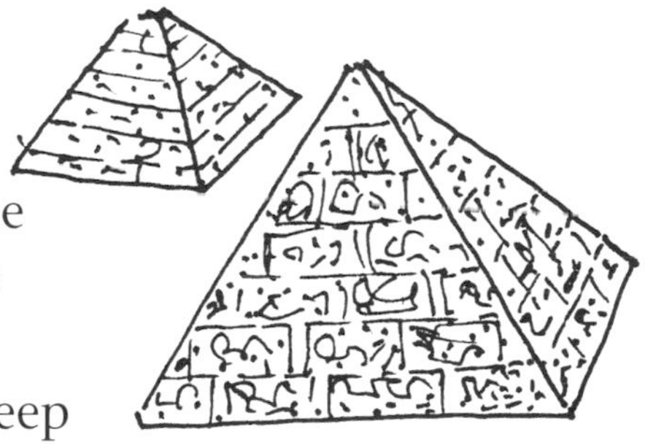
6. Glue the flaps together on one side and weight it or keep glue secured with light masking tape. This is the tricky part. After drying time, carefully remove the securing tape and admire the handsome pyramid.

More than 80 pyramids of different shapes and sizes have been discovered in Egypt. The most famous is the Great Pyramid of Khufu at Giza. It is one of the Seven Wonders of the Ancient World. It was built in 2570 B.C. It was covered with limestone, a hard shiny surface, and had a capstone of gold that reflected the sun's rays. Later, pyramids had stepped sides that were made smooth. The burial chamber was inside the shape. By the late Old Kingdom it was clear that pyramids took too much labor and material. Pharaohs began to be buried in rock-cut tombs in the Valley of the Kings. It was here the Tutankhamen tomb was discovered in 1922 by Howard Carter.

Jan M. Mike has written ***Gift of the Nile,*** Troll Assoc. 1999.

An Introduction to Islam

Born in the seventh century A.D. in **Saudi Arabia**, Islam is a monotheistic religion focusing on the glorification of the One Supreme Being, Allah, and around a Holy Book, the Qur'an revealed between 610 and 632 A.D. to the Prophet Muhammad. Islam was founded at a time when moral and spiritual laxity was at its height in the region of Mecca and further north in Medina. Muhammad's followers and successors soon spread the word of Islam in the surrounding areas and beyond Arabia. To Muslims, the followers of Islam, their religion became a way of life, forming and guiding their entire culture and society.

wooden holder of the Qur'an

The Five Pillars of Islam are known as duties and together support the structure of Islam. **The Qur'an,** which means "recitation," has 114 chapters. Muslims believe that it expresses precisely the word of God.
The Shahada means "bearing witness" and is a declaration of faith that there is only one God (Allah) and that Muhammad is his messenger. **The Salat** is the ritual prayer, said five times a day while a person kneels in the direction of the Ka'bah in Mecca.
The Zakat is a form of charity and is 2.5% of one's wealth. The **Sawm** is the fast from sunrise to sunset during the month of Ramadan. The Fifth and final pillar is **Hajji**, a special pilgrimage to Mecca which brings millions of Muslims together for common worship. It is expected that all adult Muslims must try to make the journey once in their lifetime if physically and financially able. Some symbols of Islam are shown below:

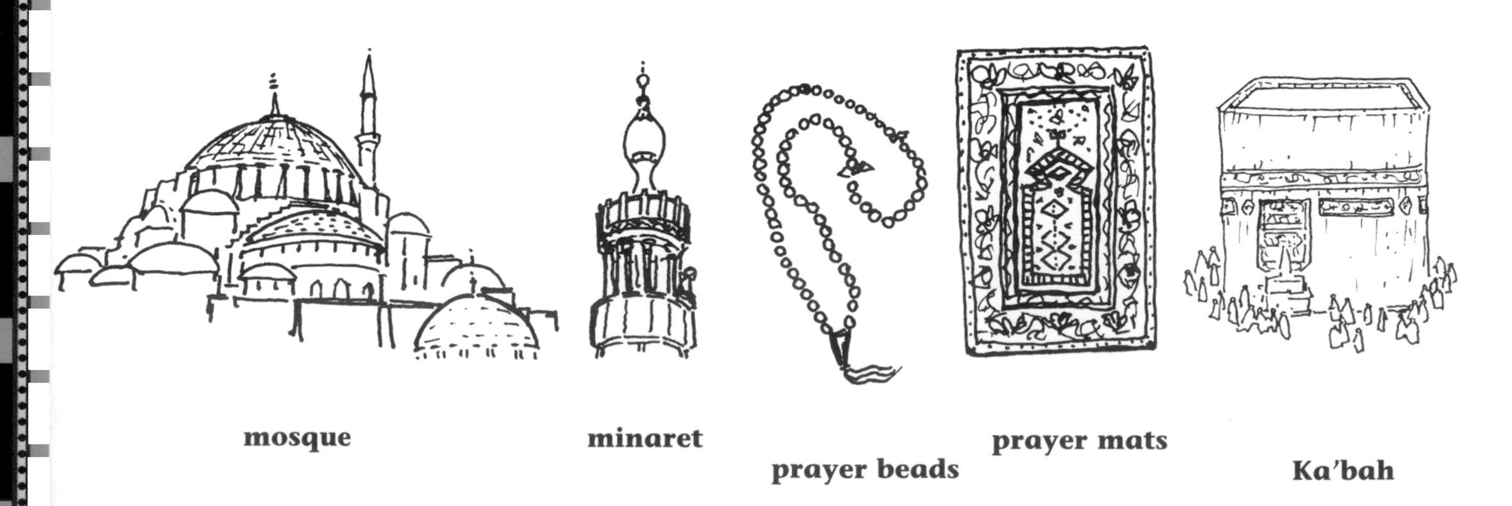

mosque **minaret** **prayer beads** **prayer mats** **Ka'bah**

Art in the Islamic World

Islamic design has a spiritual importance because it is considered by Muslims to be a way for humans to reflect the glory of nature as created by Allah. From early days the idea of portraying humans and animals was rejected as idol worship.

Five Characteristics of Islamic Art

1. **Tessellations:** Squares, triangles, and hexagons are shapes that will fit together with all sides connecting. These are called tessellations. They imply infinity.

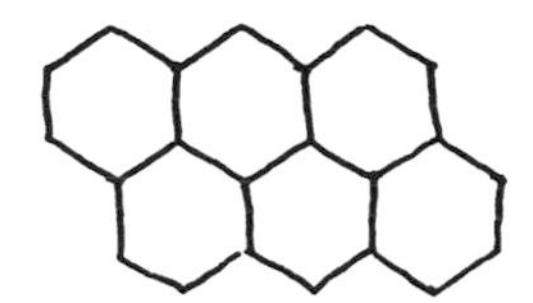
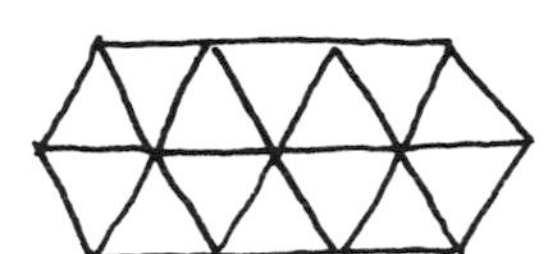
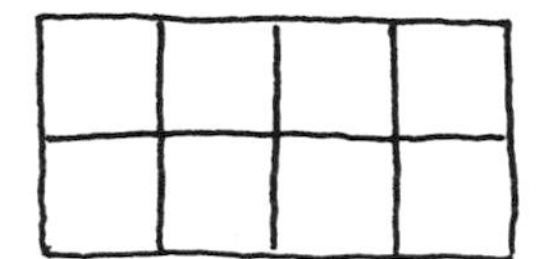

2. **Complex Star Polygons:** Before computers, these complex patterns were drawn with a ruler and compass.

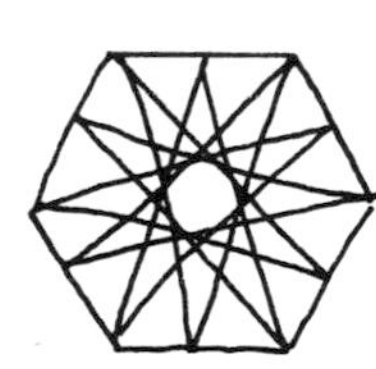

3. **Linear Repeat Patterns:** These are often borders around blocks of pattern. They add a rich effect. Often several borders are combined.

4. **Arabesques:** These are plant-world in form but stylized. Often the arabesque weaves in and out and around things. The arabesque symbolizes the organized earth with its underlying structures.

5. **Calligraphy in the Arabic Alphabet:** Calligraphy in Arabic is referred to as "the geometry of line", line meaning writing or letters. Since the rise of Islam, calligraphy has been a major art form. Numerous manuscripts have survived describing the preparation or inks, colors and paper. Here is the essential calligraphed form which reads "al-salaam" which means peace.
This is the heart of Islamic art. It is the most important of all unifying characteristics and is, to this day, the most treasured and revered art form. It is through calligraphy that the Divine Intention is expressed explicitly. Arabic is read from right to left and the alphabet has 28 letters.

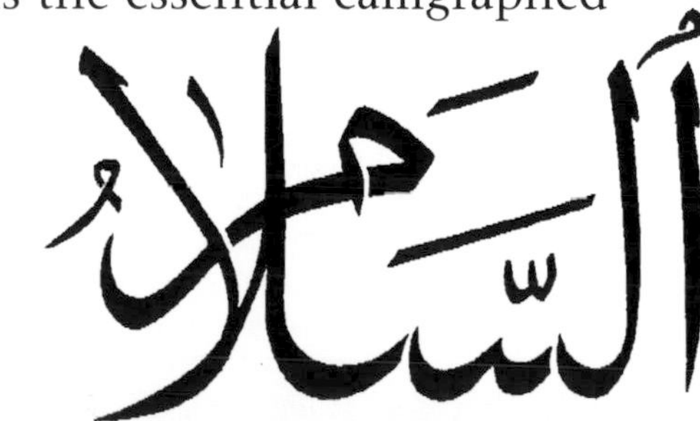

The Eye of Good Fortune

THE EYE OF GOOD FORTUNE

Materials: Light cardboard, circle templates such as lids, cup tops or bottoms etc., pencil, scissors, dark blue, light blue and white paint, small brush, strong black marker, hole punch (making bricks, like the photo, with plaster of paris is optional).

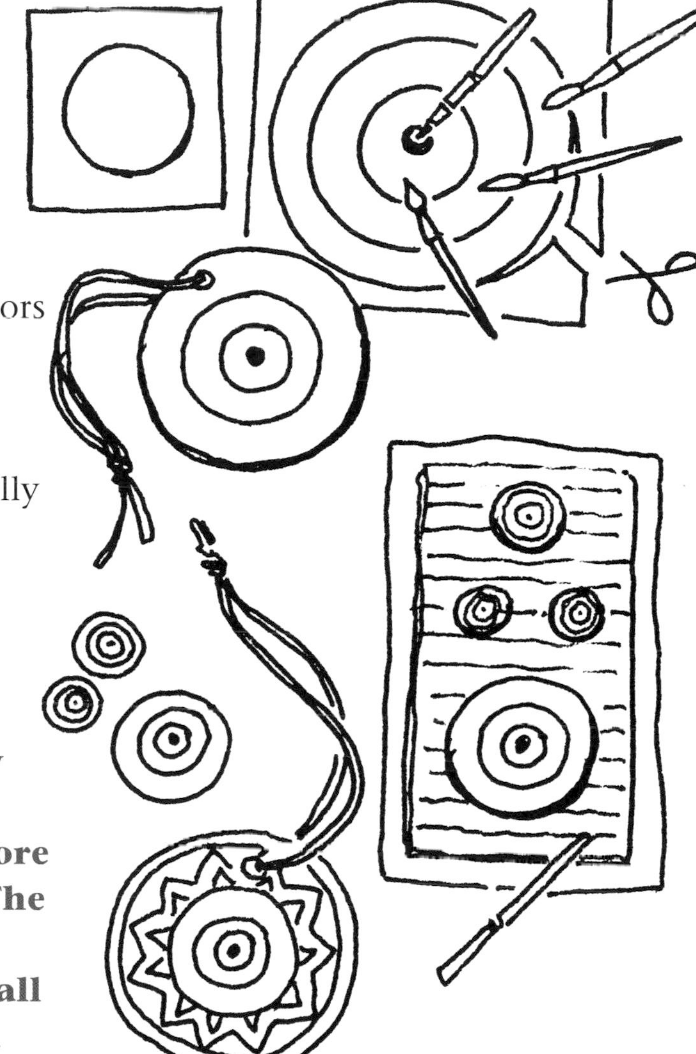

1. Think about how the "eyes" are going to be used: a necklace, glued to a surface, strung on yarn, put above a doorway. Draw around the circles. Do not cut them out yet.

2. Paint the outside color dark blue. It can vary in thickness, but remember that three more colors will be applied. Next paint the paper white or leave a space and paint light blue. After all the colors have dried, mark the light blue circle as the eye's pupil with a black marker. Now carefully cut out each eye circle.

3. Punch a hole at the top of the eye and put it to the use you have planned.

In near Eastern countries such as Turkey people wear the "eye" or put it in their environment, as if more eyes indicate more protection from anything undesirable. The eyes are made of glass. Jewelry such as bracelets, rings, necklaces and earrings, all include the lucky eye looking out. When constructing a wall or a house, glass eyes are put in the brick material to keep bad luck away from the area. Just as Africans wear their *gris gris* charms and Mexicans have their colorful *Ojo de Dios* yarn objects, the blue eye serves the same purpose in parts of the Arab world.

Another explanation for "the evil eye" is that the evil gaze is about envy. Inciting the envy of others can be a dangerous thing. Fear of the evil eye has caused some people to do just about anything to avoid being enviable in any way. The charm is meant to deflect the evil back onto its source.

Mosaic Tiles

MOSAIC TILES: AN ANCIENT ART

Materials: One of each 10″ x 10″ and 12″ x 12″ manila cardboard or other light cardboard, ruler, pencil, acrylic paint, brushes, glue, sharp scissors, clear acrylic spray, powdered grout, water, sponge.

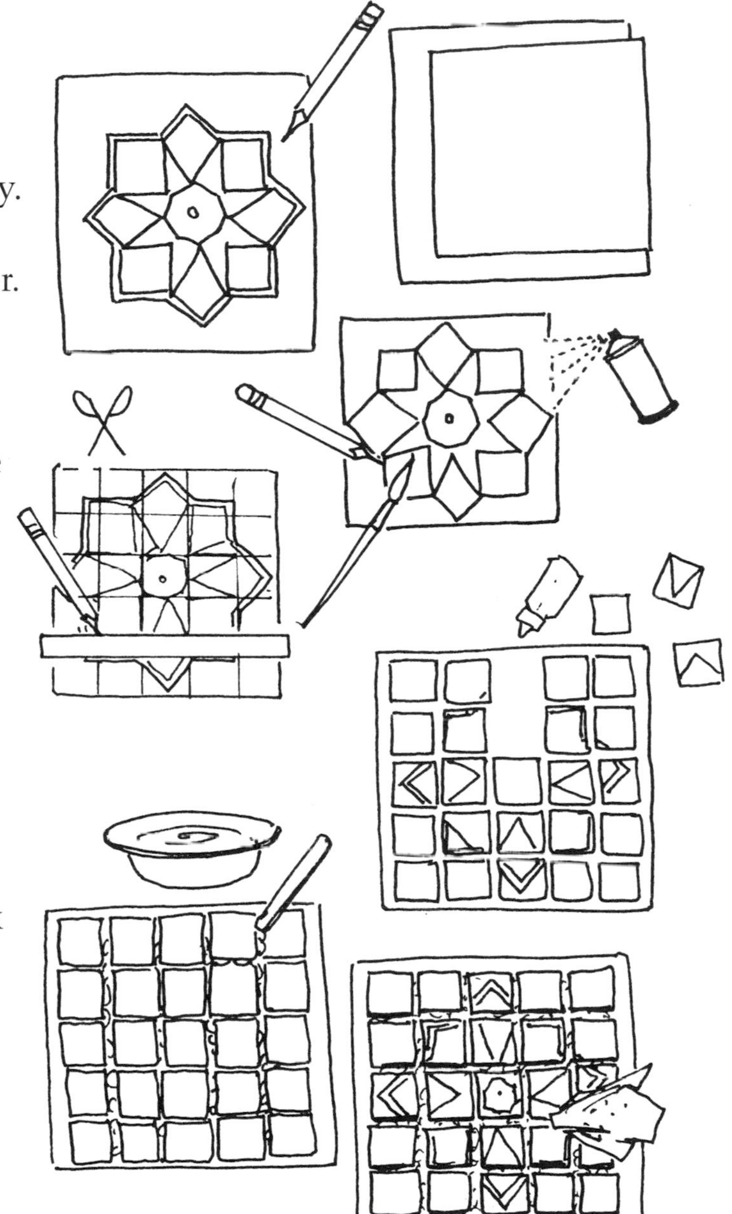

1. Look at pattern ideas on page 7. Draw the design on a practice paper.

2. Now, draw the design onto a smaller cardboard piece. Paint the design. Let it dry.

3. Spray paint the design with acrylic sealer. Several applications will give the mosaic a shiny ceramic-like shine. Let it dry.

4. With a pencil and ruler lightly mark the design into 5″ equal squares. Cut out the squares.

5. Reassemble the squares on the larger cardboard piece. Leave narrow spaces between each square. The space will hold the "grout" which is like a cement. Glue the squares in place.

6. Mix water into powdered grout and mix until smooth. With a blunt knife or craft stick carefully work the grout into spaces between the squares.

7. Gently remove excess grout with a damp (but not wet) sponge. Rinse the sponge frequently in clear water to remove all grout residue from the shiny mosaic tile.

This art form is one of the most ancient of the Middle and Near East dating back as early as 2000 B.C. Assyrians and Babylonians used enameled brick to decorate their palaces. Lapis blue and turquoise are the most common colors The process of making tiles today is almost the same as in ancient times.

Three Minarets

THREE MINARETS

Materials: Any boxes or tubes that are the correct scale (our biggest is 6" x 6" with a 12" tube our longest), plain paper, markers, crayons, oil pastels, glue, scissors, ruler, pencil. Paper strips, flour and water for making papier–mache'. Spools, glitter, buttons and any decorative trims are optional.

In researching this project over one hundred minarets were studied and composite forms were created using authentic but easily replicated patterns.

1. Gather the cardboard forms: salt, oatmeal, paper tubes were all used for the "blue minaret" and the simpler red one. Stack the boxes. A hole may have to be cut to put tubes through lids.
2. Papier–mache' for strength: Make a paste of 1 part flour to 1 1/2 parts water. Tear newspaper strips. Start making your minaret sturdy by dipping the strips Let the minaret dry overnight.
3. Cut paper strips that will fit around the boxes. They will be colored with classic designs. Think about balconies, arches and windows as they are all possible features. Think very hard about the roof. A conical form is the easiest. How will it be attached? This is the time when these architectural features are planned and added.
4. Design the colors and paper that will fit around the minaret base. Review the geometric patterns on page 7. After coloring each of the papers glue them around the minaret section. Add balconies and railings. Make a cone for the roof and decide how it is going to be attached. This should have been thought about during the papier-mache' process. After every beautiful colored and designed paper surface is in place, stand back...the minaret should be something beautiful and interesting to behold just as it is for Islamic worshippers.
5. The brown square minaret is the same process using square boxes exclusively.

The minaret is a high column designed as a platform for the muezzin (mujadhin) to call people to prayer *(the Adhan)*. It can stand alone or be part of a mosque. Angela Wood has written ***Muslim Mosque,*** Gareth Stevens Pub., Milwaukee, WI., 2000.

PAINTED PATTERNS

Materials: As many 4″ square tiles as needed. Special paint that dries hard on tile surface: DeltaCeramdecoro and PermEnamel Surface Conditioner®, a variety of brushes, water, pencil, paper for design work, grid for geometrics, page 85.

The popular and beautiful Spanish and Mexican tiles probably originated in southern Spain with the Moors, victors in peacefully occupying the south of Spain for several hundred years. Variations of the designs continue to cover walls, arches, roofs, and floors of mosques in every part of the Muslim world.

1. Clean the surface of the tile with a damp cloth. Any plain colored tile works well. Brush on the Surface Conditioner as step one if the tiles are to be used beyond a display.
2. With a 4″ square paper and pencil, design the tile. Think about the corner making a pattern of its own when the tiles are put together. Here are some traditional Muslim designs:

3. Let the tiles dry (about an hour) and glue them to the surface. Add grout to finish the tiled surface.

Tessellation has been discussed as one of the elements of design. Any shape made by combining triangles can be tessellated. A study of the architecture and sculpture and most art forms in the Arab world is rich with simple and complicated ceramic tiles.

A Prayer Rug

A Prayer Rug

Materials: Heavy white school paper 3′ x 5′, pencil, ruler, Jiffy Foam® for print-making, paint, markers.

1. Measure and cut the school paper to a rectangle 3′ x 5′. Design the borders on a smaller practice paper.

2. Mark the borders with a ruler and pencil. The inside of the rug should be at least 2′ x 3′.

3. Paint the borders and the center. Keep in mind the colors you are going to paint for contrast. See page 7 and 51 for border patterns.

4. Study shapes common to Islamic art. See page 7. Cut the shapes from cardboard or Jiffy Foam for a clean print. Prepare the paint palette (paper plate or Styrofoam meat tray). Brush on the paint or stamp it. Try the print on scrap paper. Fill the borders with the repeat painted print design.

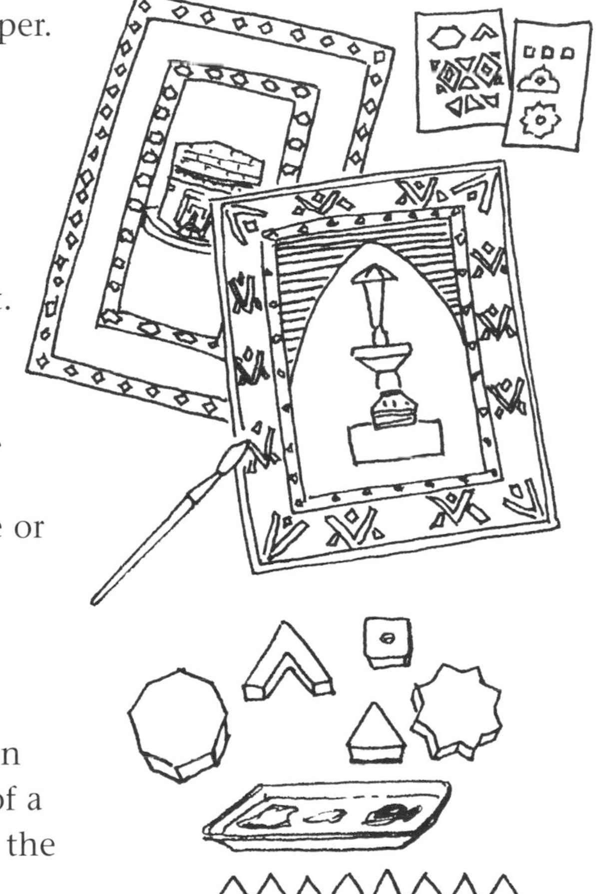

5. Cut out shapes for the center. The Ka'bah is often part of the rug design; also common is the image of a minaret. Trace around the paper pattern and paint the center of the rug with great care. The rug's central images could be painted on separate paper and glued in place.

standing for prayer **bowing** **kneeling** **prostration**

Prayer mats are laid on a surface to insure cleanliness. A Muslim does not have to kneel on a prayer mat but some have favorite prayer mats that they keep with them. A mat may be a woolen carpet or made of straw or cotton. Prayer mats often have geometric patterns or sometimes pictures of famous mosques, but they never show images of people.

THE HAND OF GOOD LUCK

THE HAND OF GOOD LUCK

Materials: White manila folder or poster board or aluminum 6" x 12", a disposable foil cookie sheet, blue bead or button, white glue, black, grey and white acrylic or tempera paint, sponges, pencil, hole punch, patterns on page 73.

1. Lay the hand on the rectangular surface. Trace around it with a pencil, indenting the foil. Look at the photograph. Notice that three of the hands have fat fingers and the big hand has cut out fingers. Decide the way you want your hand to be. Cut out your hand.

2. The hands have a decorative "relief" of dots, curves, flowers, stars, outlines. Draw the designs on the hand-shape with a pencil. Next, reinforce the pencil lines with white glue applied from a tip that makes a controlled line. Experiment on a scrap of paper. You do not want a big glob of glue. Rather, you are drawing with glue. Let the glue dry overnight. The big hand has black marker outlining the designs. Next brush on blue paint. Both looks are authentic.

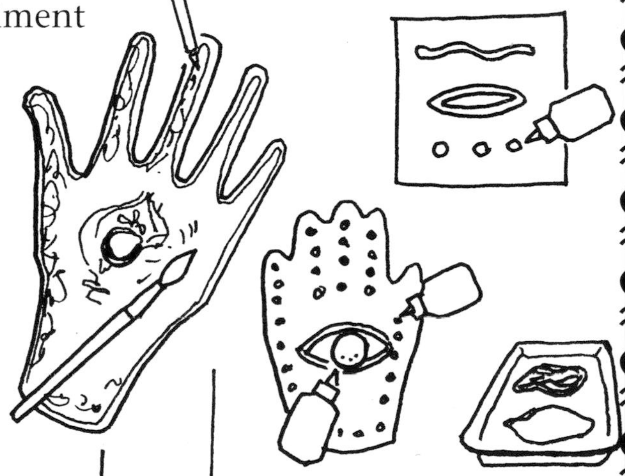

3. Put white and black paint the size of a dime on a paint dish. Use a small dry sponge piece dipped in the black and white paint and gently sponge over the glue lines. It should look patchy. Glue on the blue bead or button.

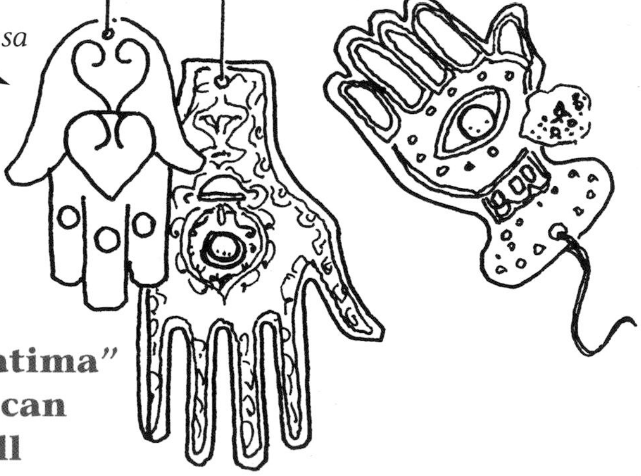

4. Punch a hole at the wrist for hanging over a door on a string or a nail. These hands are commonly found in many places.

hamsa

The downward-hanging hamsa (Arabic) hand is usually open with thumbs on each side. An alternative name for the charm is "Hand of Fatima" named for Muhammad's daughter. The hands can be suspended above doorways, included in wall paintings, and incorporated into architecture. Hamsa is also the root word for the number five in Arabic. Whether engraved or carved, realistic or stylized, it is rare when some form of the eye or hand is not displayed in an Arabic dwelling. Often it is in the form of jewelry or embroidery. People most susceptible to the evil eye or who are most likely to wear the hand charm are brides, pregnant women, and babies. ***(continued on page 81)***

A Traditional Bag

A Traditional Bag

Materials: Heavy white school paper 30" x 15" folded in half, 5-6 yarn colors (each tassel has 3 feet of yarn), buttons, bells, beads, markers or crayons, ruler, pencil, glue, stapler, scissors, big-eyed needle.

1. Cut the rectangle of paper and fold in half so your paper surface is 15" x 15". Using a ruler and pencil, plan a design which will cover the paper with color and geometric patterns. Design some bands for glued buttons. These were woven bags and used traditional zig-zag lines, diamonds, and triangles. See page 7 for ideas.

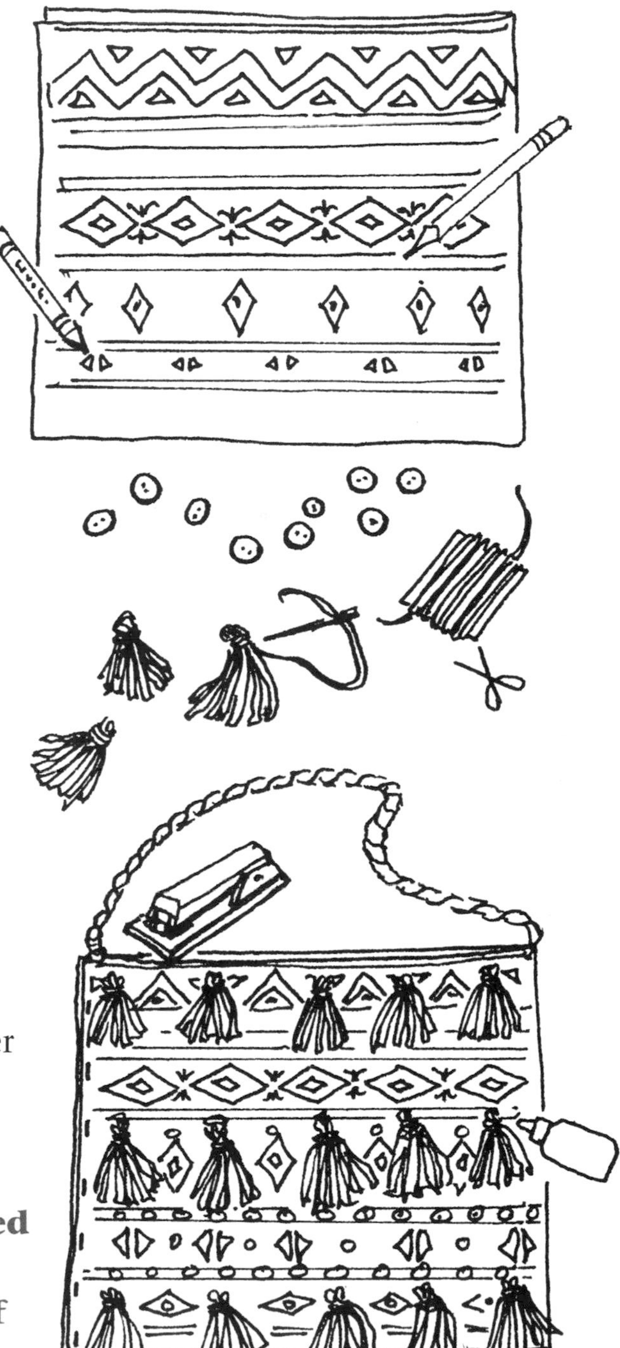

2. Color your bag and add the decorative touches.

3. Make the tassels by winding the yarn around a 3" cardboard piece. Cut the bottom of the tassel and wind one of the pieces around the top, thus making a knob. Thread the yarn through the needle-eye and push it through the wrapped section, securing the wrapping.

4. Place the tassels evenly on the bag. Staple the top row. Glue the rows in the middle. Put a book weight on the glued tassels overnight to dry.

5. Glue or staple the open side of the bag. Add a 24" handle of braided yarn or a double 1 1/2" paper band. Color the paper band; then glue the sides together and staple to each side of the bag.

These handsome bags were traditionally used as containers on camels and donkeys. They were also hung near the door on the wall of the wedding house ready to receive gifts.

ARABIC CALLIGRAPHY

Arabic Calligraphy

Materials: Paper, pencil, Arabic alphabet on page 74, any additional art supplies for Arabic writing.

ت ب ا
t b a

Guide to the Arabic alphabet

Arabic is written from right to left.
Each Arabic letter has one sound and each sound has one letter.
The 28 letters use 14 shapes mixed with 0-3 dots above or below them.

j = ج b = ب
H = ح t = ت
kh = خ th = ث

s = س sh = ش r = ر z = ز

We will concentrate on these three.

Mark مارك
KraM

Lynn ل ـ ن
nyL

Writing a Name in the Arabic alphabet

1. Print a name on a piece of paper with a blank written for each letter in the name. Number each sound in your name. For example: In English two letters often share one sound

Th sh ry ey

Put a copy of the "English to Arabic" page in front of you. Look down the list of English letters on the page, checking to be sure you are choosing the right SOUND for each numbered letter or pair of letters above, and write the Arabic letters in the blanks below, beginning on the far right:

________+__________+_________+__________+__________+

5 4 3 2 1

Connectors are used to give the calligraphy fluidity. This step is not being included as connectors come in middle, initial and final forms (almost 60 shapes) which is overwhelming to most beginners. The purpose of the study-and-do activity is to become acquainted with the alphabet and to produce a few words.

Calligraphy is an art form in the Islamic culture. It is incorporated into every aspect of life: furnishings, clothing, architecture, and household objects. Because the Muslim faith is a complete way of life, the religious values are often expressed in the form of calligraphied scriptures or wise sayings from the Qu'ran that blend into everything and are found everywhere.

PAPER CHAINS

ART MATH

PAPER CHAINS

Materials: Colored paper, scissors, pencil, glue or tape, patterns on page 75-78. Paint and markers optional.

1. Cut the paper into sections 5″– 7″ wide and as long as needed.

2. Fold your paper strip accordion-style into three to four sections. For a longer paper chain add more paper strips. Cutting this many is about the best a scissors can cut.

3. Choose a pattern from the pattern page or design your own.

4. If you want to color or paint your paper, do it now. Suggestions are to cut some out of wrapping or wallpaper or sponge paint some with color dabs. Let the paper strip dry before proceeding.

5. Refold your dry paper strip. *Trace the design onto your folded paper strip, making sure the design extends to the folded sides so that when it is cut out the shapes* ***are connected.***

6. Secure your paper for cutting by slipping a paper clip onto a section which will be cut away.

7. Repeat as many of the same or different designs as you wish. Fasten ends of your paper chains together with tape or glue.

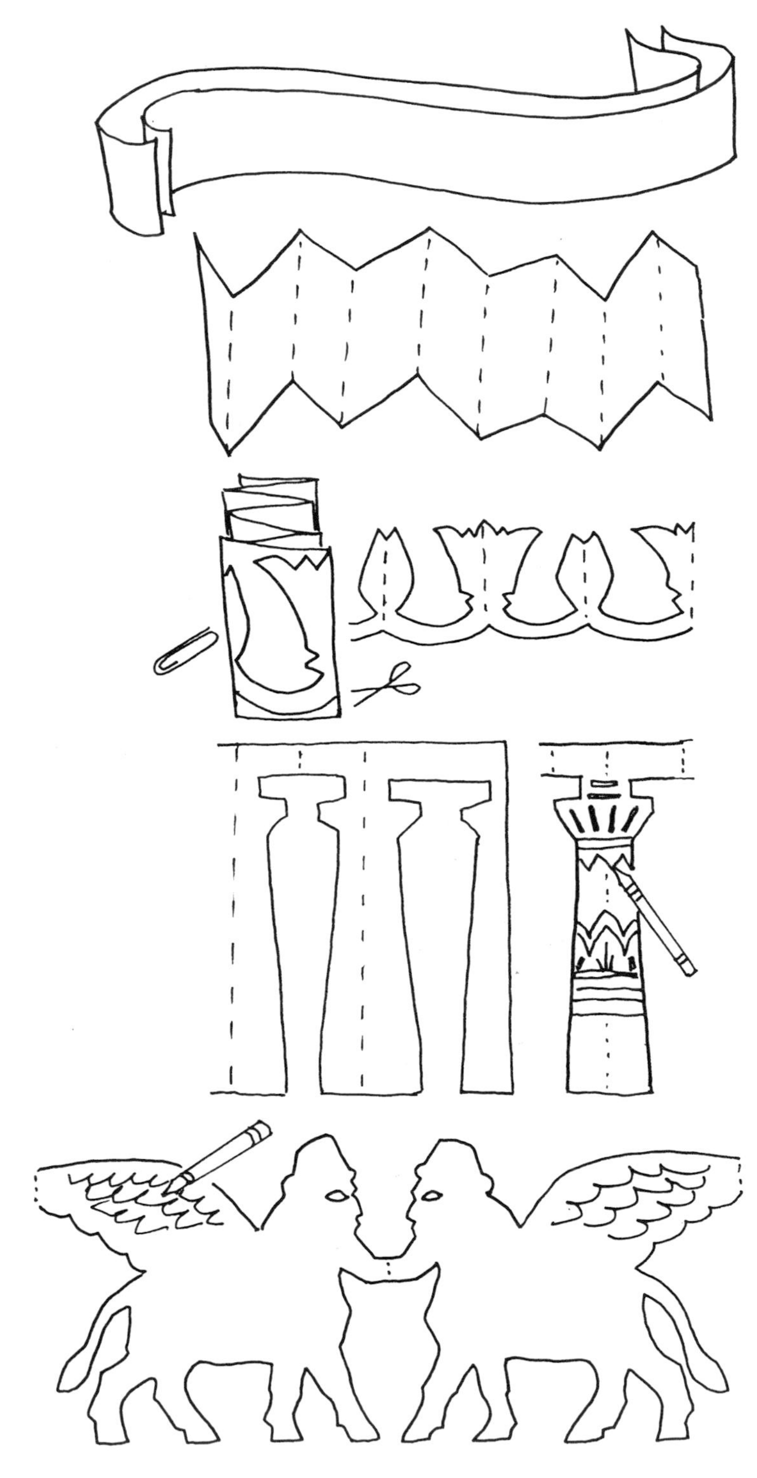

Paper chains can be used as borders for displays, book marker patterns, gift tags, any theme presentation that might need scenery motifs (when enlarged), invitations to a theme event, and stencils for a variety of purposes.

Three Sumerian Chariots - *(continued from page 15)*

The Warrior Chariot

1. Cut four wheels from cardboard 3″ in diameter. Paint and marker them to look like the real Sumerian wooden wheels. Stick two 3″ dowels through the two sets of wheels.
2. Cut a cardboard pattern like the one on page 81, doubling it in size. Add the marker lines which were often bronze strips. Paint them a second color after you have painted the body of the chariot a wood color.

The Sumerians are credited with inventing the wheel more than 6000 years ago. Heavy loads and passengers were transported in animal-drawn sledges, wagons, chariots, boats or by pack animals. As early as 2800 B.C. there is an image of a sledge with four wheels. Wheeled vehicles such as our first two projects have been found in royal tombs. Possibly the potter's wheel is also a Sumerian invention.

Cuneiform - *(continued from page 25)*

The pictures were put on prepared clay pieces perhaps 10,000 years ago by Sumerians. By 2500 B.C. pictograms had become more simplified with curves, triangles, and straight lines. This was called cuneiform (wedge shaped). The importance of cuneiform came when the symbols were used to show sounds of words.

Cuneiform was NOT a language. It was a technique for writing used by many peoples. Babylonian scribes cut ends of reeds into points and pressed them into damp clay. In 1846 experts learned how to "read" dried cuneiform clay tablets. They told mythical stories about economic dealings, wise sayings, and the history of these amazing ancient people.

Shabti Figures -*(continued from page 29)*

Every Egyptian was required to do some farming and irrigation work in the next life. Rich Egyptians paid workers to do this for them. Heaven was called the Field of Reeds and the dead Egyptian was again expected to work for Osiris. From the earliest tombs the wealthy were buried with clay worker-figures called "shabti". The Book of the Dead has this inscription:

"Oh shabti, if the deceased is called upon to do any work required there,... you will say, 'Here I am, I will do it.' "

In the New Kingdom (1500 B.C.) one shabti was enough. By 1000 B.C. 401 shabti were buried...one for each day of the year plus 36 bosses who carried whips to keep the workers on task.

Toys from the Tombs - *(continued from page 31)*

Tomb paintings throughout Egyptian history show people playing board games. Egyptian children played with homemade toys such as these leather balls, the wooden horse, and the fabric doll. There are paintings of boys playing soldiers and girls holding dolls. Some dolls were made of wood with string for hair. This doll is patterned after a toy found in a young Egyptian princess' tomb.

Scarabs - *(continued from page 33)*

The Scarab Pin: ***Materials are dough or air drying clay, the 4 Egyptian colors of paint, brush.***

Follow the procedure of the winged scarab. After baking, paint the scarab.

The Scarab Gift Bag: ***Materials are a purchased paper gift bag, pencil, ruler, paint, brushes, black marker.***

1. With your ruler and pencil mark the design on the paper bag. Paint the pattern on the bag.
2. Go over the dried paint dividing lines with black marker. Use a scarab template on page 74.

Two Stitchery Scarabs: ***Materials are a piece of handwoven fabric aged with dark tea bags (Dab used soggy tea bags on fabric. Blend. Rinse in cold water.), embroidery hoop, colorful yarn like crewel, a big-eyed needle, scissors, matte frames, masking tape.***

1.The simple embroidery stitches are a running stitch (red frame in photograph), chain, satin, French knot, and blanket stitch. Design the scarab on paper with colored marker. Be creative and use lots of color.
2. Iron the stitchery when it is finished. Tape the edges to the back of a matte board.

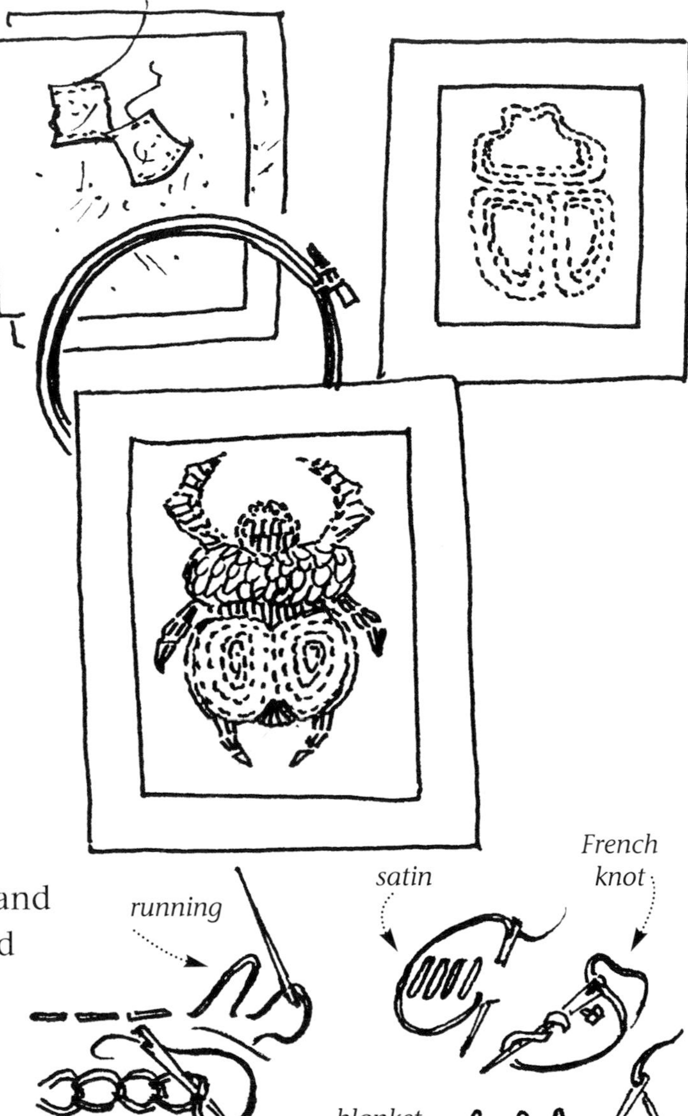

The scarab is the lowly African dung beetle. This large black-green beetle shapes animal droppings into a ball and pushes it along with its head, arms, and legs. Khepri, god of the rising sun, is painted pushing the sun out of the desert hills and into the sky. Most scarabs were globs of flattened clay but some were detailed. Thousands of scarabs have been found. Scarabs were the most common of Egyptian amulets called good-luck charms. Egyptians were burying charms with their dead 7,000 years ago. Scarabs and the Eye of Horus are the amulets found most frequently in burial places.

Four King's Crowns - *(continued from page 35)*

The Aten Crown: ***Materials are white or yellow railroad board 18" x 22", 6" paper bowl, flour, water, paper strips for papier mache', paper clips, red, gold, blue, green and turquoise paint, brushes, scissors.***

1. Cut out the crown. The tall forms are 7" each and 16" tall from the crown base. Look at the photograph.
2. Place the paper bowl in front and attach to the crown with papier-mache' strips. Let dry overnight. Paint the crown gold, the sun red, and the trim around the sun and tall forms blue. Adjust the size to fit the wearer's head.

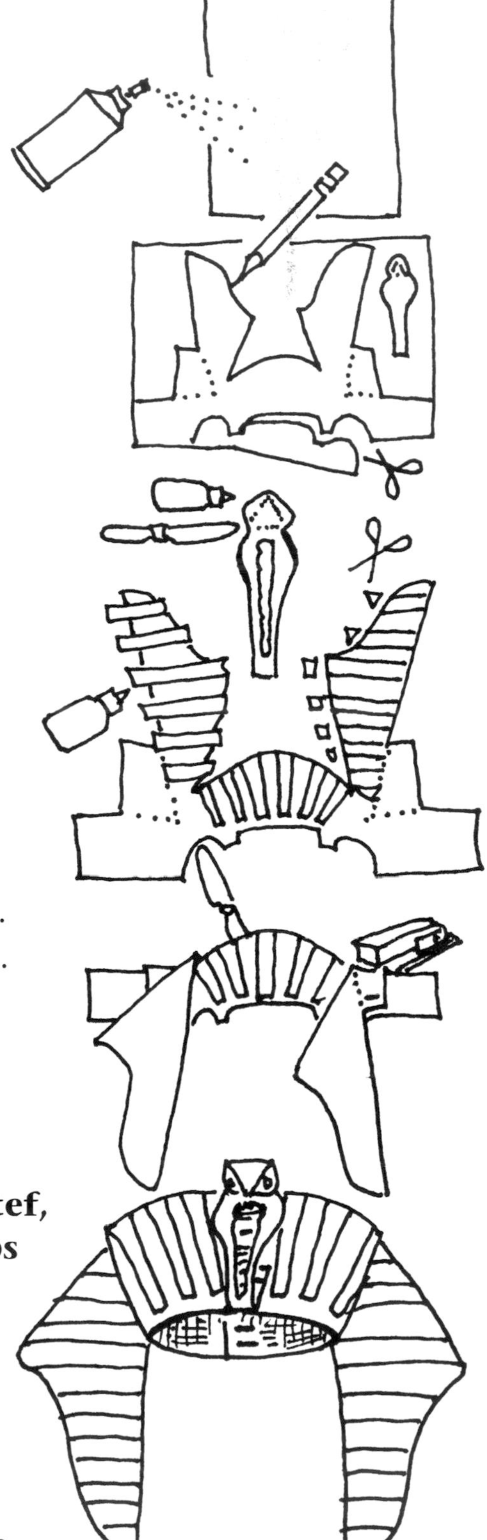

King Tut Headdress: ***Materials are half of a piece of gold railroad board 14" x 22". If gold cardboard is not available, spray paint white with gold paint, blue construction paper, glue, stapler, scissors. Patterns on pages 80 and 84.***

1. Enlarge serpent and headdress patterns to twice the size. Trace both sides onto posterboard. Cut them out.
2. With a scissor point, score along dotted lines of headdress and serpent.
3. Glue blue paper to serpent's head and belly. Draw eyes. Fold head on dotted lines.
4. Cut 1" blue paper strips for stripes for sides and top of headdress. Glue in place, trimming excess along the edges.
5. Fold sides down. Staple flaps. Adjust headband to size. Staple.
6. Curl serpent gently around pencil. Staple bottom end to crown. Arch serpent upward and staple or glue to center of the headdress.

Egyptian kings and queens wore a range of royal headdresses. By wearing one of these crowns the King was transformed into a god.

The White Crown: **Osiris is often depicted wearing the Atef, the white crown with serpents and feathers. Many tombs show dead pharaohs wearing it as they have "joined with Osiris" in the next world.**

The Blue Crown: **This headwear was like a helmet covered in gold studs or discs. It is sometimes called the "War Crown" as it was worn in and out of battle. Queens are painted wearing a similar blue helmet crown.**

The Sun Crown: **This crown was worn by Akhenaton, the Pharaoh that worshipped one god: Aten, the sun. His queen Nefertiti's famous sculpted head is shown on page 36 wearing a crown unique to her.**

Musical Instruments - *(continued from page 45)*

Harp: ***Materials are cardboard 15" x 12" for top piece, two more cardboard pieces for strengthening that are the same size cut as crescents, 6 brass brads, gold, red, green, white, blue, yellow, and orange paint and brushes, 80" of monofilament or 4" rubber bands, paring knife or exacto blade and strong scissors. Pattern on page 82.***

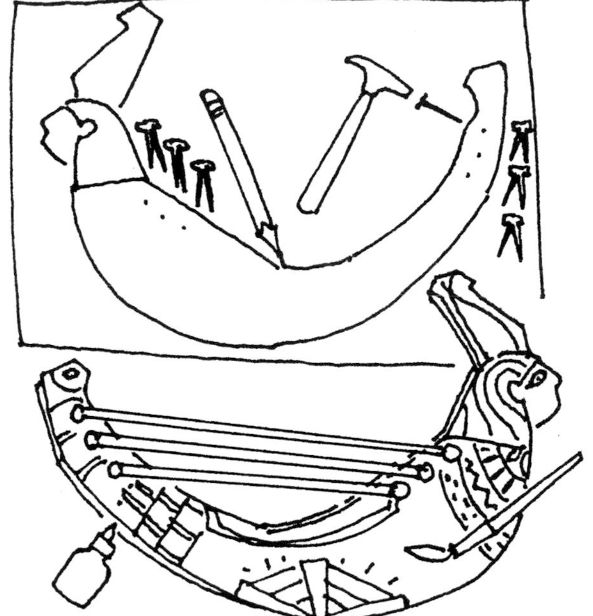

1. Using the enlarged pattern, trace it on the cardboard. Puncture the outline with a knife on a soft surface such as a carpet. Laying the top pattern on the cardboard, cut out at least one under-crescent shape and two if you need more strength. The top harp can be painted at any time.
2. Glue the cardboard layers together and let dry with a heavy object on top.
3. Hammer six holes marked on the pattern. Place the brads in each hole. Notch rubber bands around each brad. Is the harp strong enough for the tension? Use monofilament if the harp buckles with the rubber bands because of too much tension.

Clapping rhythms were important sounds for dance and song. Flutes, harps, and lutes provided music. Both men and women played instruments. The sistrum rattle was used in temple ceremonies, especially honoring Hathor, goddess of music.

ARABIC ALPHABET

ش	س	ز	ر	ذ	د	خ	ح	ج	ث	ت	ب	ا
shin	sin	zin	ra	dhal	dal	kha	ha	jim	theh	teh	beh	alif

ي	و	ه	ن	م	ل	ك	ق	ف	غ	ع	ظ	ط	ض	ص
yeh	waw	heh	nun	mim	lam	kaf	qaf	feh	ghain	ain	DHa	Ta	Dad	sad

ARABIC NUMERALS

٩	٨	٧	٦	٥	٤	٣	٢	١	٠
9	8	7	6	5	4	3	2	1	0

ENGLISH TO ARABIC

ă	ا	f, v	ف	n	ن	t	ت
ā	ـَـي	h	ح	ŏ	ـَ	u, w	و
b	ب	ĭ	—	ō	ـَو	x	كس
c, k, g	ك	ī	اي	p	ب	z	ز
d	د	j	ج	q	ق	th	ث
ĕ	—	l	ل	r	ر	sh	ش
ē, y	ي	m	م	s	س	ph	ف

SCARAB PATTERNS

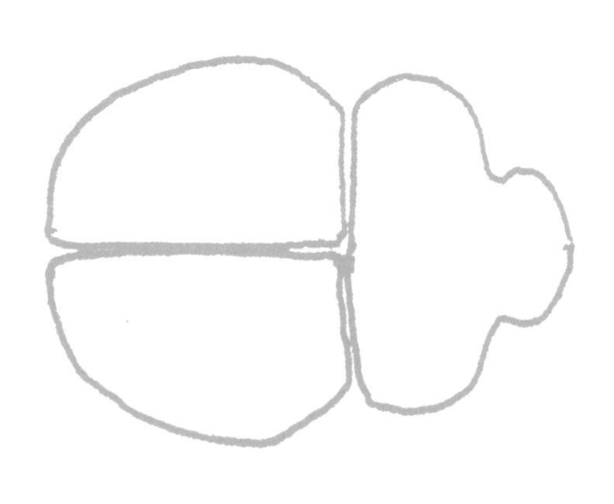

MUMMIES

A mummy is a dead body that has been preserved by drying. Ancient Egyptians developed artificial techniques for preserving their dead in this way. They decided that the dead needed their bodies in the next life. Preserving a body took 70 days. First the body was washed, then the brain was removed through the nose, and then the internal organs were removed, embalmed, and stored in canopic jars. The mummies were wrapped several times. Here are the stages of unwrapping a royal advisor:

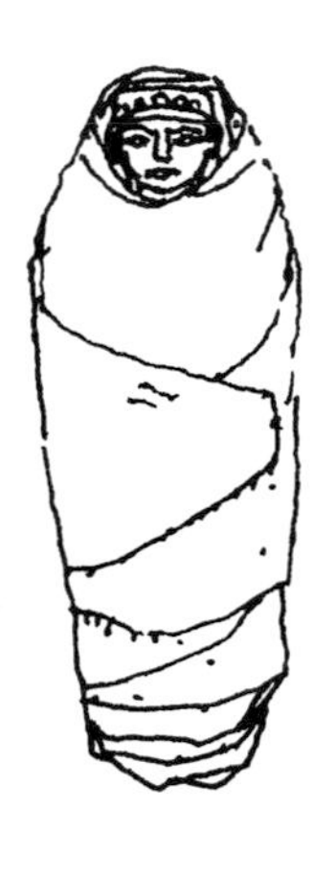
The mummy is wrapped in a shawl.

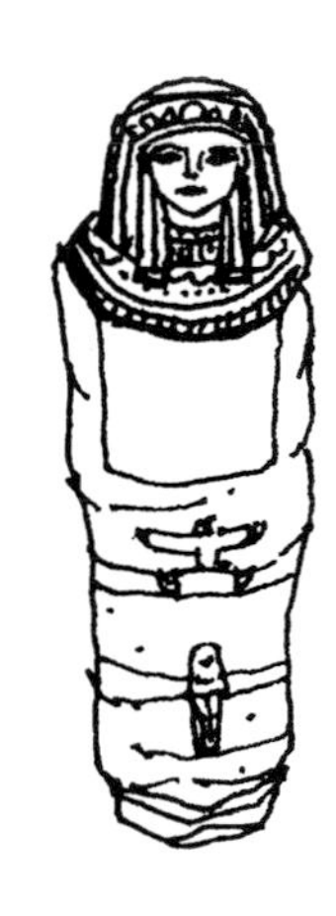
The linen-covered face is covered with a mask and collar.

The linen is covered with a hardened resin.

The removal of more linens exposes rich jewels.

After more bandages are removed the corpse has another fine collar, bracelets, anklets and good-luck charms in the bandages.

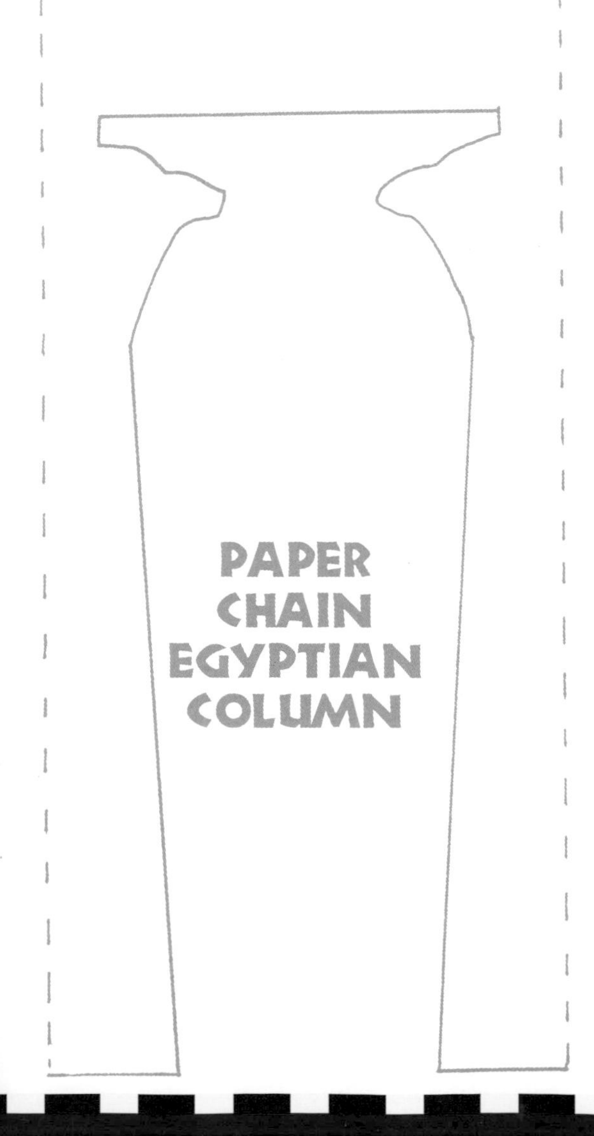

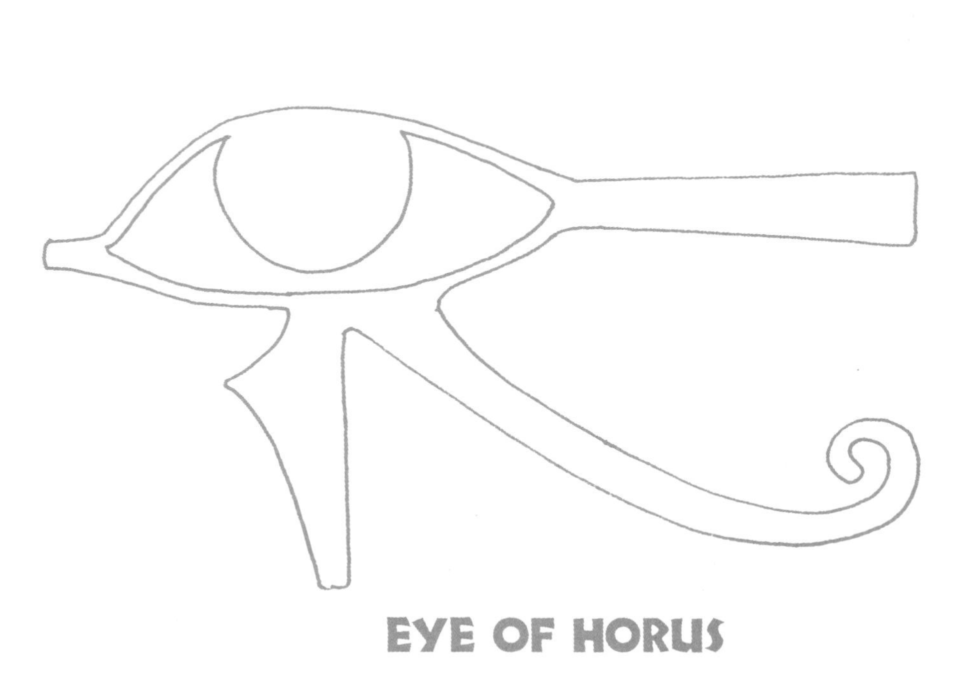

EYE OF HORUS

PAPER CHAIN PATTERNS

PAPER CHAIN PATTERNS

Animals continued from page 41

Animals were important in Egyptian life. Favorite pets were cats, dogs, monkeys, and gazelles. The importance of animals can be seen by the animal heads many of the gods and goddesses wore. When people died in ancient Egypt their bodies were mummified. To help prevent a body from decaying, the internal organs were removed and placed inside special containers known as canopic jars. The four god's heads were always used as stoppers: the ape or baboon's head oversaw the lungs; the man's head oversaw the liver; the hawk's head oversaw the intestines; and the jackal's head oversaw the stomach. Deborah Norse Lattimore has written ***The Winged Cat,*** Harper Collins, NY, 1992.

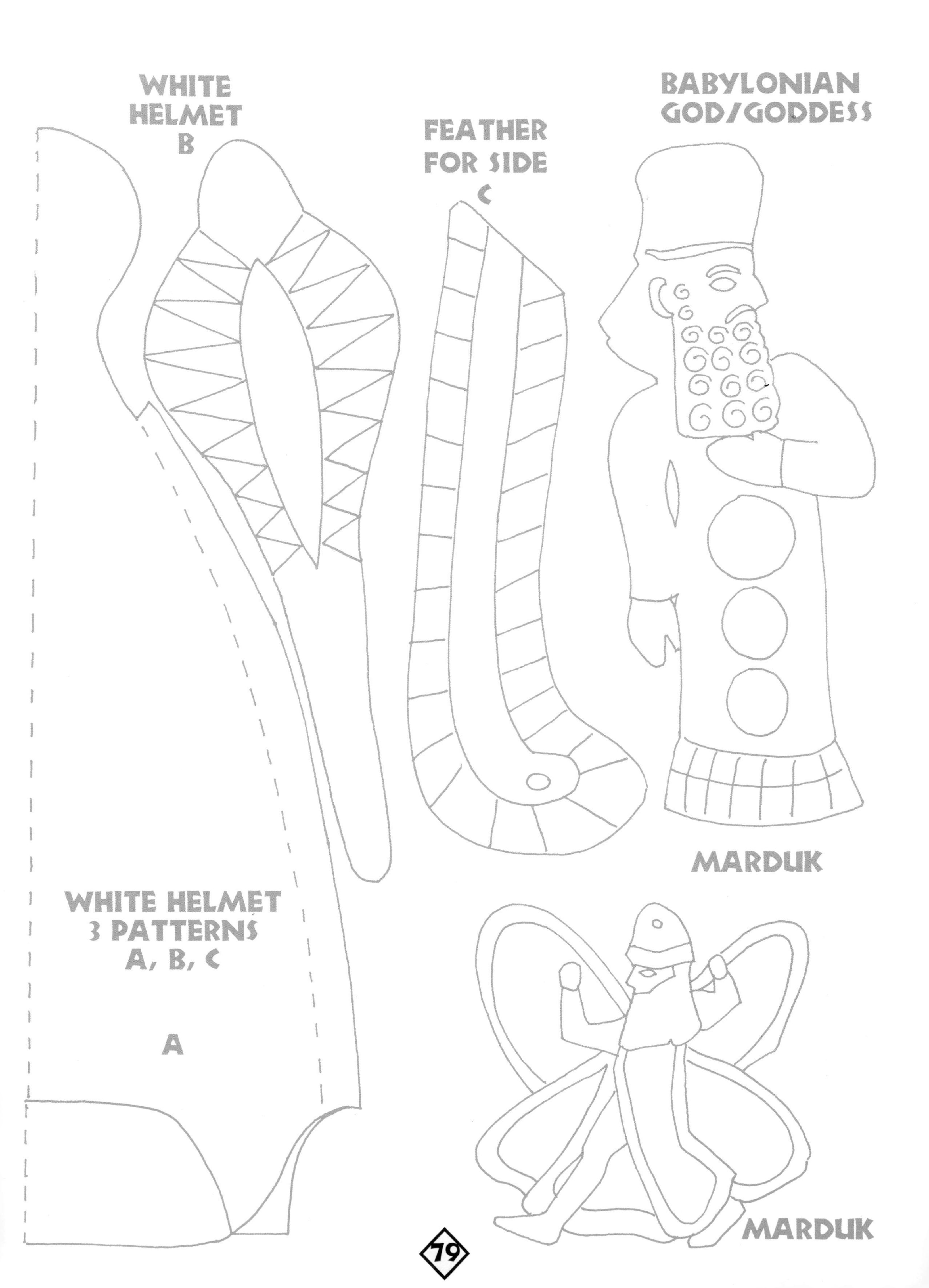
WHITE
HELMET
B
FEATHER
FOR SIDE
C
BABYLONIAN
GOD/GODDESS
MARDUK
WHITE HELMET
3 PATTERNS
A, B, C
A
MARDUK

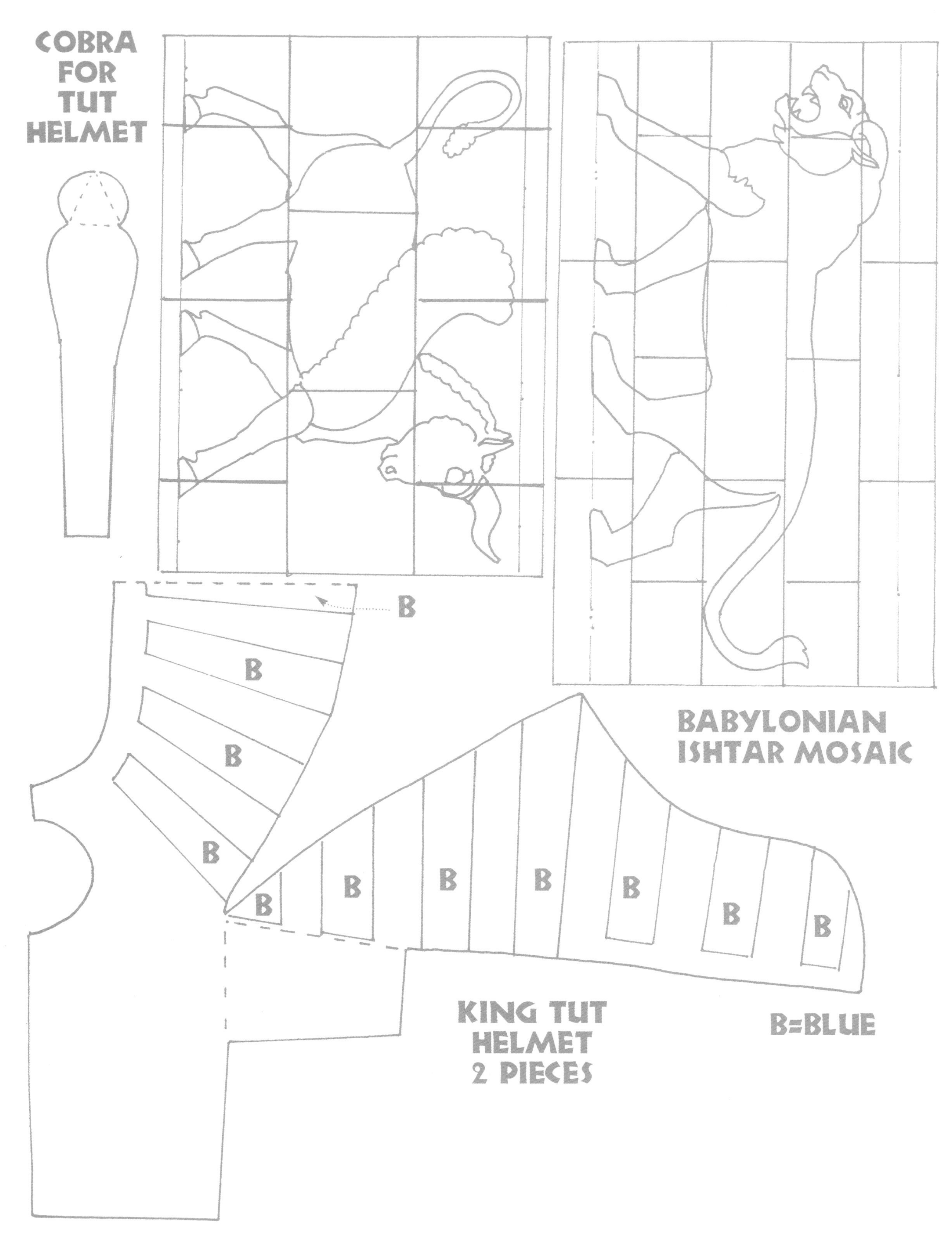
COBRA
FOR
TUT
HELMET
BABYLONIAN
ISHTAR MOSAIC
B
B
B
B
B
B
B
B
B
B
B
B
KING TUT
HELMET
2 PIECES
B=BLUE

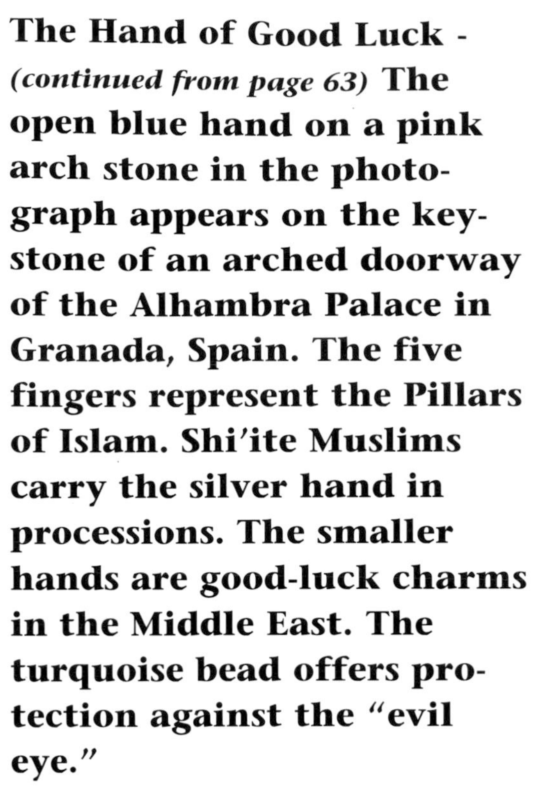

The Hand of Good Luck - *(continued from page 63)* **The open blue hand on a pink arch stone in the photograph appears on the keystone of an arched doorway of the Alhambra Palace in Granada, Spain. The five fingers represent the Pillars of Islam. Shi'ite Muslims carry the silver hand in processions. The smaller hands are good-luck charms in the Middle East. The turquoise bead offers protection against the "evil eye."**

Shelamith Levey Oppenheim and Ed Young have written ***Iblis,*** Harcourt Brace and Co. San Diego, 1994.

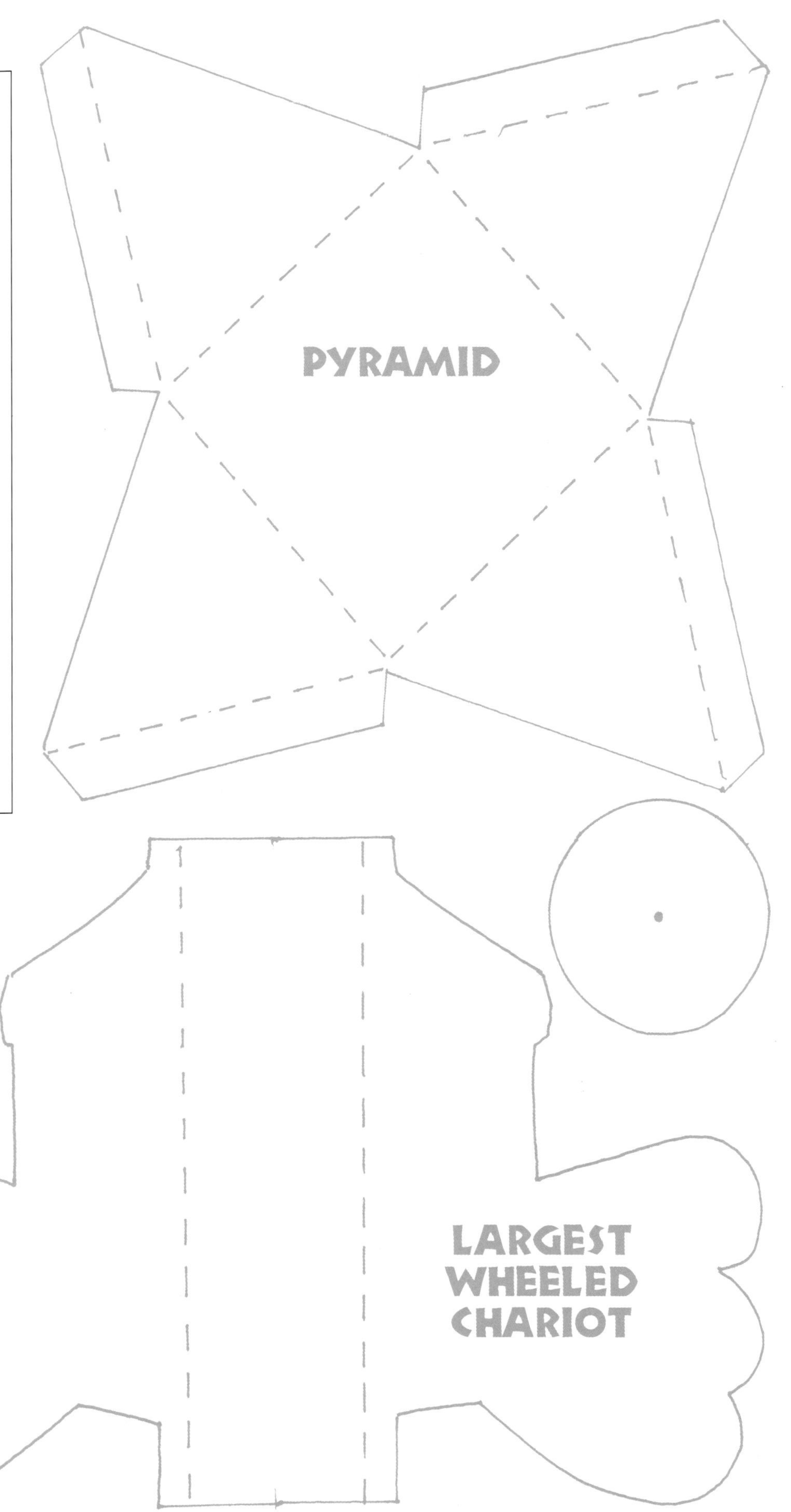

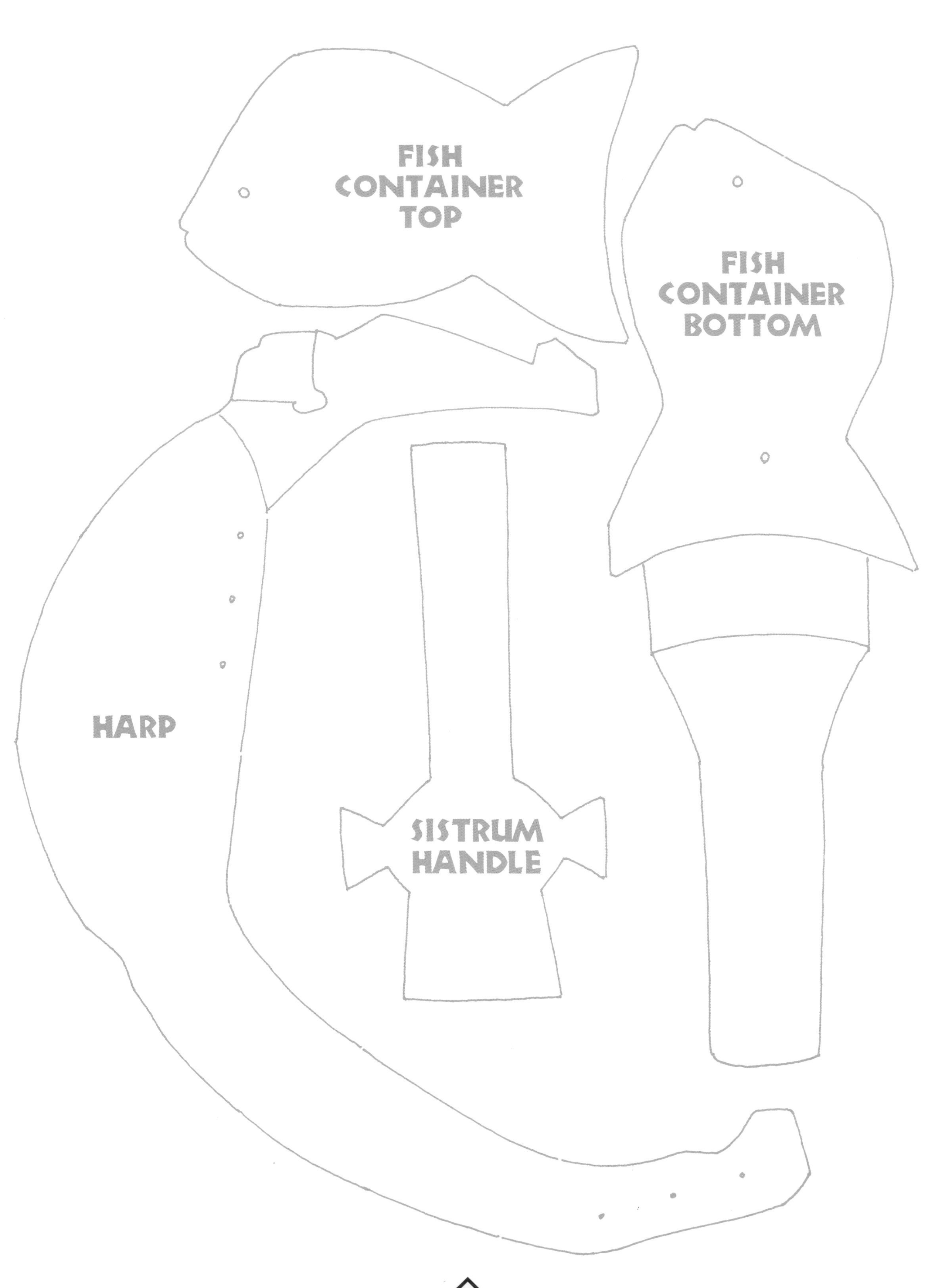
FISH CONTAINER TOP
FISH CONTAINER BOTTOM
HARP
SISTRUM HANDLE

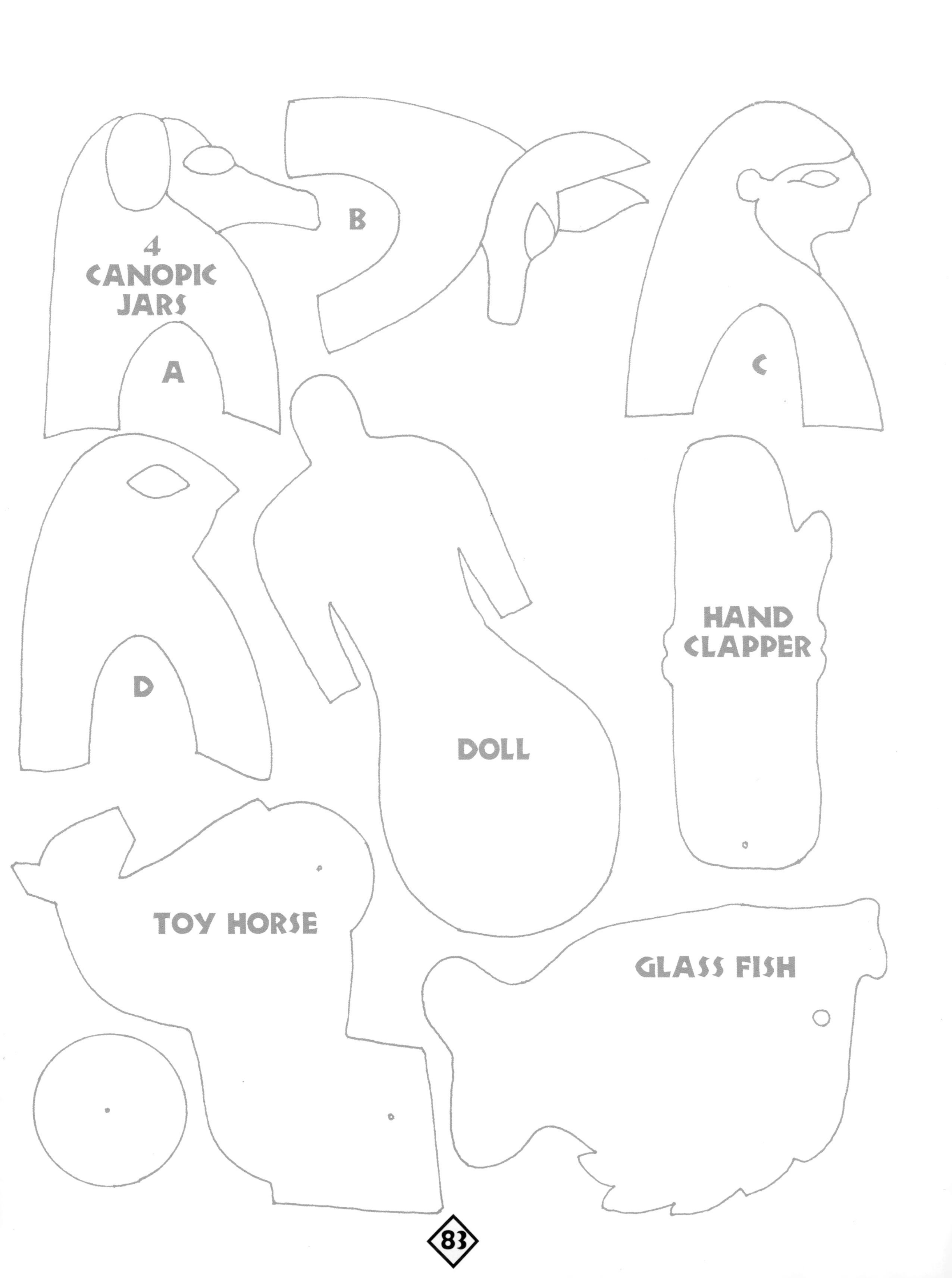
4
CANOPIC
JARS
A
B
C
D
DOLL
HAND
CLAPPER
TOY HORSE
GLASS FISH

C

COBRA
FOR
BLUE
HELMET

B

D

ISHTAR
GODDESS

BLUE HELMET
4 PIECES

A

GRID FOR TESSELLATIONS ON PAGE 59

INDEX

BIBLIOGRAPHY AND ACKNOWLEDGEMENTS

Staff from the University of Utah Center for Middle East Studies reviewed and corrected the Islam section. George Ellington and June Marvel are gratefully acknowledged.

MESOPOTAMIA

Foster, Leila Merrill, ***The Sumerians,*** Franklin Watts, NY, 1990.

Malam, John, ***Mesopotamia and the Fertile Crescent,*** Steck-Vaughn, Austin, Texas, 1999.

Moss, Carol, ***Science in Ancient Mesopotamia,*** Franklin Watts, NY, 1988.

Nardo, Don, ***The Assyrian Empire: World History Series,*** Lucent Books, Inc. San Diego, 1998.

Scarre, Chris, ***Timelines of the Ancient World, A Visual Chronology from the Origins of Life to AD 1500,*** Smithsonian, Doring Kindersley, London, 1993.

Service, Pamela F., ***Ancient Mesopotamia,*** Benchmark Books, Tarrytown, NY ,1999.

Wilson, Bernice, ***Art of the Ancient Mediterranean World,*** International Encyclopedia of Art, Cynthia Parzych Pub., Inc., NY, 1996.

EGYPT

Cavendish, Marshall, ***History of the Ancient and Medieval World, Mesopotamia and Egypt: Volume 2,*** Marshall Cavendish, NY, 1996.

Harris, Geraldine and Delia Pemberton, ***Illustrated Encyclopedia of Ancient Egypt,*** Peter Bedrick Books, Chicago, 1999.

Hart, George, ***Ancient Egypt: Eyewitness Books,*** Knopf, NY, 1990.

ISLAM

Ahsan, M.M., ***Muslim Festivals,*** Rourke Enterprises, Vero Beach, Ca. 1987.

Burckhardt, Titus, ***Art of Islam: Language and Meaning,*** World of Islam Festival Publishing Company Ltd., Westerham, Kent, England, 1976.

Chebel, Malek, ***Symbols of Islam,*** Editions Assouline, Paris, 1997.

Clevenot, Domnique, ***Splendors of Islam: Architecture, Decoration and Design,*** The Vendome Press, NY, 2000.

Husain, Shahrukh, ***What do We Know About Islam?,*** Peter Burdrick Books, NY, 1995.

Morris, Neil, ***Islam: World of Beliefs,*** Peter Burdrick Books, Columbus, OH, 2002.

Nardo, Don, ***The Persian Empire,*** Lucent Books, San Diego, 1998.

Paz, Octavio, ***In Praise of Hands,*** World Crafts Council, McClelland and Stewart Limited and New York Graphic Society, Greenwich, Ct., 1974.

Tames, Richard, ***The Rise of Islam,*** Crystal Lake, IL., 1996.

Hands-on Alaska
(ISBN 0-9643177-3-7)

Hands-on America Vol. I
(ISBN 0-9643177-6-1)

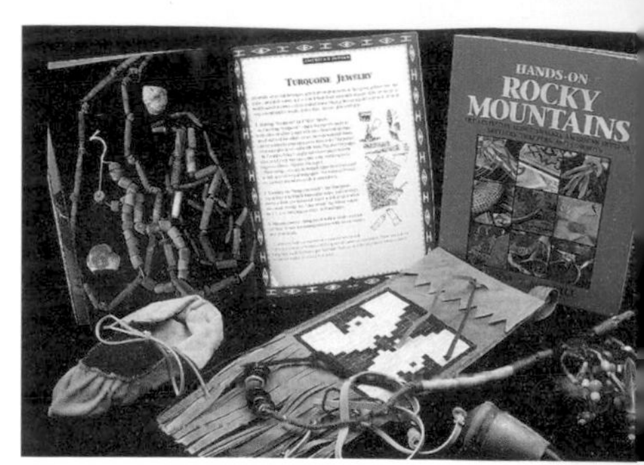

Hands-on Rocky Mountains
(ISBN 0-9643177-2-9)

Hands-on Latin America
(ISBN 0-9643177-1-0)

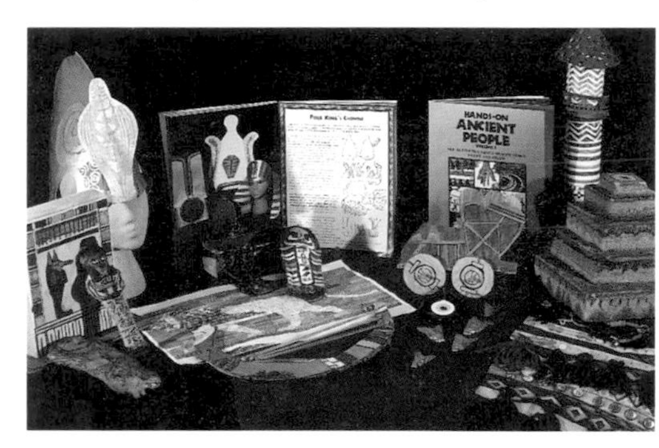

Hands-on Ancient People - Vol. I
(ISBN 0-9643177-8-8)

Hands-on Celebrations
(ISBN 0-9643177-4-5)

Hands-on Pioneers
(ISBN 1-57345-085-5)

Hands-on Africa
(ISBN 0-9643177-7-X)

Hands-on Asia
(ISBN 0-9643177-5-3)

KITS PUBLISHING **Consider these books for:** *the library • teaching social studies art • ESL progra multicultural programs • museum programs • community youth events • home schoolin*

ORDER FORM

SEND TO: ______________________________

ADDRESS: ______________________________

____

CITY: ____________ STATE: ________ ZIP ________

CONTACT NAME: ____________ PHONE: ____________

PO # ____________ FAX ____________

Books are $20.00 each.

Shipping - $2.00 per book

All books shipped media rate unless otherwise requested.

Make checks payable to:

KITS PUBLISHING • 2359 E. Bryan Avenue • Salt Lake City, Utah 84108

1-801-582-2517 fax: (801) 582-2540

e-mail - info@hands-on.com

Kits Publishing Web site: www.hands-on.com

- ❒ ____ Hands-on Africa
- ❒ ____ Hands-on Alaska
- ❒ ____ Hands-on America Vol I
- ❒ ____ Hands-on Ancient People V
- ❒ ____ Hands-on Asia
- ❒ ____ Hands-on Celebrations
- ❒ ____ Hands-on Latin America
- ❒ ____ Hands-on Pioneers
- ❒ ____ Hands-on Rocky Mountains

______ Total Quantity Ordered

3.00 Handling

______ Shipping

______ Total Enclosed/PO

THE BEST-EVER STEP-BY-STEP

EGG COOKBOOK

THE BEST-EVER STEP-BY-STEP
EGG COOKBOOK

OVER 90 RECIPES FOR OMELETTES, PANCAKES, SOUFFLÉS, CUSTARDS, MERINGUES, CAKES, SOUPS, SALADS AND MORE, WITH OVER 350 STEP-BY-STEP PHOTOGRAPHS

ALEX BARKER

This edition is published by Hermes House, an imprint of Anness Publishing Ltd, Hermes House, 88–89 Blackfriars Road, London SE1 8HA; tel. 020 7401 2077; fax 020 7633 9499

www.hermeshouse.com; www.annesspublishing.com

Publisher: Joanna Lorenz
Managing Editor: Linda Fraser
Editor: Susannah Blake
Editorial Reader: Jonathan Marshall
Designer: Nigel Partridge
Photography: Amanda Heywood (recipes) and Steve Moss (reference)
Food for Photography: Joy Skipper (recipes) and Alex Barker and Stephanie England (reference)

ETHICAL TRADING POLICY

PUBLISHER'S NOTE

Although the advice and information in this book are believed to be accurate and true at the time of going to press, neither the authors nor the publisher can accept any legal responsibility or liability for any errors or omissions that may have been made nor for any inaccuracies nor for any loss, harm or injury that comes about from following instructions or advice in this book.
The very young, the elderly, pregnant women and those in ill-health or with a compromised immune system are advised against consuming raw eggs or dishes and drinks containing raw eggs.

NOTES

Bracketed terms are intended for American readers.
For all recipes, quantities are given in both metric and imperial measures and, where appropriate, in standard cups and spoons.
Follow one set of measures, but not a mixture, because they are not interchangeable.
Standard spoon and cup measures are level. 1 tsp = 5ml, 1 tbsp = 15ml, 1 cup = 250ml/8fl oz.
Australian standard tablespoons are 20ml. Australian readers should use 3 tsp in place of 1 tbsp for measuring small quantities.
American pints are 16fl oz/2 cups. American readers should use 20fl oz/2.5 cups in place of 1 pint when measuring liquids.
Electric oven temperatures in this book are for conventional ovens. When using a fan oven, the temperature will probably need to be reduced by about 10–20°C/20–40°F. Since ovens vary, you should check with your manufacturer's instruction book for guidance.
Medium (US large) eggs are used unless otherwise stated.

Main front cover image shows Baked Custard with Burnt Sugar – for recipe, see page 80.

Previously published as *Take One Egg...*

Contents

Egg Basics

Eggs are one of nature's convenience foods: neatly "packaged" in single portions, readily available, inexpensive and easily digested. They are packed with protein and contain vitamins A, B and D and important minerals such as iron and calcium. They are wonderfully versatile, form the basis of a vast range of savoury and sweet dishes, and make a quick and tasty meal if served on their own or with a simple vegetable accompaniment. Eggs are used in cuisines throughout the world and are popular with both children and adults. Ideal for vegetarians and meat-eaters alike, the egg is every cook's stand-by.

GRADING

Eggs are graded and checked at the packing station. A light is shone through them so the contents can be checked without cracking the shell. Any eggs that have imperfections are removed.

Only grade A (EU) or grade A and AA (US) eggs reach the stores. In the US, eggs are washed and, as this removes their protective bloom, a light mineral oil is usually applied before packing. This is not permitted in the EU.

SIZING

Eggs are sized according to weight. Size does not make any difference when you are cooking eggs individually, for example when frying, poaching or boiling them. However, in baking, the size of egg can be important because the success of many recipes depends on accurate proportions of ingredients.

DATE MARKING

Producers outside EU or US inspection areas are governed by laws in their own country or state. In the EU and US, all boxes of eggs are date marked. The date of packing is used in the US. Each day of the year has a number: 1 refers to eggs packed on 1 January and 365 refers to those packed on 31 December. Boxes may also carry an expiry date after which the eggs cannot be sold. This "best before" date allows for seven days after purchase when the eggs are safe to eat. The laying date and "sell by" or packing date can be stamped on the shells in the EU and US.

Above: Eggs should be stored unwashed and with the pointed end down to reduce evaporation.

CHOOSING AND STORING EGGS

With the existing quality controls, there is little need for thorough checking, but it is worth making sure that the eggs are intact and not cracked. Also check the date stamped on the box or eggs. Try to buy from a store with a fast turnover so that the eggs are fresh. Avoid buying eggs that are already two weeks old.

Egg shells are porous, so eggs are vulnerable to bacteria and can absorb odours, which may affect their flavour. Always store in an egg compartment in the refrigerator at or below 4°C/40°F, where fresh eggs can be kept safely for 3–4 weeks.

Remove eggs from the refrigerator a short while before using them for cooking, especially when making meringues or other whisked dishes, as a better result is often achieved if the eggs are at room temperature.

Left: Although there are a large number of edible bird's eggs, the majority of eggs used in the kitchen are hen's eggs.

SIMPLE COOKING TECHNIQUES

Eggs are delicious when combined with other ingredients, but they are also very good cooked on their own. The basic techniques of egg cooking are easy to master and will help you with more complex methods and mixtures.

SEPARATING EGGS

Many egg dishes, such as soufflés and meringues, require the yolk and white to be separated.

1 To crack the egg, using a single, sharp movement, tap the egg firmly on the side of the bowl as near to the middle of the shell as possible. Alternatively, make an indent in the shell by tapping the egg with the blade of a knife.

2 Use your thumbs to prise the shell halves apart gently, trying to break the shell as little as you possibly can. Turn the shell half containing the yolk upright and let the white from both halves drop into the bowl below.

3 Tilt the shell halves to slip the yolk from one to the other, being careful not to break it. Let the excess white fall into the bowl. Repeat until most of the white has been transferred to the bowl. Slip the yolk into a second bowl and check that there is no white left in the shell.

BOILING EGGS

Eggs are delicious soft-boiled (soft-cooked) and eaten on their own for breakfast or hard-boiled and in used in salads and as a sandwich filling.

1 When cooking chilled eggs, it is best to put them into a pan of cold water.

2 Alternatively, lower the eggs on a spoon into simmering water, taking care not to let them drop on to the base of the pan or they will crack.

3 Heat the water until bubbling gently, then begin timing the cooking, using the table below.

Cooking times

This is a guide to cooking eggs added to hot water. Start timing when the water boils gently. Reduce the time for eggs added to cold water by about 30 seconds.

Cooking time in minutes	*Small	Medium	Large
Soft	3	4	4½–5
Semi-firm (yolks still soft)	4	5–6	6–7
Hard	7	8–10	10–12

*(US medium, large and extra large)

POACHING EGGS

This simple cooking method produces a delicious egg with a wonderful, soft texture. Poached eggs can be enjoyed on their own, in salads or as part of a dish, such as eggs Florentine.

1 Pour about 2.5–4cm/1–1½in water into a frying pan. Add 15ml/1 tbsp vinegar and bring to the boil. Reduce the heat to a gentle simmer. Crack the egg into a cup or small dish so that you can control its position easily when adding it to the pan, then gently tip it into the bubbling water.

2 Cook the egg very gently for 1 minute undisturbed, then gently spoon a little water over the centre to cook the yolk.

3 Use a skimmer, slotted spoon or fish slice (spatula) to lift out the egg.

CODDLING EGGS

This gentle cooking method cooks gives delicate results and cooks eggs evenly. To coddle in the shell, add eggs to the pan as for boiling and bring the water to a gentle boil, then cover and remove the pan from the heat. Leave the eggs to stand for about 5 minutes for a soft egg or 7 minutes for a firmer set.

Using an Egg Coddler

Butter the dish and crack an egg into it. Season, replace the lid and put in a pan of simmering water for 6–10 minutes, depending on the size of the egg. For a very soft egg, turn off the heat and leave to stand for 6–10 minutes.

BAKING EGGS

Delicate, oven-baked eggs are quick and easy to prepare and can be flavoured with a variety of ingredients. Cover the eggs with foil to prevent the yolks from overcooking.

1 Preheat the oven to 180°C/350°F/ Gas 4. Lightly butter some ramekins and crack an egg into each. Top with a knob (pat) of butter and season.

2 Stand the ramekins in a roasting pan, half filled with hot water. Bake for about 15 minutes, or until the whites are set.

FRYING EGGS

Eggs can be shallow fried or deep-fried. Shallow frying with little or no oil is the healthier method, but when deep-fried briefly and well drained, eggs are wonderfully crisp. The fat must be hot enough for the eggs to bubble and cook as soon as they are added to the pan, but not so hot that they break up.

Shallow Frying Eggs

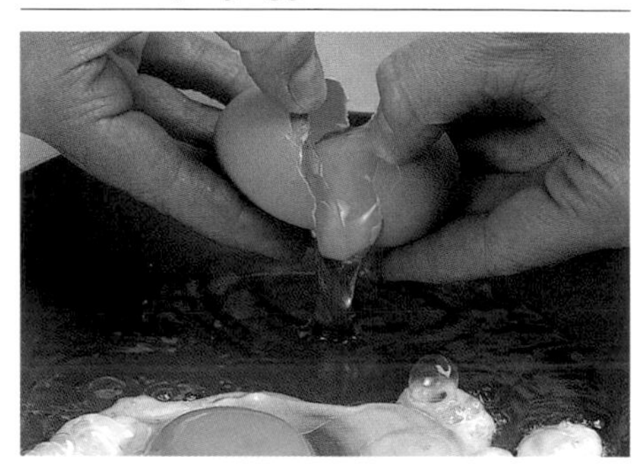

1 Heat 30–45ml/2–3 tbsp oil in a heavy frying pan over a medium heat. Crack the egg into the pan and allow it to settle and start bubbling gently around the edges before basting with hot oil or adding another egg.

2 After 1 minute, spoon a little hot oil over the yolk to cook the egg evenly.

3 Cook for a further 1 minute, until the white has become totally opaque and the edges are just turning brown. For a firmer yolk, cook the egg for a further minute. Lift the egg out of the pan, with a fish slice (spatula), carefully draining off the oil.

4 Alternatively, if you would prefer a firmer, crisper egg still, gently flip the egg over, using a fish slice, and cook for a further minute on the other side.

Deep-frying Eggs

1 Crack the egg into a cup or small bowl so that you can slip it quickly and easily into the pan without splashing yourself with hot oil or breaking up the egg yolk.

2 Heat about 2.5cm/1in vegetable or sunflower oil in a deep frying pan to 180°C/350°F, or until it is hot enough to turn a cube of day-old bread brown in about 45 seconds. Gently tip the egg into the hot oil.

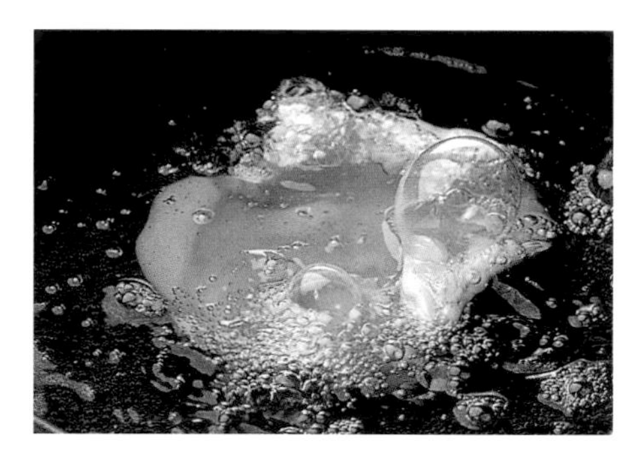

3 Cook the egg for 30 seconds, then use a slotted spoon to turn or fold it over carefully.

4 Cook for a further 30 seconds, or until the egg white is crisp and golden on both sides. Remove with a slotted spoon and drain on kitchen paper.

SCRAMBLING EGGS

Lightly beaten eggs are gently stirred in hot butter until they set. They can be soft and creamy or cooked until firm and dry. Milk or water may be added.

Making Scrambled Eggs

1 Lightly beat 3 eggs per serving and season to taste. Heat 15g/½oz/1 tbsp butter in a small non-stick pan until sizzling. Pour in the eggs and stir.

2 Stir frequently over a medium heat for 1–2 minutes until the eggs are lightly set but still very moist and creamy.

3 For more firmly set scrambled egg, stir less frequently for about 4 minutes.

4 For a chunkier texture, stir the eggs occasionally with a flat-ended wooden spoon or spatula.

OMELETTES

Lightly beaten eggs, seasoned and fried to form a light omelette, provide a meal in about 3 minutes. Any number of seasonings, fillings or toppings can be added to make an omelette more substantial. Thick, set omelettes can be served cold, cut into small portions to make finger food. When the whites are whisked and folded into the yolks, a plain omelette is elevated to soufflé omelette status. With a rich fruit filling, soufflé omelettes make luxurious, yet light desserts.

Although special omelette pans are available, any heavy, medium-size, non-stick frying pan will do. Prepare the flavourings and fillings first. Have a warmed serving plate ready and do not cook the omelette until you are ready to eat it. Traditionally rolled or folded to enclose a filling, an omelette can also be served flat and topped with flavouring ingredients.

Making a Classic Omelette

1 Allow 3 eggs per omelette. In a bowl, lightly beat the eggs with seasonings.

2 Heat 15g/½ oz/1 tbsp butter in an omelette or frying pan until very hot and sizzling, but not smoking or browning. Pour in the eggs, tilting the pan slightly.

3 Cook the eggs for a few seconds until the base has set, then use a fork to push in the sides or stir gently. The idea is to ensure that the unset egg mixture runs on to the hot pan and starts cooking. Cook for about 1 minute, or until the egg is just beginning to set. For a firmer set, cook for a little longer.

4 Use a large flat spatula to fold over a third of the omelette.

5 Tilting the pan away from you, flip the omelette over again and immediately slide it out on to a warmed serving plate in a single smooth action.

COOK'S TIP

In a perfect omelette, the egg in the middle should still be slightly runny or creamy when served, but the omelette can be completely set if you like.

Breakfasts and Brunches

Eggs make a perfect start to the day, providing plenty of energy to keep you going. They first became important breakfast food in the Victorian era and have become a key ingredient, both for breakfasts and lazy weekend brunches, and are used to create enticing dishes that are a far cry from plain boiled eggs or poached eggs on toast. This chapter includes classic breakfast and brunch dishes, such as Poached Eggs Florentine, Chive Scrambled Eggs in Brioches, and Bacon, Egg and Chanterelle Baps, as well as contemporary recipes, such as Stuffed Thai Omelette, and Vegetable Pancakes with Tomato Salsa.

SAVOURY SCRAMBLED EGGS

ALSO KNOWN AS "SCOTCH WOODCOCK", THESE EGGS ARE FLAVOURED WITH A HINT OF ANCHOVY AND WERE POPULAR IN ENGLAND AT THE BEGINNING OF THE 20TH CENTURY. THEY WOULD HAVE BEEN SERVED AS A SAVOURY INSTEAD OF CHEESE AT THE END OF A MEAL, RATHER THAN FOR BREAKFAST.

SERVES TWO

INGREDIENTS

- 2 slices bread
- 40g/1½oz/3 tbsp butter, plus extra for spreading
- anchovy paste, such as Gentleman's Relish, for spreading
- 2 eggs and 2 egg yolks, beaten
- 60–90ml/4–6 tbsp single (light) cream or milk
- salt and ground black pepper
- anchovy fillets, cut into strips, and paprika, to garnish

COOK'S TIP

These creamy scrambled eggs make a great brunch dish. Serve with a glass of crisp white wine and follow with a fresh fruit salad.

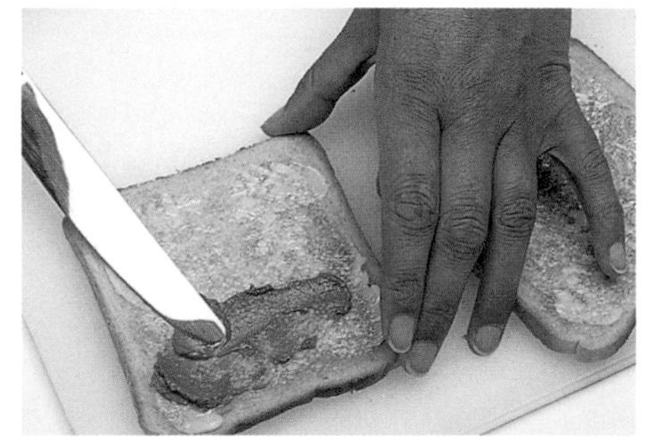

1 Toast the bread, spread with butter and anchovy paste, then remove the crusts and cut into triangles. Keep warm.

2 Melt the rest of the butter in a medium non-stick pan, then stir in the beaten eggs, cream or milk, and a little salt and pepper. Heat very gently, stirring constantly, until the mixture begins to thicken.

3 Remove the pan from the heat and continue to stir until the mixture becomes very creamy, but do not allow it to harden.

4 Divide the scrambled eggs among the triangles of toast and garnish each with strips of anchovy fillet and a generous sprinkling of paprika. Serve the eggs immediately, while still hot.

PIPÉRADE WITH CROSTINI

THIS MIXTURE OF SWEET PEPPERS, TOMATOES AND EGGS HAS ALL THE FLAVOURS OF THE MEDITERRANEAN. IT IS PERFECT FOR A LAZY WEEKEND BRUNCH OR A LIGHT LUNCHTIME SNACK.

SERVES SIX

INGREDIENTS

- 60ml/4 tbsp bacon fat, duck fat or olive oil
- 2 small onions, coarsely chopped
- 4 red, orange or yellow (bell) peppers, seeded and chopped
- 2 large garlic cloves, finely chopped
- pinch of chilli or hot cayenne pepper
- 675g/1½lb ripe plum tomatoes, peeled, seeded and chopped
- 15ml/1 tbsp chopped fresh oregano or 5ml/1 tsp dried
- 1 long French stick
- 60–90ml/4–6 tbsp olive oil
- 25g/1oz/2 tbsp butter
- 6 eggs, beaten
- salt and ground black pepper
- basil leaves, to serve

1 Heat the fat or oil in a large heavy frying pan. Add the onions and cook over a gentle heat, stirring occasionally, for about 5 minutes until softened but not coloured.

2 Add the peppers, garlic and chilli or cayenne. Cook for a further 5 minutes, stirring, then add the plum tomatoes, seasoning and oregano, and cook over a moderate heat for 15–20 minutes until the peppers are soft and most of the liquid has evaporated.

COOK'S TIP

To make a quick party version, cut the bread into thick slices and mix about 200ml/7fl oz/scant 1 cup ready-made sweet (bell) pepper and tomato pasta sauce into the eggs and continue as above.

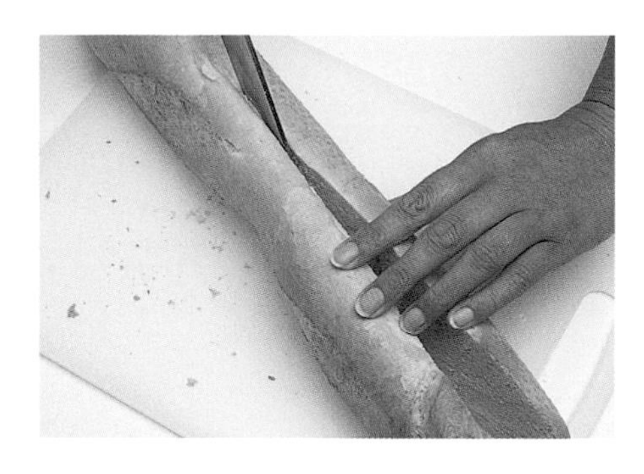

3 Preheat the oven to 200°C/400°F/Gas 6. Cut the bread in half lengthways, trim off the ends, then cut into six equal pieces and brush with olive oil. Place on baking sheets and bake for 8 minutes until crisp and just turning golden.

4 Heat the butter until it bubbles, add the eggs and stir until softly scrambled. Turn off the heat and stir in the pepper mixture. Divide evenly among the pieces of bread and sprinkle with the basil leaves. Serve hot or warm.

SWEET PERSIAN BREAKFAST OMELETTE

THIS VERSION OF A SIMPLE OMELETTE IS POPULAR THROUGHOUT THE MIDDLE EAST AND IS EXCELLENT EATEN WITH A FRUITY HOME-MADE JAM OR CONSERVE.

SERVES ONE

INGREDIENTS
- 3 eggs
- 10ml/2 tsp caster (superfine) sugar
- 5ml/1 tsp plain (all-purpose) flour
- 10g/¼oz/½ tbsp unsalted (sweet) butter
- bread and jam, to serve

COOK'S TIP
Continue the Middle Eastern theme when choosing a jam to serve with this omelette. Pick one made from fruits such as fig or apricot that are popular in the Middle East. Alternatively, you could use raspberry or strawberry jam.

1 Break the eggs into a large bowl, add the sugar and flour and beat until really frothy. Heat the butter in an omelette pan until it begins to bubble, then pour in the egg mixture and cook, without stirring, until it begins to set.

2 Run a wooden spatula around the edge of the omelette, then carefully turn it over and cook the second side for 1–2 minutes until golden. Serve hot or warm with thick slices of fresh bread and fruity jam.

CHIVE SCRAMBLED EGGS IN BRIOCHES

SCRAMBLED EGGS ARE DELICIOUS AT ANY TIME OF DAY BUT, WHEN SERVED WITH FRANCE'S FAVOURITE BREAKFAST BREAD, THEY BECOME THE ULTIMATE BREAKFAST OR BRUNCH TREAT. THESE SCRAMBLED EGGS ARE SOFTER AND CREAMIER THAN OTHER VERSIONS, AND TASTE GOOD SERVED COLD.

SERVES FOUR

INGREDIENTS
- 4 individual brioches
- 6 eggs, beaten
- 30ml/2 tbsp chopped fresh chives, plus extra to serve
- 25g/1oz/2 tbsp butter
- 45ml/3 tbsp cottage cheese
- 60–75ml/4–5 tbsp double (heavy) cream
- salt and ground black pepper

COOK'S TIP
If you do not happen to have brioches to hand, these wonderful herbed eggs taste delicious on top of thick slices of toasted bread. Try them piled high on warm focaccia, or on toasted ciabatta, Granary (whole-wheat) bread or English muffins.

1 Preheat the oven to 180°C/350°F/ Gas 4. Cut the tops off the brioches and set aside. Carefully scoop out the centre of each brioche, leaving a bread shell. Put the brioche cases and lids on a baking sheet and bake for 5–6 minutes until hot and crisp.

COOK'S TIP
Save the scooped-out brioche centres and freeze them in an airtight container. Partly thaw and blend or grate them to make crumbs for coating fish or pieces of chicken before frying.

2 Lightly beat the eggs and season to taste. Add about half the chives. Heat the butter in a medium pan until it begins to foam, then add the eggs and cook, stirring with a wooden spoon until semi-solid.

3 Stir in the cottage cheese, cream and the rest of the chives and continue to cook for 1–2 minutes, making sure that the eggs remain soft and creamy.

4 To serve, spoon the eggs into the crisp brioche shells and sprinkle with the extra chives.

BACON, EGG AND CHANTERELLE BAPS

THE DELICATE CHANTERELLE MUSHROOM WITH ITS SLIGHT FRUITINESS COMBINES BEAUTIFULLY WITH EGGS AND BACON FOR THIS RATHER SOPHISTICATED BREAKFAST BAP.

SERVES FOUR

INGREDIENTS

- 350g/12oz unsmoked bacon rashers (strips)
- 50g/2oz/4 tbsp unsalted (sweet) butter, plus extra for spreading
- 115g/4oz/1½ cups chanterelle mushrooms, trimmed and halved
- 60ml/4 tbsp sunflower oil
- 4 eggs
- 4 large baps, split
- salt and ground black pepper

COOK'S TIP

Other varieties of mushroom can be used instead of chanterelles. Try brown cap mushrooms, chestnut mushrooms or, better still, freshly picked field (portabello) mushrooms.

1 Place the bacon in a large non-stick frying pan and fry in its own fat until crisp. Transfer to a heatproof plate, cover and keep warm in a low oven.

2 Melt 25g/1oz/2 tbsp of the butter in the pan, add the chanterelles and fry over a gentle heat until soft, without letting them colour. Transfer to a plate, cover and keep warm.

3 Melt the remaining butter, add the oil and heat to a moderate temperature. Break the eggs into the pan, two at a time, if necessary. Fry them, turning to cook both sides if you like.

4 Toast the baps, spread with butter, then top each with bacon, chanterelles and a fried egg. Season, add the bap lids and serve immediately.

POACHED EGGS FLORENTINE

FLORENTINE DISHES, WHICH ARE COOKED IN "THE STYLE OF FLORENCE", ALWAYS CONTAIN SPINACH AND MAY ALSO BE TOPPED WITH A CREAMY SAUCE.

SERVES FOUR

INGREDIENTS
- 675g/1½lb spinach, washed and drained
- 25g/1oz/2 tbsp butter
- 60ml/4 tbsp double (heavy) cream
- pinch of freshly grated nutmeg

For the topping
- 25g/1oz/2 tbsp butter
- 25g/1oz/¼ cup plain (all-purpose) flour
- 300ml/½ pint/1¼ cups hot milk
- pinch of ground mace
- 115g/4oz/1 cup grated Gruyère cheese
- 4 eggs
- 15ml/1 tbsp freshly grated Parmesan cheese
- salt and ground black pepper

COOK'S TIP

This dish can be prepared with any other green vegetable that is in season, such as chard, fennel or Chinese cabbage.

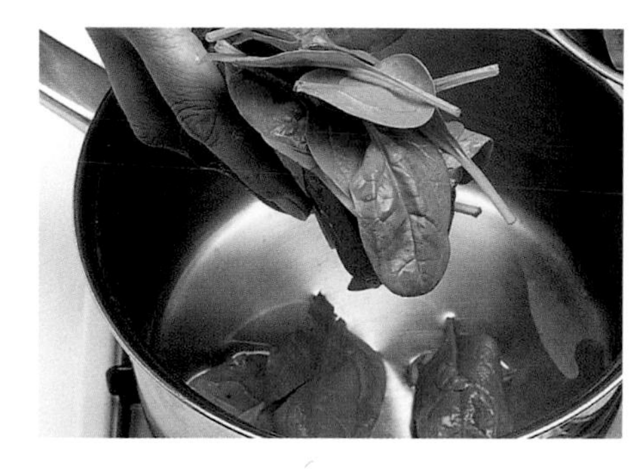

1 Preheat the oven to 200°C/400°F/ Gas 6. Place the spinach in a large pan with a little water. Cook for 3–4 minutes, then drain well and chop finely. Return to the pan, add the butter, cream, nutmeg and seasoning and heat through. Spoon into four small gratin dishes, making a well in the middle of each.

2 To make the topping, heat the butter in a small pan, add the flour and cook for 1 minute, stirring. Gradually blend in the hot milk, beating well.

3 Cook for 2 minutes, stirring. Remove from the heat and stir in the mace and 75g/3oz/¾ cup of the Gruyère cheese.

4 Break each egg into a cup and slide it into a pan of lightly salted simmering water. Poach for 3–4 minutes. Lift out the eggs using a slotted spoon and drain on kitchen paper. Place a poached egg in the middle of each dish and cover with the cheese sauce. Sprinkle with the remaining cheeses and bake for 10 minutes or until just golden.

Omelette Arnold Bennett

Created for the author, Arnold Bennett, who frequently dined at the Savoy Hotel in London, this creamy, smoked haddock soufflé omelette is now served all over the world.

SERVES TWO

INGREDIENTS

- 175g/6oz smoked haddock fillet, poached and drained
- 50g/2oz/4 tbsp butter, diced
- 175ml/6fl oz/¾ cup whipping or double (heavy) cream
- 4 eggs, separated
- 40g/1½oz/⅓ cup grated mature (sharp) Cheddar cheese
- ground black pepper
- watercress, to garnish

COOK'S TIP

Try to buy smoked haddock that does not contain artificial colouring for this recipe. Besides being better for you, it gives the omelette a lighter, more attractive colour.

1 Remove the skin and any bones from the haddock fillet and discard. Carefully flake the flesh using a fork.

2 Melt half the butter with 60ml/4 tbsp of the cream in a fairly small non-stick pan over a low heat, then add the flaked fish and stir together gently. Cover the pan with a lid, remove from the heat and set aside to cool.

3 Mix the egg yolks with 15ml/1 tbsp of the cream. Season with pepper, then stir into the fish. Mix the cheese and the remaining cream in another bowl. Stiffly whisk the egg whites, then fold into the fish mixture. Heat the remaining butter in an omelette pan, add the fish mixture and cook until browned underneath. Pour the cheese mixture over and grill (broil) until bubbling. Garnish and serve.

Stuffed Thai Omelettes

Thai food often cleverly combines hot chilli with sweet flavours, as in the filling for the omelettes. It makes an interesting contrast to the delicate flavour of the egg.

SERVES FOUR

INGREDIENTS

- 5–6 eggs
- 15ml/1 tbsp Thai fish sauce
- 30ml/2 tbsp vegetable oil
- sprigs of coriander (cilantro) and red chillies, sliced, to garnish

For the filling

- 30ml/2 tbsp vegetable oil
- 2 garlic cloves, finely chopped
- 1 small onion, finely chopped
- 225g/8oz/2 cups minced (ground) pork
- 30ml/2 tbsp Thai fish sauce
- 5ml/1 tsp granulated sugar
- 2 tomatoes, peeled and chopped
- 15ml/1 tbsp chopped fresh coriander (cilantro)
- ground black pepper

1 Heat the oil in a wok, add the garlic and onion and fry for 3–4 minutes until soft. Add the pork and fry for about 8 minutes until lightly browned.

2 Stir in the fish sauce, sugar, tomatoes and pepper; simmer until slightly thickened. Mix in the fresh coriander.

3 To make the omelettes, whisk together the eggs and fish sauce.

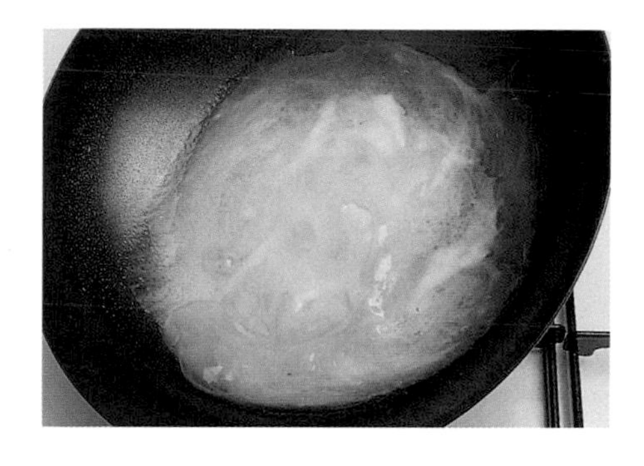

4 Heat 15ml/1 tbsp of the oil in an omelette pan or wok. Add half the beaten egg mixture and tilt the pan to spread the egg into a thin, even sheet.

5 Cook until the omelette is just set, then spoon half the filling into the centre. Fold into a neat square parcel by bringing the opposite sides of the omelette towards each other – first the top and bottom, then the right and left sides.

6 Slide the parcel on to a warm serving dish, folded side down. Repeat with the rest of the oil, eggs and filling to make a second omelette parcel. Garnish with sprigs of coriander and red chillies. Cut each omelette in half to serve.

COOK'S TIP

For a milder flavour, discard the seeds and membrane of the chillies where most of their heat resides. Always remember to wash your hands immediately after handling chillies.

Omelettes Foo Yung

These unusual breakfast omelettes are served with a traditional Chinese filling.

SERVES FOUR

INGREDIENTS
- 15ml/1 tbsp groundnut (peanut) oil
- 40g/1½oz/3 tbsp spring onions (scallions), chopped
- 2 celery sticks
- 10ml/2 tsp chopped fresh root ginger
- 1 garlic clove, crushed
- 40g/1½oz/¼ cup diced cooked ham
- 75g/3oz/½ cup crab meat
- 75g/3oz/½ cup peeled cooked small prawns (shrimp)
- 25ml/1½ tbsp chopped fresh coriander (cilantro)
- 15–30ml/1–2 tbsp soy sauce, plus extra for serving
- 8–12 eggs, beaten
- 80g/3oz/6 tbsp butter
- salt and ground black pepper
- sprigs of coriander (cilantro), to garnish

1 Heat the oil in a large frying pan over a medium heat. Add the spring onions, celery, ginger and garlic and cook for about 1 minute, stirring frequently.

2 Add the ham, crab meat, prawns, fresh coriander and soy sauce. Reduce the heat and leave the mixture to heat through gently, stirring occasionally.

3 To make the omelettes, heat 20g/¾oz/1½ tbsp butter in a pan. Season the eggs, add a quarter of the mixture to the pan and cook until it begins to set. Turn over and cook for 2 minutes. Tip on to a serving plate and keep warm. Cook another three omelettes in the same way. Divide the filling among the omelettes and roll up. Serve hot with soy sauce and garnish with coriander.

Egg Rice Cakes with Mushrooms

The creamy taste and texture of these rice cakes is set off beautifully by the earthy flavour of the wild mushrooms.

SERVES FOUR

INGREDIENTS
- 1 egg
- 15ml/1 tbsp plain (all-purpose) flour
- 60ml/4 tbsp freshly grated Parmesan, Fontina or Pecorino cheese
- 450g/1lb/2 cups cooked long grain rice
- 50g/2oz/4 tbsp unsalted (sweet) butter
- 30–45ml/2–3 tbsp olive oil
- 1 shallot or small onion, chopped
- 175g/6oz/1¾ cups assorted wild and cultivated mushrooms, such as ceps, chanterelles, horn of plenty, blewits, field (portabello) and oyster mushrooms, trimmed and sliced
- sprig of thyme, plus extra to garnish
- 30ml/2 tbsp sherry
- 150ml/¼ pint/⅔ cup sour cream or crème fraîche
- salt and ground black pepper
- paprika, for dusting (optional)

1 Beat the egg, flour and cheese together with a fork, then stir in the cooked rice. Mix well and set aside.

2 Melt half the butter and oil in a frying pan and sauté the shallot or onion until soft but not brown. Add the mushrooms and thyme and cook until the mushroom juices run. Stir in the sherry. Increase the heat to reduce the juices and concentrate the flavour. Season to taste. Remove from the heat and keep warm.

3 Heat the remaining butter and oil in a large frying pan and fry spoonfuls of the rice mixture in batches. Cook for about 1 minute, then turn over with a spatula and cook for a further 1 minute.

4 When all the rice cakes are cooked, arrange them on one large or four individual warmed plates, with the mushrooms and a spoonful of sour cream or crème fraîche. Garnish with thyme. Dust with paprika if you like.

SOFT TACOS WITH SPICED OMELETTE

SERVED HOT, WARM OR COLD, THESE TACOS MAKE EASY FOOD ON THE MOVE FOR YOUNGER MEMBERS OF THE FAMILY, WHEN THEY NEED SOMETHING NOURISHING TO TAKE ON A PICNIC, HIKE OR BIKE RIDE.

SERVES FOUR

INGREDIENTS
- 30ml/2 tbsp sunflower oil
- 50g/2oz beansprouts
- 50g/2oz carrots, cut into thin sticks
- 25g/1oz Chinese cabbage, chopped
- 15ml/1 tbsp light soy sauce
- 4 eggs
- 1 small spring onion (scallion), thinly sliced
- 5ml/1 tsp Cajun seasoning
- 25g/1oz/2 tbsp butter
- 4 soft flour tortillas, warmed in the oven or microwave
- salt and ground black pepper

COOK'S TIP
You can buy fresh soft tortillas in large supermarkets. They freeze well, so keep a packet or two in the freezer.

1 Heat the oil in a small frying pan and stir-fry the beansprouts, carrot sticks and chopped cabbage until they begin to soften. Add the soy sauce, stir to combine and set aside.

2 Place the eggs, sliced spring onion, Cajun seasoning, salt and ground black pepper in a bowl and beat together. Melt the butter in a small pan until it sizzles. Add the beaten eggs and cook over a gentle heat, stirring constantly, until almost firm.

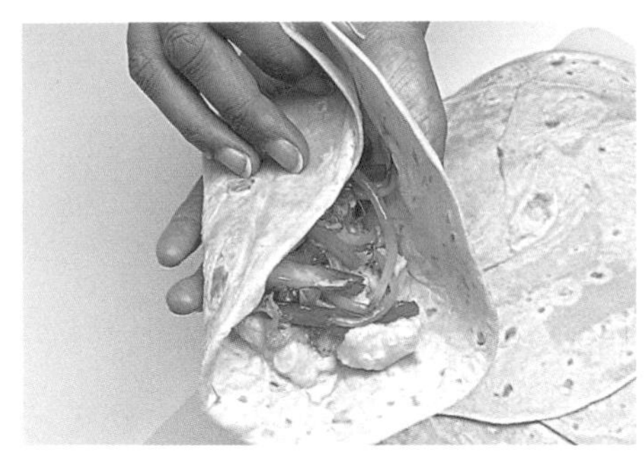

3 Divide the vegetables and scrambled egg evenly among the tortillas, fold up into cones or parcels and serve. For travelling, the tacos can be wrapped in kitchen paper and foil.

VARIATION
Fill warm pitta breads with this spicy omelette mixture. Mini pitta breads are perfect for younger children who may find the folded tacos difficult to handle.

FRENCH COUNTRY-STYLE EGGS

THIS VARIATION ON AN OMELETTE COOKS THE "FILLING" IN THE OMELETTE MIXTURE ITSELF. YOU CAN INCORPORATE LOTS OF DIFFERENT INGREDIENTS, SUCH AS LEFTOVER VEGETABLES.

SERVES TWO

INGREDIENTS
- 45–75ml/3–5 tbsp sunflower oil
- 50g/2oz thick bacon rashers (strips) or pieces, rinds removed and chopped
- 2 thick slices of bread, cut into small cubes
- 1 small onion, chopped
- 1–2 celery sticks, thinly sliced
- 115g/4oz cooked potato, diced
- 5 eggs, beaten
- 2 garlic cloves, crushed
- handful of young spinach or sorrel leaves, stalks removed, torn into pieces
- few sprigs of parsley, chopped
- salt and ground black pepper

1 Heat the oil in a large heavy frying pan, and fry the bacon and bread cubes until they are crisp and turning golden. Add the chopped onion, celery and diced potato and continue cooking gently, stirring frequently until all the vegetables are soft and beginning to turn golden brown.

2 Beat the eggs with the garlic and seasoning and pour over the vegetables. When the underside is beginning to set, add the spinach or sorrel. Cook until they have wilted and the omelette is only just soft in the middle. Fold the omelette in half and slide it out of the pan. Serve topped with the parsley.

SPANISH OMELETTE

ALMOST REGARDED AS THE NATIONAL DISH OF SPAIN, THE TRADITIONAL SPANISH OMELETTE CONSISTS SIMPLY OF POTATOES, ONIONS AND EGGS. THIS ONE HAS OTHER VEGETABLES AND WHITE BEANS, TOO, A VARIATION FROM NORTHERN SPAIN, AND MAKES A VERY SUBSTANTIAL VEGETARIAN BRUNCH.

SERVES SIX

INGREDIENTS

- 30ml/2 tbsp olive oil, plus extra for drizzling
- 1 Spanish onion, chopped
- 1 red (bell) pepper, seeded and diced
- 2 celery sticks, chopped
- 225g/8oz potatoes, peeled, diced and cooked
- 400g/14oz can cannellini beans, drained
- 8 eggs
- salt and ground black pepper
- sprigs of oregano, to garnish
- green salad and olives, to serve

1 Heat the olive oil in a 30cm/12in frying pan or paella pan. Add the onion, red pepper and celery, and cook for 3–5 minutes until the vegetables are soft, but not coloured.

2 Add the potatoes and beans and cook for several minutes to heat through.

3 In a small bowl, beat the eggs with a fork, then season well and pour over the ingredients in the pan.

4 Stir the egg mixture with a wooden spatula until it begins to thicken, then allow it to cook over a low heat for about 8 minutes. The omelette should be firm, but still moist in the middle. Cool slightly, then invert on to a serving plate.

5 Cut the omelette into thick wedges. Serve warm or cool with a green salad and olives and a little olive oil. Garnish with oregano.

COOK'S TIP

In Spain, this omelette is often served as a tapas dish or appetizer. It is delicious served cold, cut into bitesize pieces and accompanied with a chilli sauce or mayonnaise for dipping. Other sliced seasonal vegetables, baby artichoke hearts and chickpeas can also be used in this recipe.

VEGETABLE PANCAKES WITH TOMATO SALSA

THESE LITTLE SPINACH AND EGG PANCAKES CAN BE PREPARED IN ADVANCE, TO AVOID TOO MUCH LAST-MINUTE COOKING, AND SERVED AS AN UNUSUAL APPETIZER WITH THE SPICY SALSA.

MAKES TEN TO TWELVE

INGREDIENTS
- 225g/8oz spinach
- 1 small leek
- a few sprigs of fresh parsley
- 3 large (US extra large) eggs
- 50g/2oz/½ cup plain (all-purpose) flour, sifted
- oil, for frying
- 25g/1oz/⅓ cup freshly grated Parmesan cheese
- salt, ground black pepper and grated nutmeg

For the salsa
- 2 tomatoes, peeled and chopped
- ¼ fresh red chilli, finely chopped
- 2 pieces sun-dried tomato in oil, drained and chopped
- 1 small red onion, chopped
- 1 garlic clove, crushed
- 60ml/4 tbsp good olive oil
- 30ml/2 tbsp sherry
- 2.5ml/½ tsp soft light brown sugar

1 Shred or chop the spinach with the leek and parsley until fine but not puréed. Alternatively, chop them in a food processor, but do not over-process. Beat in the eggs and seasoning to taste. Gradually blend in the flour and 30–45ml/2–3 tbsp water and set aside for 20 minutes.

2 To prepare the tomato salsa, mix together all the ingredients in a bowl, then cover and leave for 2–3 hours for the flavours to infuse (steep).

3 To cook, drop small spoonfuls of the batter into a lightly oiled non-stick frying pan and fry until golden underneath. Turn and cook briefly on the other side. Drain on kitchen paper and keep warm. Sprinkle with Parmesan and serve hot with the spicy tomato salsa.

VARIATION

Use watercress, sorrel or chard or a mixture of sorrel and chard in place of the spinach.

Soups and Appetizers

Both the cooking qualities of eggs and their decorative appearance make them the ideal ingredient for tempting soups and appetizers. Eggs can be used to enrich or thicken soups, such as Egg and Cheese Soup, and Avgolemono, and can be used as attractive garnishes in soups, such as Cauliflower Cream Soup and Prawn and Egg-knot Soup. Some cold appetizers, such as Asparagus and Egg Terrine, rely on eggs for setting, and they are ideal for dinner parties because they can be prepared in advance. Delicate and elegant appetizers, such as Quail's Eggs in Aspic with Prosciutto, and Vegetable Tempura, will whet the appetite at the beginning of a meal, while more substantial dishes, such as Twice-baked Soufflés and Leek and Onion Tartlets, will delight guests who have heartier appetites.

CAULIFLOWER CREAM SOUP

THIS DELICATELY FLAVOURED, THICK WINTER SOUP IS ENRICHED AT THE LAST MINUTE WITH CHOPPED EGGS AND CRÈME FRAÎCHE.

SERVES FOUR

INGREDIENTS
- 1 cauliflower, cut into large pieces
- 1 large onion, roughly chopped
- 1 large garlic clove, chopped
- bouquet garni
- 5ml/1 tsp ground coriander
- pinch of mustard powder
- 900ml/1½ pints/3¾ cups vegetable or chicken stock
- 5–10ml/1–2 tsp cornflour (cornstarch)
- 150ml/¼ pint/⅔ cup milk
- 45ml/3 tbsp crème fraîche
- 2 eggs, hard-boiled (hard-cooked) and roughly chopped
- 15ml/1 tbsp chopped fresh coriander (cilantro)
- salt and ground black pepper

VARIATION
Use one or two large heads of broccoli in place of the cauliflower.

1 Place the cauliflower in a large pan with the onion, garlic, bouquet garni, coriander, mustard, salt and pepper and stock. Simmer for 10–15 minutes until the cauliflower is tender. Cool slightly.

2 Remove the garlic and bouquet garni, then blend the cauliflower and onion with some of the cooking liquid in a food processor, or press through a sieve for a really smooth result. Return to the pan along with the rest of the liquid.

3 Blend the cornflour with a little of the milk, then add to the soup with the rest of the milk. Return to the heat and cook until thickened, stirring all the time. Season to taste and, just before serving, turn off the heat and blend in the crème fraîche. Stir in the chopped egg and coriander and serve immediately.

COOK'S TIP
Garlic croûtons would make a delicious accompaniment to this smooth soup.

AVGOLEMONO

THE NAME OF THIS POPULAR GREEK SOUP MEANS "EGG AND LEMON", THE TWO KEY INGREDIENTS. IT IS A LIGHT, NOURISHING SOUP MADE WITH ORZO, A GREEK RICE-SHAPED PASTA, BUT YOU CAN USE ANY VERY SMALL PASTA SHAPE IN ITS PLACE.

SERVES FOUR TO SIX

INGREDIENTS
- 1.75 litres/3 pints/7½ cups chicken stock
- 115g/4oz/½ cup orzo pasta
- 3 eggs
- juice of 1 large lemon
- salt and ground black pepper
- lemon slices, to garnish

COOK'S TIP
To make your own chicken stock, place a chicken carcass in a large pan with 1 onion, 1 carrot, 1 celery stick, 1 garlic clove and a bouquet garni, cover with water and bring to the boil. Simmer for 2 hours, skimming occasionally. Strain the stock and use as required.

1 Pour the stock into a large pan and bring to the boil. Add the pasta and cook for 5 minutes.

COOK'S TIP
Do not allow the soup to boil once the eggs have been added or they will curdle.

2 Beat the eggs until frothy, then add the lemon juice and 15ml/1 tbsp cold water.

3 Stir in a ladleful of the hot chicken stock, then add 1–2 more. Return this mixture to the pan, remove from the heat and stir well. Season and serve immediately, garnished with lemon.

PRAWN AND EGG-KNOT SOUP

OMELETTES AND PANCAKES ARE OFTEN USED TO ADD PROTEIN TO LIGHT ASIAN SOUPS. IN THIS RECIPE, THIN OMELETTES ARE TWISTED INTO LITTLE KNOTS AND ADDED AT THE LAST MINUTE.

SERVES FOUR

INGREDIENTS
- 1 spring onion (scallion), shredded
- 800ml/1⅓ pints/3½ cups well-flavoured stock or instant dashi
- 5ml/1 tsp soy sauce
- dash of sake or dry white wine
- pinch of salt

For the prawn (shrimp) balls
- 200g/7oz/generous 1 cup raw large prawns (shrimp), peeled
- 65g/2½ oz cod fillet, skinned
- 5ml/1 tsp egg white
- 5ml/1 tsp sake or dry white wine, plus a dash extra
- 22.5ml/4½ tsp cornflour (cornstarch) or potato flour
- 2–3 drops soy sauce
- pinch of salt

For the omelette
- 1 egg, beaten
- dash of mirin
- pinch of salt
- oil, for cooking

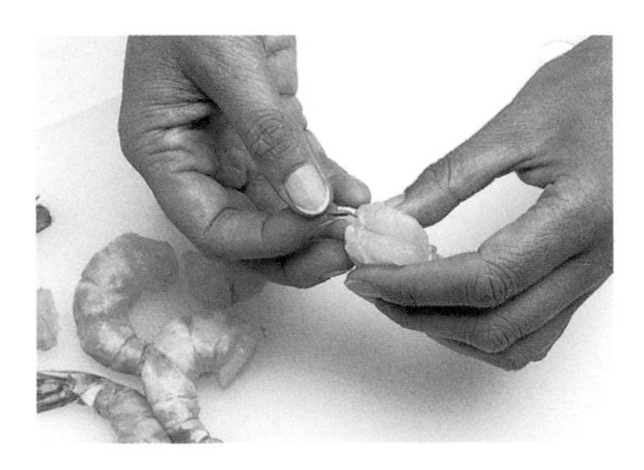

1 To make the prawn balls, use a pin to remove the black vein running down the back of each prawn. Place the prawns, cod, egg white, sake or dry white wine, cornflour or potato flour, soy sauce and a pinch of salt in a food processor or blender and process to a thick, sticky paste. Shape the mixture into four balls, place in a steaming basket and steam over a pan of vigorously boiling water for about 10 minutes.

2 To make the garnish, soak the spring onion in iced water for about 5 minutes, until it curls, then drain.

3 To make the omelette, mix the egg with the mirin and salt. Heat a little oil in a frying pan and pour in the egg mixture, coating the pan evenly. When the omelette has set, turn it over and cook for 30 seconds. Leave to cool.

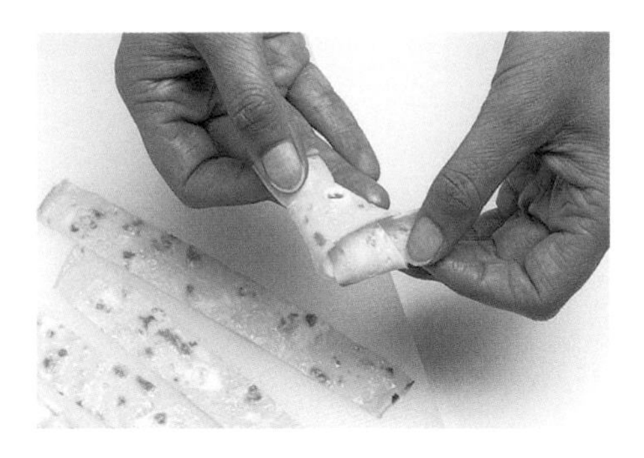

4 Cut the omelette into strips and tie each in a knot. Heat the stock or dashi, then add the soy sauce, sake or wine and salt. Divide the prawn balls and egg-knots among four bowls and add the soup. Garnish with the spring onion.

EGG AND CHEESE SOUP

In this classic Roman soup, eggs and cheese are beaten into hot soup, producing the slightly scrambled texture that is characteristic of this dish.

SERVES SIX

INGREDIENTS
- 3 eggs
- 45ml/3 tbsp fine semolina
- 90ml/6 tbsp freshly grated Parmesan cheese
- pinch of grated nutmeg
- 1.5 litres/2½ pints/6¼ cups cold meat or chicken stock
- salt and ground black pepper
- 12 rounds of country bread or ciabatta, to serve

COOK'S TIP

Once added to the hot soup, the egg will begin to cook and the soup will become less smooth. Try not to overcook the soup at this stage because it may cause the egg to curdle.

1 Beat the eggs in a bowl, then beat in the semolina and the cheese. Add the nutmeg and beat in 250ml/8fl oz/1 cup of the meat or chicken stock. Pour the mixture into a jug (pitcher).

2 Pour the remaining stock into a large pan and bring to a gentle simmer.

3 A few minutes before you are ready to serve the soup, whisk the egg mixture into the hot stock. Raise the heat slightly, and bring it barely to the boil. Season and cook for 3–4 minutes.

4 To serve, toast the rounds of country bread or ciabatta until golden, place two in each soup plate and ladle on the hot soup. Serve immediately.

QUAIL'S EGGS IN ASPIC WITH PROSCIUTTO

THESE PRETTY LITTLE EGGS IN JELLY ARE SO EASY TO MAKE, AND ARE GREAT FOR SUMMER DINING. THEY ARE EXCELLENT SERVED WITH A SALAD AND HOME-MADE MAYONNAISE.

MAKES TWELVE

INGREDIENTS

- 22g/¾oz packet aspic powder
- 45ml/3 tbsp dry sherry
- 12 quail's eggs or other small eggs
- 6 slices of prosciutto
- 12 fresh coriander (cilantro) or flat leaf parsley leaves

COOK'S TIP

Instead of dariole moulds, use small ramekins. When using larger moulds, use proportionally larger eggs as well, such as bantam, pheasant, guinea fowl or very small hen's eggs, so that the finished moulds don't have too much aspic jelly. One packet of aspic should make enough jelly to fill 8–9 small ramekins.

1 To make the aspic jelly, follow the instructions on the packet, but replace 45ml/3 tbsp of the recommended quantity of water with the dry sherry to give a greater depth of flavour. Leave the aspic jelly in the refrigerator until it begins to thicken, but do not let it become too thick or nearly set.

2 Meanwhile, put the quail's eggs in a pan of cold water and bring to the boil. Boil for 1½ minutes, then pour off the hot water and leave in cold water until completely cool. This way the yolks should still be a little soft but the eggs will be firm enough to peel.

3 Rinse 12 dariole moulds but do not dry, then place the moulds on a tray. Cut each slice of ham in half and roll or fold so that they will fit into the moulds.

4 Place a coriander or parsley leaf flat in the base of each mould, then put a peeled egg on top. As the jelly begins to thicken, spoon in enough to nearly cover each egg, holding the egg steady. Put a slice of ham on each egg and pour in the rest of the jelly to fill the moulds.

5 Transfer the tray of moulds to a cool place and leave for 3–4 hours until set and cold. When ready to serve, run a knife around the sides of the jelly to loosen. Dip the moulds into warm water and tap gently until they become loose. Invert the eggs on to small plates and serve with salad.

Asparagus and Egg Terrine

For light summer eating or a special dinner, this terrine is delicious yet very airy. Make the hollandaise sauce well in advance and warm through gently when required.

SERVES EIGHT

INGREDIENTS
- 150ml/¼ pint/⅔ cup milk
- 150ml/¼ pint/⅔ cup double (heavy) cream
- 40g/1½oz/3 tbsp butter
- 40g/1½oz/⅓ cup flour
- 75g/3oz/generous ⅓ cup herb or garlic cream cheese
- 675g/1½lb asparagus spears, cooked
- a little oil
- 2 eggs, separated
- 15ml/1 tbsp chopped fresh chives
- 30ml/2 tbsp chopped fresh dill
- salt and ground black pepper
- sprigs of fresh dill, to garnish
- mixed salad leaves, to serve

For the sauce
- 15ml/1 tbsp white wine vinegar
- 15ml/1 tbsp fresh orange juice
- 4 black peppercorns
- 1 bay leaf
- 2 egg yolks
- 115g/4oz/½ cup butter, melted

1 Put the milk and cream into a small pan and heat to just below boiling point. Melt the butter in a pan, stir in the flour and cook for 1 minute. Gradually whisk in the milk and cream and cook for about 1–2 minutes to make a very thick sauce. Stir in the cream cheese, season and leave to cool.

2 Trim the cooked asparagus spears to fit the width of a 1.3 litre/2¼ pint/5⅔ cup loaf tin (pan) or terrine. Lightly oil the tin and line the base with a piece of greaseproof (waxed) paper. Preheat the oven to 180°C/350°F/Gas 4.

3 Beat the yolks into the sauce mixture. In a separate bowl, whisk the whites until stiff then fold into the sauce mixture with the chives, dill and seasoning. Layer the asparagus and egg mixture in the tin, starting and finishing with asparagus. Cover the top with foil. Place the terrine in a roasting pan half-filled with water and bake for about 50 minutes until just firm to the touch.

4 To make the sauce, put the vinegar, orange juice, peppercorns and bay leaf in a small pan and cook for 2 minutes, or until reduced by at least half. Leave to cool slightly.

5 Whisk the egg yolks into the vinegar and orange mixture using a balloon whisk. Place the pan over a gentle heat and whisk in the butter. Season to taste and keep whisking until glossy and thick. Leave to cool, then reheat over a pan of hot water when ready to serve.

6 When the terrine is just firm to the touch remove from the oven and allow to cool, then chill. To serve, carefully invert the terrine on to a serving dish, remove the greaseproof paper and garnish with sprigs of dill. Serve cut into slices with the warm sauce.

STILTON CROQUETTES

THESE ARE PERFECT LITTLE PARTY BITES, WHICH YOU CAN MAKE IN ADVANCE AND REHEAT AT THE LAST MINUTE. FOR A REALLY CRISP RESULT, DOUBLE COAT THE CROQUETTES IN BREADCRUMBS.

MAKES ABOUT TWENTY

INGREDIENTS

- 350g/12oz floury potatoes, cooked
- 75g/3oz creamy Stilton, crumbled
- 3 eggs, hard-boiled (hard-cooked), peeled and chopped
- few drops of Worcestershire sauce
- a little plain (all-purpose) flour
- 1 egg, beaten
- 45–60ml/3–4 tbsp fine breadcrumbs
- vegetable oil, for deep-frying
- salt and ground black pepper
- dipping sauce, to serve

COOK'S TIP

You can make these croquettes in advance and freeze them before frying. To thaw, leave them to stand in a warm place for 1 hour before frying.

1 Mash the potatoes until quite smooth. Work in the crumbled Stilton cheese, chopped egg and Worcestershire sauce. Add seasoning to taste.

2 Divide the potato and cheese mixture into about 20 pieces and shape into small sausage or cork shapes, no longer than 2.5cm/1in.

3 Coat in flour, then dip into the beaten egg and coat evenly in breadcrumbs. Reshape, if necessary. Chill for about 30 minutes then deep-fry, 7–8 at a time, in hot oil turning frequently until they are golden brown all over. Drain on kitchen paper, transfer to a serving dish and keep warm for up to 30 minutes. Serve with a dipping sauce.

VEGETABLE TEMPURA

TEMPURA ARE JAPANESE SAVOURY FRITTERS. THEY ARE TRADITIONALLY MADE WITH PRAWNS, BUT MONKFISH AND VEGETABLES CAN ALSO BE USED. THE SECRET OF MAKING THE INCREDIBLY LIGHT BATTER IS TO USE REALLY COLD WATER, AND TO HAVE THE OIL FOR FRYING AT THE RIGHT TEMPERATURE.

SERVES FOUR

INGREDIENTS

- 2 courgettes (zucchini)
- ½ aubergine (eggplant)
- 1 large carrot
- ½ small Spanish onion
- 1 egg
- 120ml/4fl oz/½ cup iced water
- 115g/4oz/1 cup plain (all-purpose) flour
- vegetable oil, for deep-frying
- salt and ground black pepper
- sea salt flakes, lemon slices and Japanese soy sauce (shoyu), to serve

1 Using a vegetable peeler, pare strips of peel from the courgettes and aubergine.

2 Using a large, sharp knife, cut the courgettes, aubergine and carrot into strips about 7.5–10cm/3–4in long and 6mm/¼in wide.

3 Put the courgettes, aubergine and carrot strips into a colander and sprinkle liberally with salt. Put a small plate over the vegetables, weight it down and leave for about 30 minutes, then rinse thoroughly under cold running water. Drain thoroughly, then dry the vegetables with kitchen paper.

4 Thinly slice the onion from top to bottom, discarding the plump pieces in the middle. Separate the layers so that there are lots of fine, long strips. Mix all the vegetables together and season with salt and pepper.

5 Make the batter immediately before frying. Mix the egg and iced water in a bowl, then sift in the flour. Mix briefly with a fork or chopsticks. Do not overmix; the batter should remain lumpy. Add the vegetables to the batter and mix to coat.

VARIATION

Other suitable vegetables for tempura include mushrooms and (bell) peppers.

6 Half-fill a wok with oil and heat to 180°C/350°F. Scoop up 1 heaped tablespoon of the mixture at a time and carefully lower it into the oil. Deep-fry in batches for about 3 minutes until golden brown and crisp. Drain on kitchen paper.

7 Serve each portion with salt, slices of lemon and a tiny bowl of Japanese soy sauce for dipping.

STEAMED THAI EGGS WITH PRAWNS

THIS GENTLY COOKED EGG DISH CONTAINS A SURPRISING KICK OF CHILLI, GINGER AND GARLIC. BE SURE YOU HAVE A STEAMER, COLANDER OR SIEVE WITH A TIGHT-FITTING LID OTHERWISE THE EGGS WILL TAKE MUCH LONGER TO COOK.

SERVES FOUR

INGREDIENTS
- a little oil
- 175g/6oz/1 cup peeled prawns (shrimp)
- 5ml/1 tsp grated fresh root ginger
- 5ml/1 tsp fish sauce
- 1 large garlic clove, thinly sliced
- 15–30ml/1–2 tbsp soy sauce
- 2 large spring onions (scallions), thinly sliced
- 4 eggs
- 50ml/2fl oz/¼ cup vegetable stock
- 5ml/1 tsp sesame oil
- 5ml/1 tsp very finely chopped fresh red chilli, plus extra to garnish
- salt and ground black pepper
- shredded Chinese cabbage and thinly sliced cucumber, to serve (optional)

1 Lightly oil four large ramekin dishes. Put the prawns in a large bowl and stir in the ginger, fish sauce, garlic, soy sauce and half the spring onions.

COOK'S TIP
If the steamer does not have a tightly fitting lid, cook for a few more minutes to ensure the eggs are cooked through.

2 Put the eggs into another bowl, whisk in the stock, oil and chilli, without letting the eggs get too frothy. Add the prawn mixture and divide among the ramekins.

3 Place the ramekins in a steamer over a pan of simmering water, cover and cook for 15 minutes until set. Remove from the heat and leave to cool.

EGGS IN RED WINE

THIS IS A VARIATION ON A CLASSIC FRENCH RECIPE OEUFS EN MEURETTE *BUT IS MUCH LIGHTER AND LESS RICH. TRADITIONALLY, THE EGGS ARE POACHED IN THE WINE RATHER THAN WATER.*

SERVES SIX

INGREDIENTS
- 40g/1½oz/3 tbsp butter
- 150g/5oz streaky (fatty) bacon, rinds removed, and roughly chopped
- 1 large onion, chopped
- 2 shallots, chopped
- 1 large garlic clove, chopped
- 750ml/1¼ pints/3 cups red wine
- 1 clove
- 5ml/1 tsp sugar
- 1 bay leaf
- 1 sprig fresh thyme or 5ml/1 tsp dried
- 25g/1oz/¼ cup plain (all-purpose) flour
- 6 slices of French bread
- 15g/½oz/1 tbsp butter, softened or melted
- 6 eggs
- salt and ground black pepper
- sprigs of thyme, to garnish

1 Melt half the butter in a pan and fry the bacon gently for 5 minutes. Then add the onion, shallots and garlic, and cook, stirring, for a further 5 minutes.

2 Add the wine, clove, sugar and herbs and simmer for about 15 minutes to reduce by about one-third.

3 Leave the sauce to cool until you can pick out the bacon to reserve. Remove the bay leaf, thyme and clove, then sieve the sauce or purée in a blender.

4 Melt the rest of the butter in a pan and stir in the flour to make a roux. On a very low heat, gradually whisk in the wine purée and cook for 2–3 minutes until thickened, whisking all the time. Add 30–45ml/2–3 tbsp water to give a lighter consistency and whisk well. Return the bacon to the sauce.

5 Meanwhile, brush the bread on both sides with the soft or melted butter and grill (broil) until golden on both sides.

6 Break the eggs, two at a time, into cups and slide into a pan of gently simmering water. Poach for 3 minutes, then remove and drain well on kitchen paper. To serve, spoon a little sauce on to the toast, top with the eggs and garnish with thyme.

LEEK AND ONION TARTLETS

THESE ATTRACTIVE LITTLE TARTLETS MAKE A WONDERFUL APPETIZER AND ARE PERFECT FOR BUFFETS. SMALLER VERSIONS CAN ALSO BE MADE AND MAKE FABULOUS PARTY FOOD.

SERVES SIX

INGREDIENTS

- 25g/1oz/2 tbsp butter, plus extra for greasing
- 1 onion, thinly sliced
- 2.5ml/½ tsp dried thyme
- 450g/1lb/4 cups leeks, thinly sliced
- 50g/2oz/½ cup grated Gruyère cheese
- 3 eggs
- 300ml/½ pint/1¼ cups single (light) cream
- pinch of freshly grated nutmeg
- salt and ground black pepper
- mixed salad leaves, to serve

For the pastry

- 175g/6oz/1½ cups plain (all-purpose) flour
- 75g/3oz/6 tbsp cold butter
- 1 egg yolk
- 30–45ml/2–3 tbsp cold water
- 2.5ml/½ tsp salt

1 To make the pastry, sift the flour into a large bowl. Rub in the butter with your fingertips until the mixture resembles fine breadcrumbs.

2 Make a well in the flour mixture. Beat together the egg yolk, water and salt. Pour into the well and mix lightly to form a stiff dough. Form into a flattened ball. Wrap and chill for 30 minutes.

3 Butter six 10cm/4in tartlet tins (muffin pans). Roll out the dough on a floured surface to 3mm/⅛in thick. Cut out rounds with a 12.5cm/5in cutter. Ease the rounds into the tins, pressing into the base and sides. Reroll the trimmings and line the remaining tins. Prick the bases and chill for 30 minutes.

4 Preheat the oven to 190°C/375°F/Gas 5. Line the pastry cases with foil and fill with baking beans. Place them on a baking sheet and bake for 6–8 minutes until golden at the edges. Remove the foil and beans, and bake for 2 minutes until the bases appear dry. Transfer to a wire rack to cool. Reduce the oven temperature to 180°C/350°F/Gas 4.

5 In a large frying pan, melt the butter over a medium heat, then add the onion and thyme and cook for 3–5 minutes until the onion is just softened, stirring frequently. Add the leeks and cook for 10–12 minutes until they are soft and tender. Divide the mixture among the pastry cases and sprinkle each with cheese, dividing it evenly.

6 In a medium bowl, beat the eggs, cream, nutmeg and salt and pepper. Place the pastry cases on a baking sheet and pour on the egg mixture. Bake for 15–20 minutes until set and golden. Transfer the tartlets to a wire rack to cool slightly, then remove them from the tins and serve warm or at room temperature with salad leaves.

EGG AND SALMON PUFF PARCELS

THESE ELEGANT PARCELS HIDE A MOUTHWATERING COLLECTION OF FLAVOURS, AND MAKE A DELICIOUS APPETIZER OR LUNCH DISH. SERVE WITH CURRY-FLAVOURED MAYONNAISE OR HOLLANDAISE SAUCE.

SERVES SIX

INGREDIENTS

- 75g/3oz/scant ½ cup long grain rice
- 300ml/½ pint/1¼ cups fish stock
- 350g/12oz tail piece of salmon
- juice of ½ lemon
- 15ml/1 tbsp chopped fresh dill
- 15ml/1 tbsp chopped fresh parsley
- 10ml/2 tsp mild curry powder
- 6 small (US medium) eggs, soft-boiled (soft-cooked) and cooled
- 425g/15oz flaky or puff pastry
- 1 small egg, beaten
- salt and ground black pepper

1 Cook the rice in the fish stock according to the packet instructions, then drain and set aside to cool. Preheat the oven to 220°C/425°F/Gas 7.

2 Place the salmon in a large pan and cover with cold water. Gently heat until almost simmering and cook for about 8 minutes until it flakes easily. Lift the salmon out of the pan with a fish slice (spatula). Remove the bones and skin. Flake the fish into the rice, add the lemon juice, herbs, curry powder and seasoning and mix well. Peel the eggs.

3 Roll out the pastry and cut into six 14–15cm/5½–6in squares. Brush the edges with the beaten egg. Place a spoonful of the rice mixture in the middle of each square, push a boiled egg into the centre and top with a little more of the rice mixture. Pull over the pastry corners to the middle to form a square parcel, pressing the joins together firmly to seal.

4 Brush the parcels with more beaten egg, place on a baking sheet and bake for 20 minutes, then reduce the oven temperature to 190°C/375°F/Gas 5 and cook for a further 10 minutes or until golden and crisp underneath. Cool slightly before serving.

TWICE-BAKED SOUFFLÉS

These little soufflés are served upside down. They are remarkably simple to make and can be prepared up to a day in advance, then reheated in the sauce just before serving. They are perfect for easy, stress-free entertaining.

SERVES SIX

INGREDIENTS

- 20g/¾ oz/1½ tbsp butter
- 30ml/2 tbsp plain (all-purpose) flour
- 150ml/¼ pint/⅔ cup milk
- 1 small bay leaf
- 2 eggs, separated, plus 1 egg white
- 115g/4oz/1 cup grated Gruyère cheese
- 1.5ml/¼ tsp cream of tartar
- 250ml/8fl oz/1 cup double (heavy) cream
- 25g/1oz/¼ cup flaked (sliced) almonds
- salt, ground black pepper and grated nutmeg
- sprigs of parsley, to garnish

1 Preheat the oven to 190°C/375°F/Gas 5. Lightly grease six 175ml/6fl oz/¾ cup ramekins. Line the bases with buttered greaseproof (waxed) paper.

2 In a small pan, melt the butter over a medium heat, stir in the flour and cook for 1 minute, stirring. Whisk in half the milk until smooth, then whisk in the remaining milk. Add the bay leaf and seasoning. Bring to the boil and cook, stirring constantly, for 1 minute.

3 Remove the pan from the heat and discard the bay leaf. Beat the egg yolks, one at a time, into the hot sauce, then stir in the cheese until it is completely melted. Set aside.

4 In a large, clean, grease-free bowl, whisk the egg whites slowly until they become frothy. Add the cream of tartar, then increase the speed and whisk until they form soft peaks that just flop over at the top.

5 Whisk a spoonful of beaten egg whites into the cheese sauce to lighten it. Pour the cheese sauce over the remaining whites. Using a rubber spatula or large metal spoon, gently fold the sauce into the whites, cutting down through the centre to the bottom, then along the side of the bowl and up to the top.

VARIATION

Other strong cheeses could be used in place of the Gruyère. Try mature (sharp) Cheddar, blue Stilton, Emmenthal or farmhouse Lancashire cheese.

6 Spoon the soufflé mixture into the prepared ramekins, filling them about three-quarters full. Put the ramekins in a shallow ovenproof dish and pour in boiling water to come halfway up their sides. Bake for about 18 minutes until puffed and golden brown. Let the soufflés cool in the ramekins just long enough for them to deflate.

7 Increase the oven temperature to 220°C/425°F/Gas 7. Run a knife around the edge of the soufflés and invert on to an ovenproof dish or individual dishes. Remove the lining paper.

8 Lightly season the cream and pour over the soufflés, sprinkle with almonds and bake for 10–15 minutes until well risen and golden. Serve immediately, garnished with sprigs of parsley.

COOK'S TIP

If you are making these soufflés in advance, cool the once-cooked soufflés, then cover and chill. It is important to bring the soufflés back to room temperature before baking, so remove them from the refrigerator in good time.

LUNCHES AND LIGHT SUPPERS

Eggs can be combined with other ingredients to create all sorts of quick and delicious light meals. Poached or boiled eggs or strips of omelette can be added to mixed salad leaves or wholesome grains to make a perfect lunch or supper. Alternatively, eggs can be used to fill pastries, such as Cheese and Onion Flan or Egg and Spinach Pie, or to top pizzas, such as Fiorentina Pizza. They can also be used to make wonderful batter dishes, such as Baked Mediterranean Vegetables and Baked Herb Crêpes, which are delicious for a light but warming supper. All the dishes in this chapter are either quick and easy to make or can be prepared in advance, making them ideal for speedy weekday lunches and suppers.

EGG AND FENNEL TABBOULEH WITH NUTS

TABBOULEH IS A MIDDLE EASTERN SALAD OF STEAMED BULGUR WHEAT, FLAVOURED WITH LOTS OF PARSLEY, MINT, LEMON JUICE AND GARLIC. IT IS PERFECT AT A SUMMER BARBECUE.

SERVES FOUR

INGREDIENTS

- 250g/9oz/1¼ cups bulgur wheat
- 4 small (US medium) eggs
- 1 fennel bulb
- 1 bunch of spring onions (scallions), chopped
- 25g/1oz/½ cup drained sun-dried tomatoes in oil, sliced
- 45ml/3 tbsp chopped fresh parsley
- 30ml/2 tbsp chopped fresh mint
- 75g/3oz/½ cup black olives
- 60ml/4 tbsp olive oil, preferably Greek or Spanish
- 30ml/2 tbsp garlic oil
- 30ml/2 tbsp lemon juice
- 50g/2oz/½ cup chopped hazelnuts, toasted
- 1 open-textured loaf or 4 pitta breads, warmed
- salt and ground black pepper

1 Put the bulgur wheat into a bowl. Pour over boiling water and leave to soak for about 15 minutes.

2 Drain the bulgur wheat in a metal sieve and place the sieve over a pan of boiling water. Cover the pan and sieve with a lid and steam for 10 minutes. Fluff up the grains with a fork and spread them out on a metal tray. Set aside to cool.

3 Hard-boil (hard-cook) the eggs for 8 minutes. Cool under running water, peel and quarter, or, using an egg slicer, slice not quite all the way through.

4 Halve and thinly slice the fennel. Boil in salted water for 6 minutes, drain and cool under running water.

5 Combine the eggs, fennel, spring onions, sun-dried tomatoes, parsley, mint and olives with the bulgur wheat. Dress with olive oil, garlic oil and lemon juice and sprinkle with hazelnuts. Season well and serve with bread.

COOK'S TIP

If you are short of time, simply soak the bulgur wheat in boiling water for about 20 minutes until the grains are tender. Drain and rinse under cold water to cool, then drain thoroughly.

WARM DRESSED SALAD WITH POACHED EGGS

SOFT POACHED EGGS, CHILLI, HOT CROÛTONS AND COOL, CRISP SALAD LEAVES MAKE A LIVELY AND UNUSUAL COMBINATION. THIS DELICIOUS SALAD IS PERFECT FOR A SUMMER LUNCH.

SERVES TWO

INGREDIENTS
- ½ small Granary (whole-wheat) loaf
- 45ml/3 tbsp chilli oil
- 2 eggs
- 115g/4oz mixed salad leaves
- 45ml/3 tbsp extra virgin olive oil
- 2 garlic cloves, crushed
- 15ml/1 tbsp balsamic or sherry vinegar
- 50g/2oz Parmesan cheese, shaved
- ground black pepper (optional)

1 Carefully cut the crust from the Granary loaf and discard. Cut the bread into 2.5cm/1in cubes.

2 Heat the chilli oil in a large frying pan. Add the bread cubes and cook for about 5 minutes, tossing the cubes occasionally, until they are crisp and golden brown all over.

COOK'S TIP
If you are very sensitive to spicy flavours, cook the croûtons in olive oil or a nut oil, such as walnut or hazelnut, rather than using chilli oil.

3 Meanwhile, bring a pan of water to the boil. Break each egg into a jug (pitcher) and carefully slide into the water, one at a time. Gently poach for about 4 minutes until lightly cooked.

4 Divide the salad leaves among two plates. Remove the croûtons from the pan and arrange them over the leaves.

5 Wipe the pan clean with kitchen paper. Then heat the olive oil in the pan, add the garlic and vinegar and cook over high heat for 1 minute. Pour the warm dressing over the salads.

6 Place a poached egg on each salad. Top with thin Parmesan shavings and a little black pepper, if you like.

SALAD WITH OMELETTE STRIPS AND BACON

Rich duck eggs are delicious in salads and, when cooked as an omelette, they have a lovely, delicate flavour.

SERVES FOUR

INGREDIENTS
- 400g/14oz bag of mixed salad leaves
- 6 streaky (fatty) bacon rashers (strips), rinds removed and chopped
- 2 duck eggs
- 2 spring onions (scallions), chopped
- few sprigs of coriander (cilantro), chopped
- 25g/1oz/2 tbsp butter
- 60ml/4 tbsp olive oil
- 30ml/2 tbsp balsamic vinegar
- salt and ground black pepper

COOK'S TIP
Choose salad leaves that include some distinctively flavoured leaves which will add a bite to this salad. A combination that includes rocket (arugula), watercress or herbs would be ideal.

1 Warm an omelette pan over a low heat and gently fry the chopped bacon until the fat runs. Increase the heat to crisp up the bacon, stirring frequently. When the bacon pieces are brown and crispy, remove from the heat and transfer to a hot dish to keep warm.

2 Beat the eggs with the spring onions and coriander and season.

3 Melt the butter in an omelette pan and pour in the beaten eggs. Cook for 2–3 minutes to make an unfolded omelette. Cut into long strips and add to the salad with the bacon.

4 Place the salad leaves in a large bowl. Add the oil, vinegar and seasoning to the omelette pan, heat briefly and pour over the salad. Toss well before serving.

CHILLI SALAD OMELETTES WITH HUMMUS

These delicate omelettes are filled with salad and served chilled, making a refreshing lunch.

SERVES SIX

INGREDIENTS
- 4 eggs
- 15ml/1 tbsp cornflour (cornstarch)
- 15ml/1 tbsp stock or water
- 115g/4oz/1 cup shredded salad vegetables, such as crisp lettuce, carrot, celery, spring onion (scallion) and (bell) peppers
- 60ml/4 tbsp chilli salad dressing (or add a few drops of chilli sauce to your favourite salad dressing)
- 60–75ml/4–5 tbsp hummus
- 4 crisply cooked bacon rashers (strips), chopped
- salt and ground black pepper

VARIATIONS
These omelettes can be filled with a whole range of ingredients. Try using taramasalata instead of hummus, or fill the omelettes with ratatouille.

1 Break the eggs into a bowl. Add the cornflour and stock or water and beat well. Heat a lightly oiled frying pan and pour a quarter of the egg mixture into the pan, tipping it to spread it out to a thin, even layer. Cook the omelette gently to avoid it colouring too much or becoming bubbly and crisp. When cooked, remove from the pan and make a further three omelettes in the same way. Stack them between sheets of baking parchment, then cool and chill.

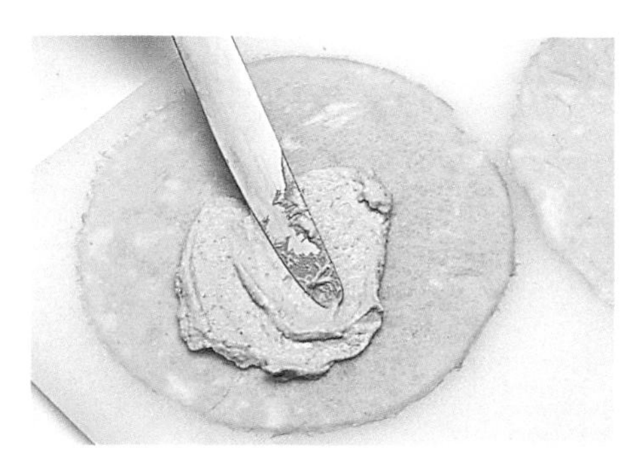

2 When ready to serve, toss the shredded salad vegetables together with 45ml/3 tbsp of the dressing. Spread half of each omelette with hummus, top with the salad vegetables and chopped bacon and fold in half. Drizzle the rest of the dressing over the filled omelettes before serving.

COOK'S TIP
These wafer-thin omelettes can be made in advance and stored in the refrigerator.

BAKED MEDITERRANEAN VEGETABLES

CRUNCHY GOLDEN BATTER SURROUNDS THESE VEGETABLES, MAKING THEM DELICIOUS AND FILLING. SERVE WITH SALAD AS A LIGHT LUNCH, OR SAUSAGES FOR A MORE SUBSTANTIAL MEAL.

SERVES SIX

INGREDIENTS
- 1 small aubergine (eggplant), trimmed, halved and thickly sliced
- 1 egg
- 115g/4oz/1 cup plain (all-purpose) flour
- 300ml/½ pint/1¼ cups milk
- 30ml/2 tbsp fresh thyme leaves
- 1 red onion
- 2 large courgettes (zucchini)
- 1 red (bell) pepper
- 1 yellow (bell) pepper
- 60–75ml/4–5 tbsp sunflower oil
- 30ml/2 tbsp freshly grated Parmesan cheese
- salt and ground black pepper
- fresh herbs, to serve

1 Place the aubergine in a colander or sieve, sprinkle generously with salt and leave for 10 minutes. Drain, rinse well and pat dry on kitchen paper.

2 Meanwhile, beat the egg in a bowl, then gradually beat in the flour and a little milk to make a smooth thick paste. Gradually blend in the rest of the milk, add the thyme leaves and seasoning to taste and stir until smooth. Leave the batter in a cool place until required. Preheat the oven to 220°C/425°F/Gas 7.

COOK'S TIP
As with Yorkshire pudding, it is essential to get the oil in the dish really hot before adding the batter, which should sizzle slightly as it goes in. If the fat is not hot enough, the batter will not rise well. Use a pan that is not too deep.

3 Quarter the onion, slice the courgettes and seed and quarter the peppers. Put the oil in a roasting pan and heat in the oven at 220°C/425°F/Gas 7. Add the prepared vegetables, toss in the oil to coat thoroughly and return to the oven for 20 minutes.

4 Give the batter another whisk, then pour it over the vegetables and return the pan to the oven for 30 minutes. When puffed up and golden, reduce the heat to 190°C/375°F/Gas 5 for 10–15 minutes until crisp around the edges. Sprinkle with Parmesan and herbs and serve.

Fiorentina Pizza

An egg adds the finishing touch to this spinach pizza; try not to overcook it though, as it's best when the yolk is still slightly soft in the middle.

SERVES TWO TO THREE

INGREDIENTS

- 45ml/3 tbsp olive oil
- 1 small red onion, thinly sliced
- 175g/6oz fresh spinach, stalks removed
- 1 pizza base, about 25–30cm/10–12in in diameter
- 1 small jar pizza sauce
- freshly grated nutmeg
- 150g/5oz mozzarella cheese
- 1 egg
- 25g/1oz/¼ cup grated Gruyère cheese

1 Heat 15ml/1 tbsp of the oil and fry the onion until soft. Add the spinach and fry until wilted. Drain any excess liquid.

2 Preheat the oven to 220°C/425°F/ Gas 7. Brush the pizza base with half the remaining olive oil. Spread the pizza sauce evenly over the base, using the back of a spoon, then top with the spinach mixture. Sprinkle over a little freshly grated nutmeg.

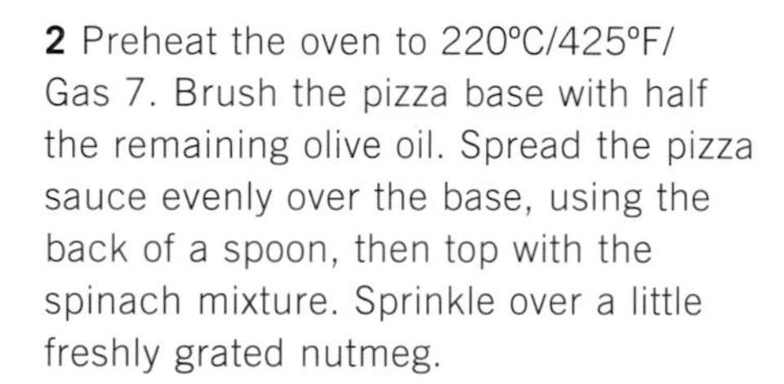

3 Thinly slice the mozzarella and arrange over the spinach. Drizzle over the remaining oil. Bake for 10 minutes, then remove from the oven.

4 Make a small well in the centre of the pizza topping and carefully break the egg into the hole.

5 Sprinkle over the grated Gruyère cheese and return to the oven for a further 5–10 minutes until crisp and golden. Serve immediately.

VARIATION

Italians make a folded pizza called calzone. It is made in the same way as a pizza, but is folded in half to conceal the filling. Add the egg with the rest of the pizza topping, fold over the dough, seal the edges and bake for 20 minutes.

CHEESE AND ONION FLAN

THE USE OF YEAST DOUGHS FOR TARTS AND FLANS IS POPULAR IN VARIOUS REGIONS OF FRANCE. CHOOSE A STRONG CHEESE SUCH AS LIVAROT, MUNSTER OR PORT SALUT IN THIS RECIPE.

SERVES FOUR

INGREDIENTS
- 15g/½oz/1 tbsp butter
- 1 onion, halved and sliced
- 2 eggs
- 250ml/8fl oz/1 cup single (light) cream
- 225g/8oz strong semi-soft cheese, rind removed, sliced
- salt and ground black pepper
- salad leaves, to serve

For the yeast dough
- 10ml/2 tsp dried yeast
- 120ml/4fl oz/½ cup milk
- 5ml/1 tsp sugar
- 1 egg yolk
- 225g/8oz/2 cups plain (all-purpose) flour, plus extra for kneading
- 2.5ml/½ tsp salt
- 50g/2oz/4 tbsp butter, softened

1 To make the dough, place the yeast in a bowl. Warm the milk in a small pan until it is lukewarm and then stir into the yeast with the sugar. Continue stirring until the yeast has dissolved completely. Leave the yeast mixture to stand for about 3 minutes, then beat in the egg yolk.

COOK'S TIP
If you prefer to use easy-blend (rapid-rise) dried yeast, omit step 1. Beat the egg yolk and milk together in a jug (pitcher). Add the yeast to the flour and salt in a food processor and pulse to combine. Pour in the egg and milk mixture, and proceed with the recipe.

2 Put the flour and salt in a food processor fitted with a metal blade and pulse to combine. With the machine running, slowly pour in the yeast mixture. Scrape down the sides and continue processing for 2–3 minutes. Add the softened butter and process for another 30 seconds.

3 Transfer the dough to a lightly greased bowl. Cover the bowl with a dishtowel and leave to rise in a warm place for about 1 hour until the dough has doubled in bulk.

4 Remove the dough from the bowl and place on a lightly floured surface. Knock back (punch down) the dough. Sprinkle a little more flour on the work surface and roll out the dough to a round about 30cm/12in in diameter.

5 Line a 23cm/9in flan tin (quiche pan) or dish with the dough. Gently press it into the tin or dish and trim off any overhanging pieces, leaving a 3mm/⅛in rim around the pastry case. Cover with a dishtowel, set aside in a warm place and leave to rise for about 30 minutes, or until puffy.

6 Meanwhile, melt the butter in a heavy pan and add the onion. Cover the pan and cook over a medium-low heat for about 15 minutes, until the onion has softened, stirring occasionally. Remove the lid and continue cooking, stirring frequently, until the onion is very soft and has caramelized.

7 Preheat the oven to 180°C/350°F/ Gas 4. Beat together the eggs and cream. Season and stir in the cooked onion.

8 Arrange the cheese on the base of the flan case. Pour over the egg mixture and bake for 30–35 minutes until the base is golden and the centre is just set. Cool slightly on a wire rack and serve warm with salad leaves.

EGG AND SPINACH PIE

THIS PIE WAS ORIGINALLY COOKED FOR GREEK EASTER CELEBRATIONS. IT IS TRADITIONALLY MADE WITH 33 LAYERS OF FILO PASTRY, EACH ONE REPRESENTING A YEAR OF CHRIST'S LIFE. IT MAKES AN EXCELLENT PICNIC DISH, AS IT CAN BE MADE IN ADVANCE AND TRAVELS WELL IN ITS COOKING TIN.

SERVES TEN TO TWELVE

INGREDIENTS
- oil, for greasing
- 675g/1½lb fresh or frozen spinach, cooked and chopped
- 115g/4oz/½ cup butter, melted
- 1 bunch spring onions (scallions), finely chopped
- 30ml/2 tbsp fresh marjoram, chopped
- 350g/12oz/1½ cups ricotta cheese
- 45ml/3 tbsp freshly grated Parmesan cheese
- 60ml/4 tbsp double (heavy) cream, whipped
- 5ml/1 tsp grated fresh nutmeg
- 450g/1lb filo pastry
- 2 egg whites, stiffly whisked
- 8 eggs, hard-boiled (hard-cooked) and peeled
- salt and ground black pepper

1 Lightly grease a deep 20 × 25cm/8 × 10in roasting pan. Preheat the oven to 190°C/375°F/Gas 5.

2 Make sure the spinach is well cooked and thoroughly dried. Return it to the pan and cook gently, stirring until all the excess liquid has evaporated.

COOK'S TIP
This pie makes perfect picnic food. Partially cool it in the pan, then invert it on to a large board. Clean the pan and return the pie to the pan for easy transporting. You may find it easier to cut the pie into portions before going on your picnic.

3 Heat 30ml/2 tbsp butter in a pan and fry the spring onions until softened. Stir in the spinach and marjoram, and season with salt and ground black pepper to taste. Mix until well blended and the spinach is quite soft and smooth.

4 Place the ricotta, Parmesan, cream, nutmeg and seasoning in a bowl and beat until really smooth.

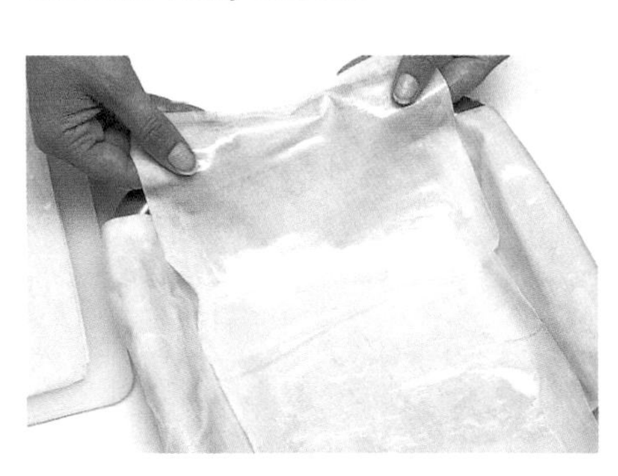

5 Use just over half the sheets of filo pastry for the base: brush each sheet with melted butter and layer neatly in the pan, allowing any excess pastry to hang over the edges. Filo pastry is very delicate, so you may find it simpler to cut very large sheets in half for easier handling. Keep the rest of the pastry covered with a damp cloth to prevent it from drying out.

VARIATION
For a pie with a slightly sharper, tangy taste, replace the ricotta cheese with the same weight of feta cheese. Crumble the cheese and mix with the cream, nutmeg and seasoning in step 4.

6 Whisk the egg whites, then fold into the cheese. Fold in the spinach until evenly mixed. Spoon half the mixture into the pan and arrange the eggs on top. Cover with the rest of the filling and fold over any excess pastry edges.

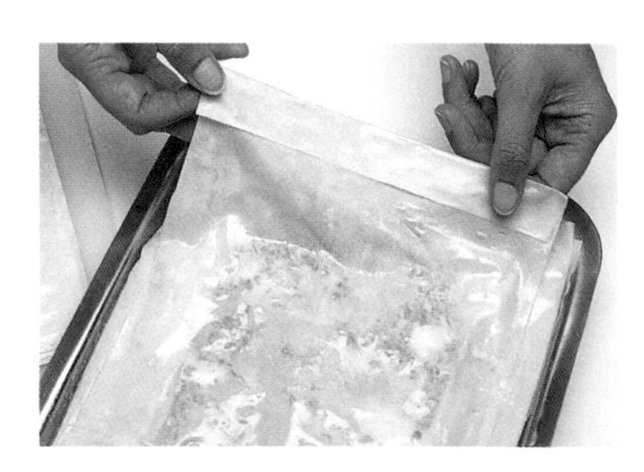

7 Brush the remaining sheets of pastry with butter and place over the top in an even layer. Brush with more butter, then bake for about 1 hour until the pastry is golden and the pie feels quite firm.

8 Allow the pie to cool slightly, then carefully invert it on to a clean surface and serve warm or leave to cool completely and serve cold.

Roasted Ratatouille Moussaka

Based on the classic Greek dish, this moussaka really has a taste of the Mediterranean. Roasting brings out the deep rich flavours of the vegetables, which give a colourful contrast to the light and mouthwatering egg-and-cheese topping. This dish is perfect as a hearty winter side dish or as a vegetarian main course.

SERVES FOUR TO SIX

INGREDIENTS
- 2 red (bell) peppers, seeded and cut into large chunks
- 2 yellow (bell) peppers, seeded and cut into large chunks
- 2 aubergines (eggplants), cut into large chunks
- 3 courgettes (zucchini), thickly sliced
- 45ml/3 tbsp olive oil
- 3 garlic cloves, crushed
- 400g/14oz can chopped tomatoes
- 30ml/2 tbsp sun-dried tomato paste
- 45ml/3 tbsp chopped fresh basil
- 15ml/1 tbsp balsamic vinegar
- 1.5ml/¼ tsp light brown sugar
- salt and ground black pepper
- basil leaves, to garnish

For the topping
- 25g/1oz/2 tbsp butter
- 25g/1oz/¼ cup plain (all-purpose) flour
- 300ml/½ pint/1¼ cups milk
- 1.5ml/¼ tsp freshly grated nutmeg
- 250g/9oz/generous 1 cup ricotta cheese
- 3 eggs, beaten
- 25g/1oz/⅓ cup freshly grated Parmesan cheese

1 Preheat the oven to 230°C/450°F/Gas 8. Arrange the peppers, aubergines and courgettes in an even layer in a large roasting pan. Season well with salt and ground black pepper.

2 Mix together the oil and crushed garlic cloves and pour them over the vegetables. Shake the roasting pan to coat the vegetables thoroughly in the garlic mixture.

3 Roast in the oven for 15–20 minutes until slightly charred, lightly tossing the vegetables once during the cooking time. Remove the pan from the oven and set aside. Reduce the oven temperature to 200°C/400°F/Gas 6.

4 Put the chopped tomatoes, sun-dried tomato paste, chopped basil, balsamic vinegar and brown sugar in a large, heavy pan and heat to boiling point. Reduce the heat and simmer gently, uncovered, for about 10–15 minutes until thickened, stirring occasionally. Season with salt and freshly ground black pepper to taste.

5 Carefully tip the roasted vegetables out of their pan and into the pan of tomato sauce. Mix well, coating the vegetables thoroughly in the tomato sauce. Spoon into an ovenproof dish.

6 To make the topping, melt the butter in a large, heavy pan over a gentle heat. Stir in the flour and cook for 1 minute. Pour in the milk, stirring constantly, then whisk until blended. Add the nutmeg and continue whisking over a gentle heat until thickened. Cook for a further 2 minutes, then remove from the heat and leave to cool slightly.

7 Mix in the ricotta cheese and beaten eggs thoroughly. Season with salt and plenty of freshly ground black pepper to taste.

8 Level the surface of the roasted vegetable mixture with the back of a spoon. Spoon the moussaka topping over the vegetables and sprinkle with the Parmesan cheese. Bake for 30–35 minutes until the topping is golden brown. Serve immediately, garnished with basil leaves.

VARIATION

Rather than baking this recipe in one large dish, divide the roasted vegetables and topping among individual gratin dishes. Reduce the baking time to 25 minutes. Individual portions can also be frozen and, when needed, simply removed from the freezer, left to thaw and baked for 30–35 minutes – ideal for those with a vegetarian in the family, or for unexpected guests.

BAKED HERB CRÊPES

TURN LIGHT HERB CRÊPES INTO SOMETHING SPECIAL. FILL WITH A SPINACH, CHEESE AND PINE NUT FILLING, THEN BAKE AND SERVE WITH A DELICIOUS TOMATO SAUCE.

SERVES FOUR

INGREDIENTS

- 25g/1oz/⅔ cup chopped fresh herbs
- 15ml/1 tbsp sunflower oil, plus extra for frying
- 120ml/4fl oz/½ cup milk
- 3 eggs
- 25g/1oz/¼ cup plain (all-purpose) flour
- pinch of salt

For the sauce

- 30ml/2 tbsp olive oil
- 1 small onion, chopped
- 2 garlic cloves, crushed
- 400g/14oz can chopped tomatoes
- pinch of light brown sugar

For the filling

- 450g/1lb fresh spinach, cooked and drained
- 175g/6oz/¾ cup ricotta cheese
- 25g/1oz/¼ cup pine nuts, toasted
- 5 sun-dried tomato halves in olive oil, drained and chopped
- 30ml/2 tbsp shredded fresh basil
- salt, nutmeg and ground black pepper
- 4 egg whites
- oil, for greasing

1 To make the crêpes, place the herbs and oil in a food processor and blend until smooth. Add the milk, eggs, flour and salt and process again until smooth. Leave to rest for 30 minutes.

2 Heat a small non-stick frying pan and add a very small amount of oil. Pour out any excess oil and pour in a ladleful of the batter. Swirl to cover the base. Cook for 2 minutes, turn over and cook for a further 1 minute. Make the remaining seven crêpes in the same way.

3 To make the sauce, heat the oil in a small pan, add the onion and garlic and cook gently for 5 minutes. Add the tomatoes and sugar and cook for about 10 minutes until thickened. Process in a blender, then sieve and set aside.

4 To make the filling, mix together the spinach with the ricotta, pine nuts, tomatoes and basil. Season with salt, nutmeg and pepper.

5 Preheat the oven to 190°C/375°F/ Gas 5. Whisk the four egg whites until stiff. Fold one-third into the spinach mixture, then gently fold in the rest.

6 Place one crêpe at a time on a lightly oiled baking sheet, add a spoonful of filling and fold into quarters. Bake for 12 minutes until set. Reheat the sauce and serve with the crêpes.

BAKED COD WITH HOLLANDAISE SAUCE

SIMPLY COOKED FRESH FISH NEEDS LITTLE ASSISTANCE OTHER THAN A SPOONFUL OF CLASSIC HOLLANDAISE SAUCE. THIS RECIPE ALSO INCLUDES SOME VARIATIONS TO THE CLASSIC SAUCE.

SERVES FOUR

INGREDIENTS

- 4 cod steaks or cutlets
- a little olive oil
- a squeeze of lemon juice
- 15ml/1 tbsp fresh white breadcrumbs
- 15ml/1 tbsp roughly ground hazelnuts
- salt and ground black pepper
- a few sprigs of dill, to garnish
- chips (French fries) and mixed leaf salad, to serve

For the sauce

- 30ml/2 tbsp lemon juice
- 2 egg yolks
- 115g/4oz/½ cup butter, melted and cooled slightly

1 Preheat the oven to 200°C/400°F/Gas 6. Brush both sides of the cod with oil and lemon juice. Season, then mix together the crumbs, nuts and seasoning and press on to the fish. Place on a baking sheet and bake for 20 minutes.

2 Meanwhile, prepare the hollandaise sauce. Simmer the lemon juice with 30ml/2 tbsp water in a small pan for a couple of minutes until reduced by at least half. Cool slightly.

3 Whisk in the egg yolks, then, over a very gentle heat, add the butter in a slow stream, whisking all the time. Keep whisking until glossy and thick, then season to taste. Keep warm over a pan of hot water, until ready to serve.

4 Top the fish with the sauce and garnish with dill. Serve with chips and a mixed leaf salad.

VARIATIONS

To make anchovy sauce, whisk in 2–3 mashed anchovy fillets and keep whisking until they dissolve. Season after adding the anchovy. This sauce may only need pepper as anchovy fillets are very salty. To make herb sauce, whisk in 30ml/2 tbsp finely chopped fresh dill and leave to stand 5–10 minutes before serving for the flavour to come out. To make tomato hollandaise sauce, stir in 30ml/2 tbsp very finely chopped plum tomatoes and add extra pepper to taste.

GOAT'S CHEESE SOUFFLÉ

MAKE SURE EVERYONE IS SEATED BEFORE THIS SOUFFLÉ IS SERVED BECAUSE IT WILL BEGIN TO DEFLATE ALMOST IMMEDIATELY. THIS DISH IS DELICIOUS SERVED WITH A CRISP WHITE WINE.

SERVES FOUR

INGREDIENTS
- 25g/1oz/2 tbsp butter, plus extra for greasing
- 30ml/2 tbsp plain (all-purpose) flour
- 175ml/6fl oz/¾ cup milk
- 1 bay leaf
- freshly grated nutmeg
- freshly grated Parmesan cheese, for sprinkling
- 40g/1½oz herb and garlic soft cheese
- 150g/5oz/1¼ cups firm goat's cheese, diced
- 6 egg whites, at room temperature
- 1.5ml/¼ tsp cream of tartar
- salt and ground black pepper

VARIATION
Use a blue cheese, such as Roquefort or Stilton, instead of goat's cheese.

1 Melt the butter in a heavy pan over a medium heat. Stir in the flour and cook until slightly golden, stirring constantly. Pour in half the milk, stir until smooth, then add the remaining milk and the bay leaf. Season with salt and plenty of pepper and nutmeg. Reduce the heat to medium-low, cover and simmer gently, stirring occasionally, for 5 minutes.

2 Preheat the oven to 190°C/375°F/Gas 5. Butter a 1.5 litre/2½ pint/6¼ cup soufflé dish and sprinkle with Parmesan cheese. Remove the sauce from the heat and discard the bay leaf. Stir in the other cheeses.

3 In a clean grease-free bowl, using a balloon whisk or electric mixer, beat the egg whites slowly until they become frothy. Add the cream of tartar, increase the speed and continue beating until they form stiff peaks that just flop over a little at the top.

4 Stir a spoonful of beaten egg whites into the cheese sauce to lighten it, then pour the cheese sauce over the rest of the whites. Using a rubber spatula or large metal spoon, gently fold the sauce into the whites, cutting down through the centre to the bottom, then along the side of the bowl and up to the top, until the cheese sauce and egg whites are just combined.

5 Gently pour the soufflé mixture into the prepared dish and bake for about 30 minutes until puffed and golden brown. Serve immediately.

SPINACH AND GOAT'S CHEESE ROULADE

THIS TWICE-BAKED ROULADE IS REALLY A ROLLED SOUFFLÉ. BECAUSE IT HAS AIR TRAPPED INSIDE, IT RISES AGAIN ON REHEATING AND BECOMES QUITE CRISP ON THE OUTSIDE.

SERVES FOUR

INGREDIENTS
- 300ml/½ pint/1¼ cups milk
- 50g/2oz/½ cup plain (all-purpose) flour
- 150g/5oz/⅔ cup butter
- 100g/3¾oz chèvre (goat's cheese), chopped
- 40g/1½oz/½ cup freshly grated Parmesan cheese, plus extra for dusting
- 4 eggs, separated
- 250g/9oz/2¼ cups fresh shiitake mushrooms, sliced
- 275g/10oz baby spinach leaves, washed
- 45ml/3 tbsp crème fraîche
- salt and ground black pepper

1 Preheat the oven to 190°C/375°F/ Gas 5. Line a 30 × 20cm/12 × 8in Swiss-roll tin (jelly roll pan) with greaseproof (waxed) paper, making sure that the edge of the paper rises well above the sides of the tin. Grease lightly.

2 Combine the milk, flour and 50g/2oz/ ¼ cup of the butter in a pan. Bring to the boil over a low heat, whisking until thick. Lower the heat and simmer for 2 minutes, then mix in the chèvre and half the Parmesan. Cool for 5 minutes, then beat in the egg yolks. Season.

3 Whisk the egg whites in a grease-free bowl until soft peaks form. Carefully fold the whites into the chèvre mixture, using a large metal spoon. Spoon the mixture into the prepared tin, spread gently to level, then bake for about 15 minutes until the top feels just firm.

4 Let the roulade cool for a short time. Meanwhile, dust a sheet of greaseproof paper with a little Parmesan cheese and carefully invert the roulade on to the paper. Tear the lining paper away from the base of the roulade, in strips. Roll up in the greaseproof paper and set aside to cool completely.

5 To make the filling, melt the rest of the butter in a pan, reserving 30ml/2 tbsp. Add the mushrooms and stir-fry for 3 minutes. In a separate pan, cook the spinach until it wilts. Drain well, add to the mushrooms and stir in the crème fraîche. Season, then cool. Preheat the oven to the original temperature.

6 Unroll the roulade and spread over the filling. Roll it up again and place on a baking sheet. Brush with the reserved butter and sprinkle with the remaining Parmesan. Bake for 15 minutes until risen and golden. Serve immediately.

PARTY FOODS AND DRINKS

Beautifully presented and delicious-tasting food and drink are all that a party needs to make it a success. This chapter provides a whole host of hot and cold snacks and nibbles. Dishes such as Tapenade and Quail's Egg Canapés and Eggs Mimosa, can be made well in advance and will make a beautiful centrepiece on any table. Hot party food, such as Prawn and Tomato Canapés and Cheese Aigrettes, can also be prepared ahead of time and need only a little last-minute cooking. They are sure to impress your guests and get them in the party mood. Also included are a tempting selection of unusual egg-based party drinks, such as Brandied Eggnog and Old-fashioned Lemonade, as well as the classic morning-after remedy, Prairie Oyster.

TAPENADE AND QUAIL'S EGG CANAPÉS

POPULARLY USED IN MEDITERRANEAN COOKING, TAPENADE IS A PURÉE MADE FROM CAPERS, OLIVES AND ANCHOVIES. ITS STRONG FLAVOUR PERFECTLY COMPLEMENTS THE TASTE OF EGGS, ESPECIALLY QUAIL'S EGGS, WHICH LOOK VERY PRETTY ON THE OPEN SANDWICHES.

SERVES EIGHT

INGREDIENTS

- 4 quail's eggs
- 1 small baguette
- 45ml/3 tbsp tapenade
- a few leaves of frisée lettuce
- 3 small tomatoes, sliced and halved
- 4 canned anchovy fillets, halved lengthways
- 2 black olives, pitted and quartered
- chopped fresh parsley, to garnish

COOK'S TIP

For a crunchier base, brush each slice of bread with olive oil and grill (broil) on both sides until crisp and golden.

1 Place the quail's eggs in a pan of cold water, bring to the boil and cook for 3 minutes. Leave to cool, then peel.

2 Cut the baguette into eight slices, on the diagonal, and spread with tapenade.

3 Arrange a little frisée lettuce and a slice of tomato on top of each piece of bread.

4 Halve the quail's eggs and place half on top of each tomato slice.

5 Top each egg with a quartered olive and a halved anchovy fillet and garnish with chopped parsley.

VARIATION

Make a tuna tapenade filling for hard-boiled (hard-cooked) eggs. Put a 90g/3½oz can drained tuna in a food processor with 25g/1oz capers, 75g/3oz pitted black olives and 10 canned anchovy fillets and blend until smooth, scraping down the sides as necessary. Gradually add 60ml/4 tbsp olive oil through the feeder tube and combine. To fill the eggs, blend the tuna tapenade with the egg yolks then, using a teaspoon, pile the mixture into the halved egg whites.

Cheese Aigrettes

Choux pastry is often used to make sweet pastries, such as profiteroles, but these little savoury buns, flavoured with Gruyère and dusted with grated Parmesan, are just delicious. They make a wonderful party snack and are best made ahead of time and deep fried to serve.

MAKES THIRTY

INGREDIENTS

- 100g/3¾oz/scant 1 cup plain (all-purpose) flour
- 2.5ml/½ tsp paprika
- 2.5ml/½ tsp salt
- 75g/3oz/6 tbsp cold butter, diced
- 3 eggs, beaten
- 75g/3oz/¾ cup coarsely grated mature (sharp) Gruyère cheese
- corn oil, for deep-frying
- 50g/2oz/⅔ cup freshly grated Parmesan cheese
- ground black pepper

1 Mix together the flour, paprika and salt by sifting them on to a sheet of greaseproof (waxed) paper. Add a generous grinding of black pepper.

2 Put the butter and 200ml/7fl oz/scant 1 cup water into a pan and heat gently. As soon as the butter has melted and the liquid starts to boil, tip in all the seasoned flour at once and beat hard with a wooden spoon until the mixture forms a stiff paste and comes away from the sides of the pan in a ball.

3 Remove the pan from the heat and cool the paste for 5 minutes. This is important if the aigrettes are to rise well. Gradually beat in enough of the beaten egg to give a stiff dropping (pourable) consistency that still holds a shape on the spoon. Mix in the Gruyère.

4 Heat the oil for deep-frying to 180°C/350°F or until hot enough to turn a cube of bread brown in 1 minute. Take a teaspoonful of the choux paste and use a second spoon to slide it into the oil. Make more aigrettes in the same way. Fry for 3–4 minutes until golden brown. Drain on kitchen paper and keep warm while cooking successive batches. To serve, pile the aigrettes on a warmed serving dish and sprinkle with Parmesan.

VARIATION

Filling these aigrettes gives your guests a delightful surprise as they bite through the crisp shell. Make slightly larger aigrettes by dropping larger spoonfuls of dough into the hot oil and cooking for 1–2 minutes more. Slit them open and scoop out any soft paste that remains inside. Fill the centres with taramasalata or crumbled Roquefort mixed with a little fromage frais or natural (plain) yogurt.

EGG CANAPÉS

THESE ELEGANT PARTY PIECES TAKE A LITTLE TIME TO MAKE, BUT THEY CAN BE PREPARED IN ADVANCE WITH THE FINAL TOUCHES ADDED JUST BEFORE YOUR GUESTS ARRIVE.

EACH VARIATION MAKES 12

TRUFFLE CANAPÉS

INGREDIENTS

- 225g/8oz shortcrust (unsweetened) pastry
- 2 eggs, beaten
- 15g/½oz/1 tbsp butter
- 5ml/1 tsp truffle oil
- salt and ground black pepper
- chopped chives, to garnish

1 Preheat the oven to 190°C/375°F/ Gas 5. Roll out the pastry very thinly on a floured surface and line 12 very small tartlet or muffin tins (pans).

2 Line the base of each pastry case (shell) with greaseproof (waxed) paper and bake for 10 minutes. Remove the paper and bake for a further 5 minutes until the pastry is crisp and golden.

3 Season the beaten eggs, then melt the butter in a pan, pour in the eggs and stir constantly over a gentle heat. When the eggs are almost set, stir in the truffle oil. Spoon the mixture into the pastry cases and top with chives. Serve warm or cold.

PRAWN AND TOMATO CANAPÉS

INGREDIENTS

- 225g/8oz shortcrust (unsweetened) pastry
- 2 tomatoes, peeled and chopped
- 12 large cooked prawns (shrimp), peeled but tails left on
- 60ml/4 tbsp hollandaise sauce
- salt and ground black pepper
- fennel or chervil sprigs, to garnish

1 Preheat the oven to 190°C/375°F/ Gas 5. Roll out the pastry very thinly on a floured surface and line 12 very small tartlet or muffin tins (pans).

2 Line the base of each pastry case (shell) with greaseproof (waxed) paper and bake for 10 minutes. Remove the paper and bake for 5 minutes more.

3 Place some chopped tomato in the base of each tartlet and season with salt and pepper. Top with the prawns and spoon on some hollandaise sauce. Warm through briefly in the oven and serve garnished with fennel or chervil.

WATERCRESS AND AVOCADO CANAPÉS

INGREDIENTS

- 3–4 slices dark rye bread
- 1 small ripe avocado
- 15ml/1 tbsp lemon juice
- 45ml/3 tbsp mayonnaise
- ½ bunch watercress, chopped, reserving a few sprigs to garnish
- 6 quail's eggs, hard-boiled (hard-cooked)

1 Cut the bread into 12 rounds, using a plain or fluted biscuit (cookie) cutter.

2 Cut the avocado in half, around the stone (pit). Peel half, then slice and dip each piece in lemon juice. Put a piece of avocado on each bread round.

3 Scoop the remaining avocado into a bowl and mash. Mix in the mayonnaise and watercress. Spoon a little of the mixture on to each canapé, top with a peeled, halved quail's egg and garnish with a sprig of watercress.

SALMON AND CORIANDER CANAPÉS

INGREDIENTS

- 3–4 slices dark rye bread
- 2 eggs, hard-boiled (hard-cooked) and thinly sliced
- 115g/4oz poached salmon
- coriander (cilantro) leaves, to garnish

For the lime mayonnaise

- 45–60ml/3–4 tbsp mayonnaise
- 5ml/1 tsp chopped fresh coriander (cilantro)
- 5ml/1 tsp lime juice
- salt and ground black pepper

1 Cut the rye bread into 12 triangular pieces, using a sharp knife.

2 Make the lime mayonnaise. Combine the mayonnaise, coriander and lime juice in a small bowl. Season with salt and pepper to taste.

3 Top each bread triangle with a slice of egg, a small portion of salmon and a teaspoon of mayonnaise. Garnish with a coriander leaf. Chill until ready to serve.

Marbled Eggs

These eggs are coloured with tea leaves, an Asian method that gives a very subtle taste. You could also use the skins of 3–4 onions, which tends to give a stronger, more savoury flavour to the eggs.

SERVES FOUR

INGREDIENTS

- 4 eggs
- 30ml/2 tbsp dry strong tea leaves
- 5ml/1 tsp salt
- 2 star anise
- 2–3 cardamom pods

For the Thai fish sauce

- 2 red chillies, finely chopped
- 2 garlic cloves, crushed
- 45ml/3 tbsp hoisin sauce
- 15ml/1 tbsp soy sauce
- 15ml/1 tbsp fish sauce

COOK'S TIP

For extra flavour, add a little soy sauce to the tea before adding the eggs.

1 Place the eggs in a pan of cold water, bring to the boil and cook for about 5 minutes. Cool, then crack the shells all over. Return to the pan with the tea and seasonings, add water to cover and bring to the boil. Simmer for 1½ hours, then cool in the water and peel.

2 To make the Thai fish sauce, pound the chillies and garlic to a paste in a mortar, then blend in the rest of the sauce ingredients, discarding the chilli seeds, if you prefer a milder flavour. Chill until required. Serve the sauce with the eggs, or use as a garnish.

PICKLED QUAIL'S EGGS

THESE CHINESE EGGS ARE PICKLED IN ALCOHOL AND CAN BE STORED IN A PRESERVING JAR IN A COOL DARK PLACE FOR SEVERAL MONTHS. THEY MAKE DELICIOUS BITESIZE SNACKS AT DRINKS PARTIES AND ARE SURE TO DELIGHT GUESTS.

SERVES TWELVE

INGREDIENTS

- 12 quail's eggs
- 15ml/1 tbsp salt
- 750ml/1¼ pints/3 cups distilled or boiled water
- 5ml/1 tsp Sichuan peppercorns
- 150ml/¼ pint/⅔ cup spirit, such as Mou-tai (Chinese brandy), brandy, whisky, rum or vodka
- dipping sauce (see Cook's Tips) and toasted sesame seeds, to serve (optional)

1 Place the eggs in a pan of gently simmering water, bring to the boil and cook for 3 minutes until the yolks are soft, but not runny. Remove the eggs from the pan using a slotted spoon and set aside to cool.

2 In a large pan, dissolve the salt in the distilled or boiled water. Add the peppercorns, then allow the water to cool and add the spirit.

3 Gently tap the eggs all over to crack the shells but do not peel them. Place in a large, airtight, sterilized jar and fill up with the liquid, totally covering the eggs. Seal the jar and leave to stand in a cool, dark place for at least 7 days.

4 To serve, remove the eggs from the liquid and carefully peel off the shells. Serve whole with a dipping sauce and a bowl of toasted sesame seeds or cut each egg in half or quarters and serve as a garnish.

COOK'S TIPS

- Although you can buy Chinese dipping sauces in the supermarket, it is very easy to make your own at home. To make a quick dipping sauce, mix together equal quantities of soy sauce and hoisin sauce in a small bowl.
- Be sure to use only boiled or distilled water for the eggs. The water must be completely free of harmful bacteria because they can enter through the eggs' porous shells.

ROLLED OMELETTE

JAPANESE FOOD IS ALWAYS PREPARED AND SERVED WITH PRECISION AND ELEGANCE. THIS FIRMLY SET, ROLLED OMELETTE IS CUT INTO NEAT PIECES, SHOWING THE EXQUISITE LAYERING INSIDE. THE TEXTURE SHOULD BE SMOOTH AND SOFT, NOT LEATHERY, AND THE FLAVOUR IS SWEET-SAVOURY. SOY SAUCE IS THE PERFECT CONDIMENT TO COMPLEMENT ITS FLAVOUR AND TEXTURE.

SERVES FOUR

INGREDIENTS
- 8 eggs
- 60ml/4 tbsp sugar
- 20ml/4 tsp soy sauce
- 90ml/6 tbsp sake or dry white wine
- vegetable oil, for cooking
- soy sauce or plum sauce, to serve

For the garnish
- 8cm/3¼in piece of mooli (daikon), finely grated
- shiso leaves (optional)

1 Break the eggs into a large bowl, mix them together, using a pair of chopsticks and a cutting action.

2 In a small bowl, mix together the sugar with the soy sauce and sake or dry white wine. Lightly stir this mixture into the beaten eggs. Divide the mixture between two bowls so that it can be cooked in equal batches.

3 Heat a little oil in a medium-size frying pan and carefully wipe out the excess with kitchen paper.

COOK'S TIPS
Japanese ginger pickles can be found in chiller compartments in good supermarkets or in specialist food stores. They have a refreshing, zesty flavour, which complements this omelette perfectly.

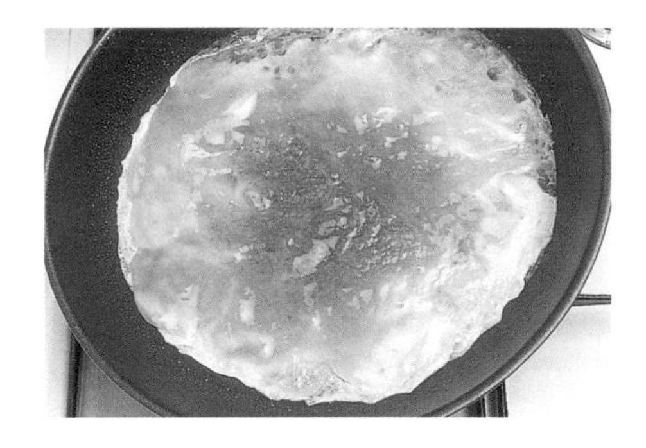

4 Pour a quarter of the mixture from one bowl into the frying pan, tilting it to coat the base in a thin layer. When the edge has set, but the middle is still moist, roll up the egg towards you.

5 Moisten a piece of kitchen paper with oil and grease the empty side of the pan. Pour in a third of the remaining egg mixture and lift up the rolled egg with your chopsticks to let the raw egg run underneath.

6 When the edges have set, roll up the omelette in the opposite direction, tilting the pan away from you so that the omelette rolls easily.

7 Slide the roll towards you again, grease the pan, using the oily kitchen paper. Pour half of the remaining egg mixture into the pan, lifting the egg roll and allowing the uncooked egg to run under it as before.

8 When set, insert the chopsticks in the side of the rolled omelette and flip it over towards the opposite side of the frying pan. Add the remaining egg and cook in the same way. Slide the roll so that the join is underneath. Cook for a further 10 seconds.

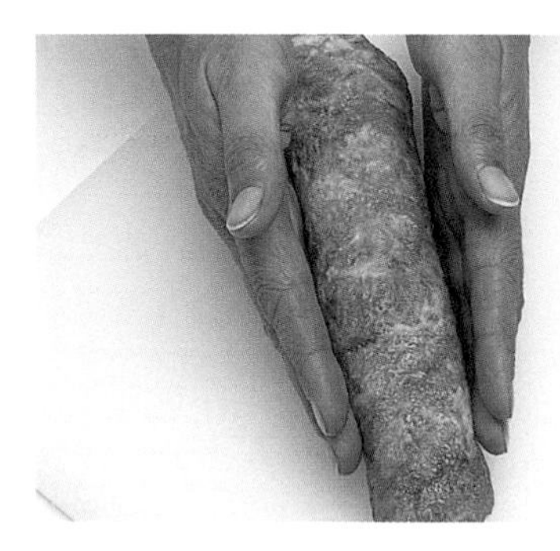

9 Slide the roll out on to a bamboo mat, if you have one, and roll up tightly, then press neatly into a rectangular shape. If you don't have a bamboo mat, simply press the omelette into a rectangle using your hands. Leave to cool.

10 Cook the remaining batch of egg mixture in the same way to make a second omelette roll. Slice the cold omelettes into 2.5cm/1in thick pieces, garnish with mooli and shiso leaves. Serve with soy or plum sauce.

EGGS MIMOSA

THE USE OF THE WORD MIMOSA DESCRIBES THE FINE YELLOW AND WHITE GRATED EGG, WHICH LOOKS VERY SIMILAR TO THE FLOWER OF THE SAME NAME. THIS PRETTY GARNISH CAN BE USED TO FINISH ANY DISH AND ADDS A LIGHT, SUMMERY TOUCH.

MAKES TWENTY-FOUR

INGREDIENTS

- 12 eggs, hard-boiled (hard-cooked) and peeled
- 2 ripe avocados, halved and stoned (pitted)
- 1 garlic clove, crushed
- a few drops of Tabasco sauce
- 15ml/1 tbsp extra virgin olive oil
- salt and ground black pepper
- basil leaves, to garnish

COOK'S TIP

You can prepare the mimosa garnish in advance, but store the egg white and yolk separately, in small airtight containers, and keep them chilled.

1 Reserve two of the hard-boiled eggs and halve the remaining ones. Carefully remove the yolks with a teaspoon and blend together with the avocados, garlic, Tabasco sauce, oil and seasoning. Pipe or spoon the mixture into the halved egg whites.

2 Sieve the remaining egg whites and sprinkle over the filled eggs. Sieve the yolks on top. Arrange the filled egg halves on a serving platter. Sprinkle a little ground black pepper over the eggs and sprinkle with basil leaves to garnish, then serve.

Cheese-Crusted Party Eggs

Similar to the popular Scotch egg, these whole small eggs are wrapped in a delicious vegetarian coating, then deep-fried. They keep well for several days and make very good party snacks. They are also ideal as picnic and travel food.

MAKES SIX

INGREDIENTS
- 115g/4oz/1⅔ cups stale white breadcrumbs
- ½ small leek, very finely chopped
- 115g/4oz/1 cup grated mild but tasty cheese
- 5ml/1 tsp garlic and herb seasoning
- 30ml/2 tbsp chopped fresh parsley
- 5ml/1 tsp mild mustard
- 2 eggs, separated
- 30–45ml/2–3 tbsp milk
- 6 small spinach or sorrel leaves, stalks removed
- 6 small eggs, such as bantam, guinea fowl, or 8–10 quail's eggs, hard-boiled (hard-cooked) and peeled
- 25–40g/1–1½oz/¼–⅓ cup flour, for coating, plus extra for dusting
- 25g/1oz/2 tbsp sesame seeds, for coating
- oil, for deep-frying
- salt and ground black pepper
- mayonnaise, to serve

1 Mix together the breadcrumbs, leeks, cheese, seasoning, parsley and mustard. Beat together the egg yolks and milk and blend into the mixture. Whisk one egg white until quite stiff and gradually work sufficient stiff egg white into the breadcrumb mixture to give a firm, dropping (pouring) consistency. Chill for about 1 hour.

COOK'S TIP
Make sure that you coat the eggs evenly first with the egg whites and then with the sesame flour to seal them completely.

2 Divide the mixture into six. Mould one portion in the palm of your hand, place a spinach leaf inside and then an egg and carefully shape the mixture around the egg to enclose it within a thin crust. Seal well and dust lightly with flour. Repeat with the remainder.

3 Beat the remaining egg white with 15ml/1 tbsp water, then pour into a shallow dish. Mix the flour with salt and pepper and the sesame seeds and place in another shallow dish. Dip the eggs first in the beaten egg white, then in the sesame flour. Cover and chill for at least 20 minutes.

4 Heat the oil in a pan until a crust of bread turns golden in about 1¼ minutes. Deep-fry the eggs in the hot oil, turning frequently, until golden brown all over. Remove with a slotted spoon, drain on kitchen paper and leave to cool. Serve, sliced in half, with a bowl of good-quality mayonnaise for dipping.

PARMESAN THINS

THESE MELT-IN-THE-MOUTH MORSELS ARE VERY MORE-ISH, SO MAKE PLENTY. DON'T JUST KEEP THEM FOR PARTIES – THEY MAKE A GREAT SNACK AT ANY TIME OF THE DAY.

MAKES SIXTEEN TO TWENTY

INGREDIENTS
- 50g/2oz/½ cup plain (all-purpose) flour
- 40g/1½oz/3 tbsp butter, softened
- 1 egg yolk
- 40g/1½oz/⅔ cup freshly grated Parmesan cheese
- pinch each of salt and mustard powder

COOK'S TIP

If you want to make large quantities of these biscuits (crackers), freeze the dough in logs, wrapped in foil. To thaw, remove from the freezer and leave for at least 1 hour before cutting and baking.

1 Rub together the flour and the butter in a bowl, then work in the egg yolk, cheese, salt and mustard. Mix to bring the dough together into a ball. Shape into a log, then wrap in foil or clear film (plastic wrap) and chill in the refrigerator for at least 10 minutes.

2 Preheat the oven to 200°C/400°F/Gas 6. Cut the dough log into very thin slices, about 3–6mm/⅛–¼in, and arrange on a baking tray. Flatten with a fork to give a pretty ridged pattern. Bake for 10 minutes or until crisp. Cool on a wire rack.

Elegant Egg Sandwiches

A well-made egg sandwich is one of the best and quickest snacks. Here are two favourite fillings, delicious at any time of day.

SERVES SIX

INGREDIENTS
- 12 thin slices white or brown bread, crusts removed
- 50g/2oz/4 tbsp butter, at room temperature
- slices of lemon, to garnish

For the egg and cress filling
- 2 small hard-boiled (hard-cooked) eggs, peeled and finely chopped
- 30ml/2 tbsp mayonnaise
- ½ small box cress
- salt and ground black pepper

For the egg and tuna filling
- 2 small hard-boiled (hard-cooked) eggs, peeled and finely chopped
- 25g/1oz canned tuna in oil, drained and mashed
- 5ml/1 tsp paprika
- squeeze of lemon juice
- 25g/1oz piece cucumber, peeled and thinly sliced

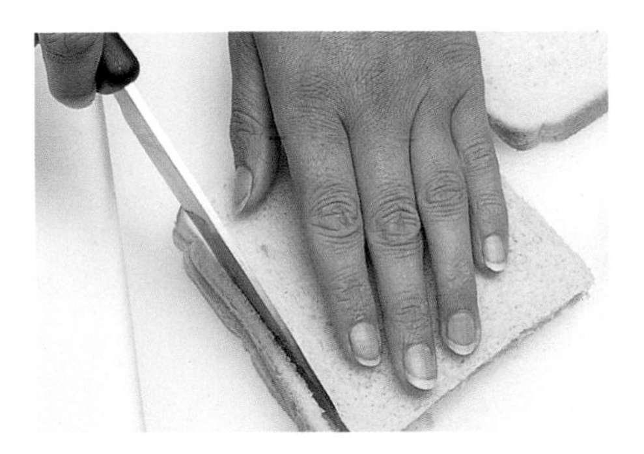

1 Carefully trim the crusts off the bread, using a sharp knife, then spread the bread thinly with softened butter.

VARIATION
For harlequin sandwiches, use a combination of white and brown bread. Use a slice of brown bread for one side of each sandwich and a slice of white for the other. Arrange them on a plate, turning the sandwiches to show alternate brown and white sides.

2 To make the egg and cress filling, mix the chopped eggs with the mayonnaise, cress and seasoning. Layer between six slices of bread. Press down gently and cut into neat triangles.

COOK'S TIP
These sandwiches will keep well for 2–3 hours. Cover with damp kitchen paper, then cover tightly in clear film (plastic wrap). Chill until required.

3 To make the egg and tuna filling, mix the chopped eggs with the tuna, paprika, lemon juice and seasoning. Put cucumber on three slices of bread, top with the tuna mixture and the rest of the bread. Press down lightly and cut each sandwich into three neat fingers.

4 Arrange all the sandwiches on a plate and garnish with lemon slices.

BANANA AND MAPLE FLIP

THIS NOURISHING AND HEALTHY BREAKFAST DRINK IS PACKED WITH SO MUCH GOODNESS THAT YOU WON'T NEED ANYTHING ELSE FOR YOUR MORNING MEAL, BUT IT IS PERFECT FOR A BRUNCH PARTY. AS IT IS MADE WITH A RAW EGG, DO BE SURE TO USE A REALLY FRESH FREE-RANGE ONE.

SERVES ONE

INGREDIENTS

- 1 small banana, peeled and halved
- 50g/2oz/¼ cup thick Greek (US strained plain) yogurt
- 1 egg
- 30ml/2 tbsp maple syrup
- 5ml/1 tsp lemon juice
- 2 ice cubes
- slice of orange, to serve (optional)

COOK'S TIPS

- To chill the glass quickly, place it in the freezer while you are preparing the drink.
- If your food processor isn't a heavy-duty model, crush the ice cubes first.

1 Put the banana, yogurt, egg, maple syrup, lemon juice and the ice cubes into a food processor or blender.

2 Blend continuously for 2 minutes until the mixture becomes really pale and frothy.

3 Pour into a tall, chilled glass and top with a slice of orange, if you like.

VARIATION

For a different fruity flavour, substitute a small, very ripe, peeled, stoned (pitted) and chopped mango for the banana.

PRAIRIE OYSTER

BASED ON THE ORIGINAL MORNING-AFTER DRINK, WHICH IS TRADITIONALLY SERVED WITH A LARGE MEASURE OF SPIRITS, THIS IS A NON-ALCOHOLIC VERSION, ALTHOUGH YOU CAN ALWAYS ADD A SMALL SPLASH OF BRANDY IF YOU REALLY FEEL THE NEED. THE DRINK CONTAINS A RAW EGG YOLK SO DO BE SURE TO USE A FRESH ONE (SEE WATCHPOINT, BELOW).

SERVES ONE

INGREDIENTS

- 5ml/1 tsp Worcestershire sauce
- 5ml/1 tsp white wine vinegar
- 5ml/1 tsp tomato ketchup or tomato sauce
- 1 egg yolk, unbroken
- cayenne pepper

WATCHPOINT

The very young, the elderly, pregnant women and those in ill-health or with a compromised immune system are advised against consuming raw eggs or dishes and drinks containing raw eggs. This is because salmonella bacteria, which can cause severe food poisoning, are sometimes found in eggs and poultry. The bacteria are destroyed when eggs are heated to a temperature of 60°C/125°F.

1 Place the Worcestershire sauce, white wine vinegar and tomato ketchup or tomato sauce in a tall, narrow glass and mix together, using a long-handled spoon or stirrer.

2 Carefully slide the unbroken egg yolk into the glass, but do not stir. Sprinkle in a little cayenne pepper and down the whole lot in a single gulp.

COOK'S TIP

If you don't like the idea of swallowing a whole raw egg yolk, try processing all the ingredients in a food processor or blender with some freshly squeezed orange juice.

OLD-FASHIONED LEMONADE

SERVES TWO

INGREDIENTS

a few large strips of lemon rind
75ml/5 tbsp lemon juice
50–75g/2–3oz/¼–generous ⅓ cup sugar, or to taste
2 egg whites
300ml/½ pint/1¼ cups boiling water
75ml/5 tbsp sherry
ice cubes, to serve
mint or lemon balm, to decorate

COOK'S TIP

Experiment with different flavours by replacing the sherry with another fortified wine, such as Madeira or vermouth.

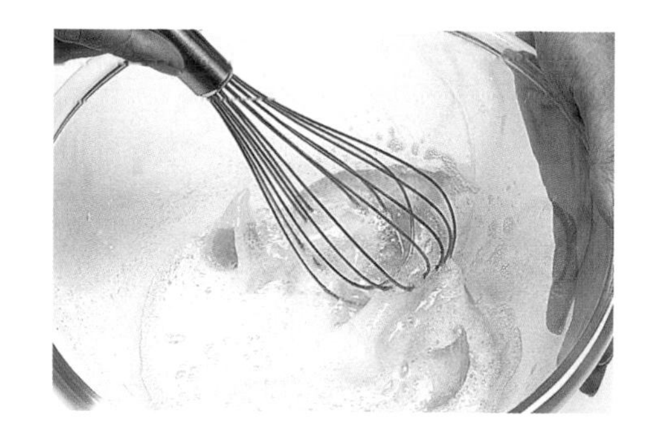

1 Put the lemon rind and juice, sugar and egg whites into a bowl or large jug (pitcher). Whisk until frothy.

2 Whisk in the water and whisk for a further 2 minutes, until the sugar has dissolved completely.

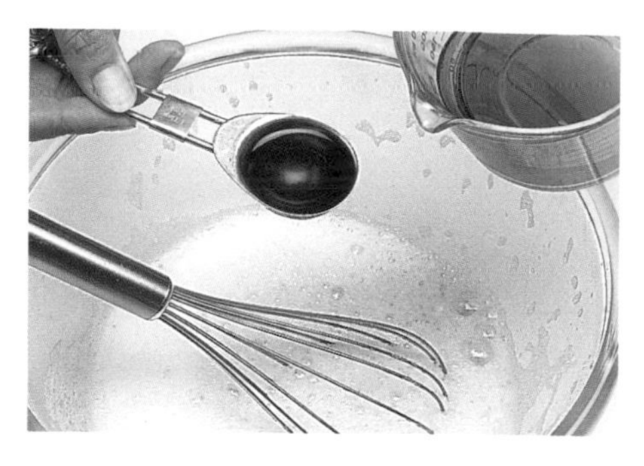

3 Pour in the sherry, a little at a time, and whisk after each addition.

4 To serve, put several ice cubes into each of two tall glasses, pour over the lemonade and decorate the glasses with a sprig of mint or lemon balm.

Brandied Eggnog

For insomniacs, this frothy blend of eggs, milk and brandy works wonders.

SERVES FOUR

INGREDIENTS

- 4 eggs, separated
- 25g/1oz/2 tbsp caster (superfine) sugar
- 120ml/4fl oz/½ cup brandy
- 300ml/½ pint/1¼ cups milk (or according to the volume of the glasses), heated to just below boiling point
- freshly grated nutmeg

COOK'S TIP

To make a cold version, use chilled single (light) cream instead of hot milk. Sprinkle with finely grated chocolate.

1 Beat the egg yolks in a bowl with the sugar. Beat the egg whites to soft peaks in a separate bowl.

2 Fold together the yolks and whites and pour into four heatproof glasses.

3 Pour 30ml/2 tbsp of brandy into each heatproof glass.

4 Top up the glasses with hot milk. Grate a little nutmeg over the top of each and serve immediately.

Cold Desserts

Many classic cold desserts depend on eggs for their light, rich or creamy textures. Whisked egg whites create the crisp, yet chewy, texture of pavlova, while the same whisked egg whites also create the light and creamy delight of Frozen Grand Marnier Soufflés. Combining egg whites with egg yolks can also produce the divinely fruity Iced Mousse with Hot Pineapple, as well as Chocolate Chestnut Roulade. A classic egg custard is often used as the base of cold desserts. Banana with Apricot Caramel Trifle is layered with thick fresh custard, while in Rich Vanilla Ice Cream the creamy vanilla custard is frozen to make a perennially popular dessert. Classic baked custards include Baked Custard with Burnt Sugar and Passion Fruit Creams.

BAKED CUSTARD WITH BURNT SUGAR

THIS DESSERT IS THOUGHT TO HAVE ORIGINATED IN ENGLAND IN THE 18TH CENTURY AND HAS STOOD THE TEST OF TIME WELL. THE SOFT AND CREAMY EGG CUSTARD IS FLAVOURED WITH VANILLA AND TOPPED WITH A BRITTLE CARAMELIZED SUGAR CRUST.

SERVES SIX

INGREDIENTS
- 1 vanilla pod (bean)
- 1 litre/1¾ pints/4 cups double (heavy) cream
- 6 egg yolks
- 90g/3½oz/½ cup caster (superfine) sugar
- 30ml/2 tbsp almond liqueur
- 75g/3oz/⅓ cup soft light brown sugar

1 Preheat the oven to 150°C/300°F/ Gas 2. Place six 125ml/4fl oz/½ cup ramekins in a roasting pan or ovenproof dish and set aside.

2 Split the vanilla pod and scrape the seeds into a pan. Add the cream and bring just to the boil, stirring frequently. Remove from the heat and cover. Set aside for 15–20 minutes.

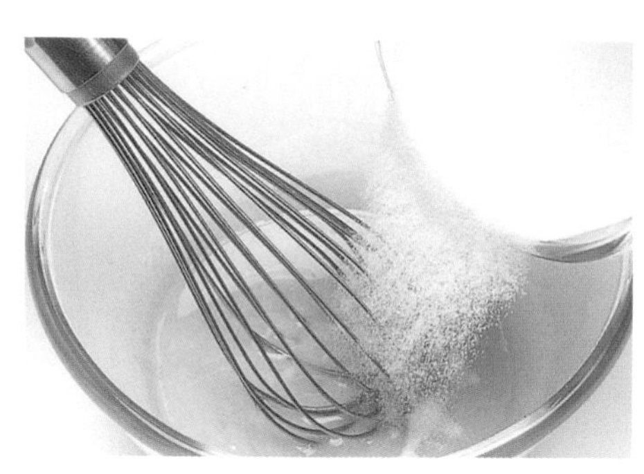

3 In a bowl, whisk the egg yolks, caster sugar and almond liqueur until well blended. Whisk in the hot cream and strain into a large jug (pitcher). Divide the custard among the ramekins.

4 Pour enough boiling water into the roasting pan to come halfway up the sides of the ramekins. Cover the pan with foil and bake for about 30 minutes until the custards are just set. To test whether the custards are ready, push the point of a knife into the centre of one – if it comes out clean, the custards are cooked. Remove the ramekins from the pan and leave to cool. Return to the dry roasting pan and chill.

5 Preheat the grill (broiler). Sprinkle the sugar over the surface of each custard and grill (broil) for 30–60 seconds until the sugar melts and caramelizes, taking care not to let the sugar burn. Place in the refrigerator to set the crust.

COOK'S TIP

It is best to make the custards the day before you wish to eat them, so that they can become really cold and firm.

PASSION FRUIT CREAMS

THESE DELICATELY PERFUMED CREAMS ARE VERY LIGHT AND THE PASSION FRUIT GIVES THEM A REFRESHING, CITRUSY FLAVOUR.

SERVES FIVE TO SIX

INGREDIENTS
- butter, for greasing
- 600ml/1 pint/2½ cups double (heavy) cream, or a mixture of single (light) and double (heavy) cream
- a few drops of vanilla essence (extract)
- 6 passion fruits
- 30–45ml/2–3 tbsp caster (superfine) sugar
- 5 eggs
- 30ml/2 tbsp lemon curd
- clotted cream and mint or geranium leaves, to serve

VARIATIONS
You can also serve these creams hot, straight from their dishes, with an extra passion fruit half on the side. To make a crème caramel-style dessert, coat each ramekin with caramel instead of paper.

1 Preheat the oven to 180°C/350°F/Gas 4. Butter six ramekins and place a circle of greaseproof (waxed) paper in the bases. Place them in a roasting pan.

2 Bring the cream and vanilla to boiling point. Sieve the flesh of four passion fruits and beat together with the sugar, eggs and lemon curd. Whisk in the hot cream. Ladle into the ramekins and half fill the roasting pan with boiling water.

3 Bake the creams for 25–30 minutes or until they are just set. Remove from the roasting pan and set aside to cool before chilling in the refrigerator.

4 Run a knife around the insides of the creams, then invert them on to serving plates, tapping the bases firmly. Peel off the greaseproof paper and chill. Just before serving, spoon on a little passion fruit flesh and add a herb leaf.

FLOATING ISLANDS

THE FRENCH NAME FOR THIS DISH IS OEUFS À LA NEIGE, MEANING SNOW EGGS. TRADITIONALLY THE MERINGUES ARE POACHED IN MILK, WHICH IS THEN USED TO MAKE THE RICH CUSTARD SAUCE. HOWEVER, THIS METHOD USES WATER FOR POACHING, WHICH GIVES A LIGHTER RESULT.

SERVES FOUR TO SIX

INGREDIENTS

- 1 vanilla pod (bean)
- 600ml/1 pint/2½ cups milk
- 8 egg yolks
- 200g/7oz/1 cup granulated sugar

For the meringues

- 4 large (US extra large) egg whites
- 1.5ml/¼ tsp cream of tartar
- 225g/8oz/1¼ cups caster (superfine) sugar

1 Using a knife with a sharp point, carefully split the vanilla pod lengthways and scrape the tiny black seeds into a pan. Add the milk and bring to the boil over a medium-high heat, stirring frequently. Remove the pan from the heat and cover with a lid. Set aside for 15–20 minutes to cool slightly.

2 In a medium bowl, whisk the egg yolks and 50g/2oz/¼ cup of the sugar for 2–3 minutes until thick and creamy. Remove the vanilla pod from the hot milk, then whisk the milk into the egg mixture and return to the pan.

3 With a wooden spoon, stir the sauce over a medium-low heat until it begins to thicken and coats the back of the spoon; do not allow the custard to boil or it may curdle.

4 Strain the custard into a chilled bowl, leave to cool, stirring occasionally, then chill until ready to serve.

5 Half-fill a large frying pan or wide pan with water and bring just to simmering point. In a clean grease-free bowl, whisk the egg whites slowly until they are frothy. Add the cream of tartar, increase the speed and continue whisking until they form soft peaks. Gradually sprinkle over the caster sugar, about 30ml/2 tbsp at a time, and whisk until the whites are stiff and glossy.

6 Using two tablespoons, form egg-shaped meringues and slide them into the water – you may need to work in batches. Poach them for 2–3 minutes, turning once, until the meringue is just firm. Use a slotted spoon to transfer the meringues from the pan to a baking sheet lined with kitchen paper to drain.

7 Pour the cold custard into shallow individual serving dishes or plates and arrange the meringues on top.

8 To make the caramel to decorate, put the remaining sugar into a small heavy pan with 45ml/3 tbsp of water. Bring the dampened sugar to the boil over a high heat, carefully swirling the pan to dissolve it. Do not allow to boil until the sugar is completely dissolved, then boil, without stirring, until the syrup turns a dark caramel colour.

9 Working quickly before it hardens, drizzle the caramel over the poached meringues and custard in a zig-zag pattern. Serve cold.

COOK'S TIP

Do not make the caramel too far ahead or it will soften as it sits on the moist meringues. If you do not have a vanilla pod, you can use 5ml/1 tsp vanilla essence (extract) instead.

BANANA WITH APRICOT CARAMEL TRIFLE

EVERYONE LOVES TRIFLE BUT IT DOESN'T NEED TO BE ALCOHOLIC TO BE DELICIOUS. GINGER CAKE MAKES A BRILLIANT BASE, BUT YOU COULD USE YOUR FAMILY'S FAVOURITE FLAVOUR, IF YOU PREFER. TOP WITH PLENTY OF WHIPPED CREAM.

SERVES SIX TO EIGHT

INGREDIENTS
- 300ml/½ pint/1¼ cups milk
- 1 vanilla pod (bean)
- 45ml/3 tbsp caster (superfine) sugar
- 20ml/4 tsp cornflour (cornstarch)
- 3 egg yolks
- ¼ packet apricot or tangerine jelly (flavoured gelatin)
- 60ml/4 tbsp apricot conserve
- 175–225g/6–8oz ginger cake, cubed
- 3 bananas, sliced, with 1 reserved for topping
- 115g/4oz/½ cup granulated sugar
- 300ml/½ pint/1¼ cups double (heavy) cream
- a few drops of lemon juice

1 Pour the milk into a small pan. Carefully split the vanilla pod down the middle and scrape the tiny seeds into the pan.

2 Add the vanilla pod to the milk and bring just to the boil over a low heat, then remove the pan from the heat. When the milk has cooled slightly, remove the vanilla pod.

COOK'S TIP
Use whatever cake you prefer in the base of the trifle. Leftover Madeira cake, with its tangy citrus flavour, makes a perfect choice. Choose a jelly and conserve that complement the flavour of your cake: strawberry jelly and raspberry conserve are good with lemon cake, or try lemon jelly and peach conserve with a chocolate sponge cake.

3 Whisk together the sugar, cornflour and eggs until pale and creamy. Whisk in the milk and return the whole mixture to the pan. Heat to simmering point, stirring constantly, and cook gently over a low heat until the custard coats the back of a wooden spoon thickly.

4 Leave to cool, covered tightly with clear film (plastic wrap). Ensure the covering is pressed against the surface of the custard to prevent a skin forming.

5 Put the jelly, apricot conserve and 60ml/4 tbsp water in a small pan and heat gently until the jelly dissolves. Set aside until cool, but not set.

VARIATION
For an adult-only version of this trifle, substitute a plainer sponge cake for the ginger cake. Before pouring the jelly (gelatin) mixture over the cubed cake, moisten the cake with a little apricot brandy and a small glass of dessert wine. If you choose to use a different flavoured jelly and conserve, try a different liqueur or brandy that will complement the flavour of the jelly and conserve.

6 Put the cubed cake in a deep serving bowl or dish and pour on the jelly mixture. Cover with sliced bananas, then the custard. Chill for 1–2 hours.

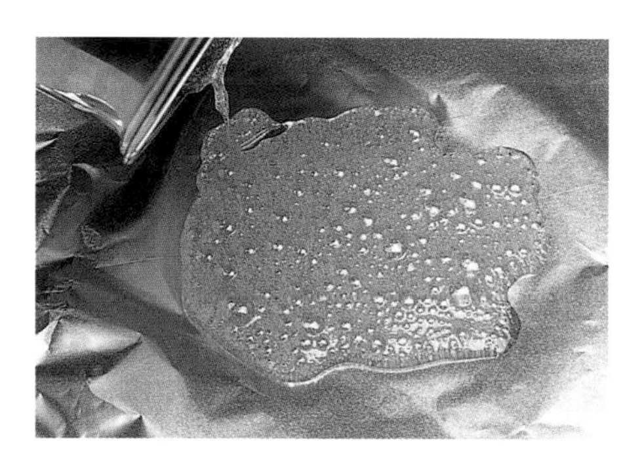

7 Melt the sugar in a small pan with 60ml/4 tbsp water and, when it has dissolved, cook until it is just turning golden. Immediately pour on to a sheet of foil and leave to harden, then break the caramel into pieces.

8 Whip the cream until it forms soft peaks and spread it over the custard. Chill for at least 2 hours, then top with the remaining sliced banana, dipped into lemon juice, and the cracked caramel pieces.

APPLE AND ROSE PETAL SNOW

This is a lovely, light and refreshing dessert, which is ideal to make when the orchards are groaning with apples. The rose petals give a delicate fragrance but other edible petals, such as honeysuckle, lavender and geranium, could also be used.

SERVES FOUR

INGREDIENTS
- 2 large cooking apples
- 150ml/¼ pint/⅔ cup thick apple juice
- 30ml/1 tbsp rose water
- 2 egg whites
- 75g/3oz/generous ⅓ cup caster (superfine) sugar, or to taste
- a few rose petals from an unsprayed rose
- crisp biscuits (cookies) or brandy snaps, to serve

COOK'S TIP
This recipe uses raw egg whites but it can also be made with a cooked meringue mixture instead.

1 Peel and chop the apples and cook with the apple juice until soft. Sieve, add the rose water and leave to cool.

2 Whisk the egg whites until peaking, then gently whisk in the sugar. Gently fold together the apple and egg whites. Stir in most of the rose petals.

3 Spoon the snow into four glasses and chill. Serve topped with the remaining petals and crisp biscuits or brandy snaps.

COOK'S TIP
To make sugared rose petals, brush each petal with beaten egg white, sprinkle with granulated sugar and leave to dry.

MANGO AND TANGERINE SORBET

Mango makes the easiest and most delicious of sorbets. It doesn't need a sugar syrup yet still gives a melt-in-the-mouth consistency. If you can, use the small, yellow Indian mangoes; their flavour is exquisite and their flesh is amazingly perfumed.

MAKES 450ML/¾ PINT/1¾ CUPS

INGREDIENTS
- 4 tangerines
- 1 lemon
- 90g/3½oz/½ cup caster (superfine) sugar
- 1 large ripe mango
- 3 egg whites
- fresh raspberries to serve

COOK'S TIP
Always treat hot syrups with great care as they can cause bad scalds if splashed on to the skin.

VARIATION
For a more elegant dessert, serve scoops of the sorbet in brandy snap baskets or chocolate cases. Sprinkle with fresh berries, to serve.

1 Squeeze the juice from the tangerines and lemon into a small pan. Stir in the caster sugar.

2 Gently heat the mixture and bring to simmering point, skimming constantly. Still stirring, simmer gently until the mixture begins to turn slightly syrupy, then remove the pan from the heat and leave to cool slightly.

3 Purée the mango in a food processor and stir in the syrup. Whisk the egg whites until holding soft peaks and fold into the mango purée. Freeze, whisking every half hour for 3–4 hours, or churn in an ice-cream machine.

4 Serve the sorbet immediately, or leave it to freeze completely, then allow 15–20 minutes at room temperature before serving with raspberries.

FROZEN GRAND MARNIER SOUFFLÉS

LIGHT AND FLUFFY YET ALMOST ICE CREAM, THESE DELICIOUS SOUFFLÉS ARE PERFECT FOR A SPECIAL DINNER. REDCURRANTS OR OTHER SMALL, SOFT FRUITS MAKE A DELICATE DECORATION.

SERVES EIGHT

INGREDIENTS

- 200g/7oz/1 cup sugar
- 6 large (US extra large) eggs, separated
- 15g/½oz/1 tbsp powdered gelatine
- 250ml/8fl oz/1 cup milk
- 450ml/¾ pint/scant 2 cups double (heavy) cream
- 60ml/4 tbsp Grand Marnier

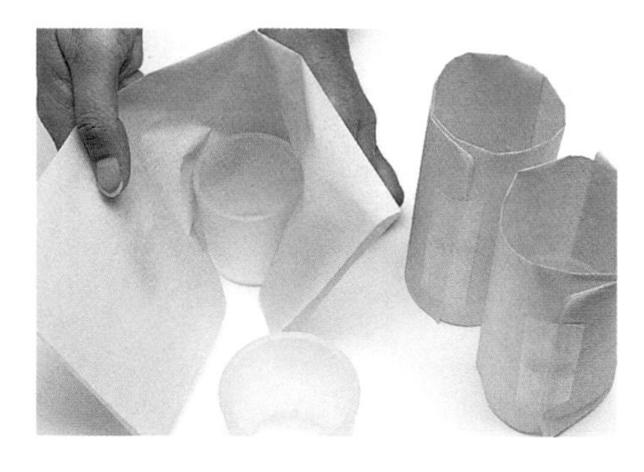

1 Wrap a double collar of greaseproof (waxed) paper around eight dessert glasses or ramekins and tie with string. Whisk together 75g/3oz/generous ⅓ cup of the sugar with the egg yolks, until the yolks are pale. This will take about 5 minutes by hand or about 3 minutes with an electric hand mixer.

2 Soak the gelatine in 45ml/3 tbsp cold water. Heat the milk until almost boiling and pour it on to the yolks, whisking constantly. Return to the pan and stir over a low heat until the custard is thick enough to coat the back of the spoon. Remove from the heat. Stir in the gelatine. Pour the custard into a bowl and leave to cool. Whisk occasionally, until on the point of setting.

3 Put the remaining sugar in a pan with 45ml/3 tbsp water and dissolve it over a low heat. Bring to the boil and boil rapidly until it reaches the soft ball stage or 119°C/238°F on a sugar thermometer. Remove from the heat. In a clean bowl, whisk the egg whites until stiff. Pour the hot syrup on to the whites, whisking constantly. Leave to cool.

COOK'S TIP

The soft ball stage of a syrup is when a teaspoon of the mixture dropped into a glass of cold water sets into a ball.

VARIATION

If you like, you can make a single, large dessert in a large soufflé dish, rather than eight individual ones.

4 Add the Grand Marnier to the cold custard. Whisk the cream until it holds soft peaks and fold into the cooled meringue, with the custard. Pour into the prepared glasses or dishes. Freeze overnight. Remove the paper collars and leave at room temperature for 15 minutes before serving.

ICED MOUSSE WITH HOT PINEAPPLE

THIS HEAVENLY COMBINATION OF COCONUT AND PINEAPPLE WILL CONJURE UP THOUGHTS OF SUN, SEA, SAND AND TROPICAL ISLANDS. IF YOU PREFER, REPLACE THE LIQUEUR WITH FRESH ORANGE JUICE.

SERVES SIX TO EIGHT

INGREDIENTS

- 4 large (US extra large) eggs
- 2.5ml/½ tsp vanilla essence (extract)
- 75g/3oz/generous ⅓ cup caster (superfine) sugar
- 175ml/6fl oz/¾ cup milk
- 90ml/6 tbsp coconut milk
- 1½ sachets powdered gelatine
- 90ml/6 tbsp coconut liqueur
- 275ml/9fl oz/generous 1 cup double (heavy) cream
- 115g/4oz fresh pineapple, grated, juice retained
- 90–105ml/6–7 tbsp pineapple jam
- 50g/2oz shredded coconut, toasted
- a few pieces of pineapple, to decorate

1 Wrap a greaseproof (waxed) paper collar around a 1.2 litre/2 pint/5 cup soufflé dish (see Cook's Tip).

2 Separate the eggs. Beat the yolks with the vanilla and sugar. Bring the milk and coconut milk to the boil, pour over the yolk mixture, whisking constantly, and return to the pan. Continue whisking over a medium heat until the custard coats the back of a wooden spoon. Sprinkle on the gelatine, leave for 20 seconds, then stir until dissolved.

COOK'S TIP

To make a dish collar, cut a piece of greaseproof (waxed) paper the length of the circumference of the dish and about 20cm/8in wide. Fold lengthways, attach one end at the rim of the dish with sticky tape, wrap it lightly around the dish and fasten the other end with tape.

3 Stir the liqueur into the custard, then place the pan in a bowl of ice to chill. Whip the cream until it stands in peaks and, in another bowl, whisk the egg whites to soft peaks. Fold them both carefully and evenly into the custard. Spoon into the prepared soufflé dish and leave to set for 2 hours. Freeze the mousse for 2–3 hours before serving.

4 Heat the pineapple and jam in a small pan with 30–45ml/2–3 tbsp water and simmer for 2–3 minutes until really hot. To serve, remove the paper collar from the soufflé and carefully press the toasted coconut against the sides. Decorate the top with more pieces of fresh pineapple and serve immediately with the hot sauce.

Rich Vanilla Ice Cream

This classic vanilla ice cream is quite superb. Serve it on its own or use as the base for other ices and desserts.

MAKES 750ML/1¼ PINTS/3 CUPS

INGREDIENTS
- 300ml/½ pint/1¼ cups single (light) cream
- 1 vanilla pod (bean)
- 3 egg yolks
- 45ml/3 tbsp caster (superfine) sugar
- 10ml/2 tsp cornflour (cornstarch)
- 300ml/½ pint/1¼ cups double (heavy) cream, whipped

VARIATION

Add 175g/6oz melted plain (semisweet) chocolate and 30ml/2 tbsp (unsweetened) cocoa powder when making the custard.

1 Put the cream in a small pan. Split the vanilla pod and scrape out the tiny seeds. Add them to the cream with the pod. Bring the cream just to the boil, then turn off the heat.

2 Whisk together the eggs, sugar and cornflour until pale and creamy. Remove the vanilla pod from the cream and whisk into the egg mixture. Return the mixture to the pan and bring to a simmer, stirring constantly. Cook gently until the custard coats the back of a wooden spoon.

3 Leave the custard to cool completely, then whisk well and fold in the whipped cream. Spoon it into a freezer container and freeze, whisking once every hour for 2–3 hours, or churn in an ice-cream maker until almost frozen, then transfer to the freezer.

ICED RASPBERRY PAVLOVA ROULADE

THIS MELT-IN-THE-MOUTH MERINGUE, ROLLED AROUND VANILLA CREAM AND LUSCIOUS RASPBERRIES, IS A STAR DINNER-PARTY ATTRACTION, AND IS SURPRISINGLY QUICK AND SIMPLE TO MAKE.

SERVES SIX TO EIGHT

INGREDIENTS

- 10ml/2 tsp cornflour (cornstarch)
- 225g/8oz/generous 1 cup caster (superfine) sugar
- 4 egg whites, at room temperature
- icing (confectioners') sugar, sifted
- 300ml/½ pint/1¼ cups double (heavy) cream or whipping cream
- drops of vanilla essence (extract)
- 175g/6oz/1 cup raspberries, partly frozen, plus extra to serve

1 Line a 33 × 23cm/13 × 9in Swiss-roll tin (jelly-roll pan) with baking parchment. Sift the cornflour into a bowl and blend evenly with the sugar.

2 Using a balloon whisk or hand-held electric beaters, whisk the egg whites in a clean mixing bowl until they form stiff peaks, but are not dry and crumbly.

3 Gradually whisk in the caster sugar, a few spoonfuls at a time, until the mixture becomes stiff and glossy.

4 Spoon the mixture into the prepared tin and flatten the top. Place in a cold oven and turn it to 150°C/300°F/Gas 2. Cook for 1 hour until the top is crisp and the meringue still feels springy (if it appears to be colouring too early while cooking, reduce the temperature).

5 Turn out on to a double sheet of greaseproof (waxed) paper sprinkled with sifted icing sugar and leave to cool.

6 Meanwhile, whip the cream with the vanilla essence and stir in the partly frozen raspberries. Freeze the mixture until required.

7 When the meringue has cooled, carefully spread the cream over it, then roll up, using the paper as a support. Freeze for about 1 hour before serving, sprinkled with more icing sugar and extra raspberries.

COOK'S TIP

The filling can be as varied as you wish. Try flavouring the cream with liqueur or home-made lemon curd, or fill with softened ice cream, then return the roulade to the freezer immediately.

Chocolate Chestnut Roulade

This combination of intense flavours produces a very rich dessert, so serve it well chilled and in thin slices. It can be sliced more easily when it is very cold.

SERVES TEN TO TWELVE

INGREDIENTS

- oil, for greasing
- 175g/6oz dark (bittersweet) chocolate, chopped
- 30ml/2 tbsp (unsweetened) cocoa powder, sifted, plus extra
- 50ml/2fl oz/¼ cup strong coffee
- 6 eggs, separated
- 75g/3oz/6 tbsp caster (superfine) sugar
- pinch of cream of tartar
- 5ml/1 tsp vanilla essence (extract)
- glacé (candied) chestnuts, to decorate

For the filling

- 475ml/16fl oz/2 cups double (heavy) cream
- 30ml/2 tbsp coffee-flavoured liqueur
- 350g/12oz can chestnut purée
- 115g/4oz dark chocolate, grated
- thick cream, to serve

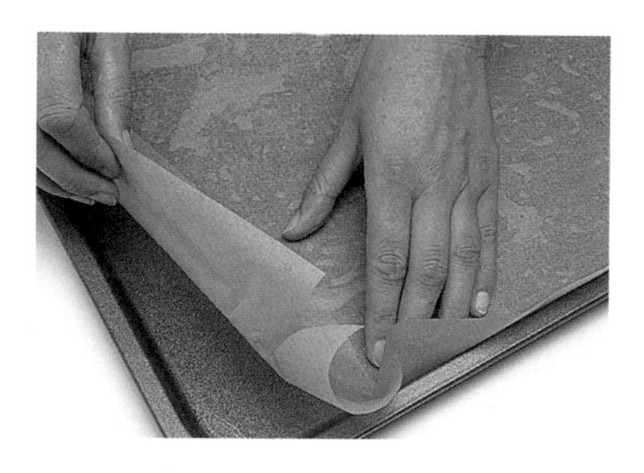

1 Preheat the oven to 180°C/350°F/Gas 4. Grease the base and sides of a 39 × 27 × 2.5cm/15½ × 10½ × 1in Swiss-roll tin (jelly-roll pan). Line with baking parchment, allowing a 2.5cm/1in overhang.

2 Melt the chocolate in the top of a double boiler over a low heat, stirring frequently. Set aside. Dissolve the cocoa in the freshly brewed coffee. Stir to make a smooth paste. Set aside.

COOK'S TIP

Beating egg whites should always be the last step in the preparation of cake mixtures. Once they are beaten, they should be folded in immediately.

3 With an electric mixer or in a bowl using a whisk, beat the egg yolks with half the sugar for about 3–5 minutes until pale and thick. Slowly beat in the melted chocolate and cocoa-coffee paste until just blended.

4 In another bowl, beat the egg whites and cream of tartar until stiff peaks form. Sprinkle the remaining sugar over in two batches and beat until stiff and glossy, then beat in the vanilla.

5 Stir a spoonful of the whisked whites into the chocolate mixture to lighten it, then fold in the remainder.

6 Spoon the mixture into the tin and level the top. Bake for 20–25 minutes or until the cake springs back when lightly pressed with the fingertips.

7 Meanwhile, dust a clean dishtowel with the extra cocoa powder. As soon as the cake is cooked, carefully turn it out on to the dishtowel and gently peel off the lining paper from the base. Starting at a narrow end, roll the cake and the dishtowel together Swiss-roll fashion. Cool completely.

8 To make the filling, whip the cream and liqueur until soft peaks form. Beat a spoonful of cream into the chestnut purée to lighten it, then fold in the remaining cream and most of the grated chocolate. Reserve a quarter of the chestnut cream mixture.

9 To assemble the roulade, unroll the cake and spread with the filling, to within 2.5cm/1in of the edges. Gently roll it up, using the dishtowel for support.

10 Place the roulade, seam side down, on a serving plate. Spoon the reserved chestnut cream into a small icing (pastry) bag and pipe rosettes along the top. Dust with cocoa and decorate with glacé chestnuts and grated chocolate.

Hot Desserts

There is nothing better than a hot dessert at the end of a meal. The classic French batter pudding, Black Cherry Clafoutis, or a wonderful steamed Chocolate Pudding with Rum Custard are great on a cold winter evening. Warm and fluffy Zabaglione, and Grilled Peaches with Meringues offer a lighter, yet equally tempting, alternative. Children love hot desserts, too, and this chapter includes a whole range of recipes that are sure to be popular with the whole family. Apricot Panettone Pudding provides a twist on the traditional bread and butter pudding, and Rhubarb Meringue Pie combines the sharp, tangy flavour of rhubarb with mouthwatering meringue and crisp pastry.

Grilled Peaches with Meringues

Although ripe peaches need little to set them off, these mini meringues, made with brown sugar, make a perfect accompaniment for the sweet grilled peaches.

SERVES SIX

INGREDIENTS
- 2 egg whites
- 115g/4oz/½ cup soft light brown sugar, reserving 5ml/1 tsp for the peaches
- pinch of ground cinnamon
- 6 ripe peaches, or nectarines
- 15–30ml/1–2 tbsp orange juice
- 5ml/1 tsp finely grated orange rind, to serve
- crème fraîche, to serve

COOK'S TIP
Use leftover egg whites to make these little cinnamon-flavoured meringues. The meringues can be stored in an airtight container for about 2 weeks. Serve them after dinner with coffee or with desserts in place of biscuits (cookies).

1 Preheat the oven to 140°C/275°F/ Gas 1. Line two large baking trays with non-stick baking parchment.

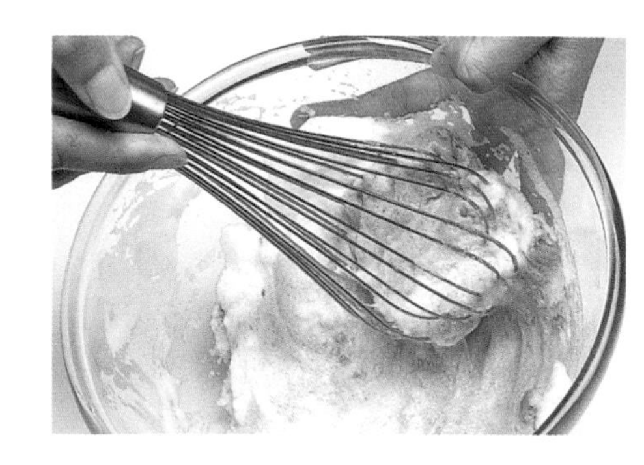

2 Whisk the egg whites until they form stiff peaks. Gradually whisk in the sugar and ground cinnamon until the mixture is stiff and glossy. Pipe 18 very small meringues on to the trays and bake for 40 minutes. Leave in the oven to cool.

3 Meanwhile, halve and stone (pit) the peaches. Brush the cut sides of the fruit with orange juice and sprinkle on a little sugar. Grill (broil) for 4–5 minutes until just beginning to caramelize.

4 Stir the orange rind into the crème fraîche with 15ml/1 tbsp orange juice. Serve the peaches topped with a little crème fraîche and three meringues.

ZABAGLIONE

LIGHT AS AIR AND WONDERFULLY ALCOHOLIC, THIS WARM EGG CUSTARD IS A MUCH-LOVED ITALIAN DESSERT. THOUGH TRADITIONALLY MADE WITH MARSALA, THIS FORTIFIED WINE CAN BE REPLACED BY MADEIRA OR SWEET SHERRY.

SERVES FOUR

INGREDIENTS
- 4 egg yolks
- 50g/2oz/¼ cup caster (superfine) sugar
- 60ml/4 tbsp Marsala, Madeira or sweet sherry
- amaretti, to serve

VARIATION
To make a chocolate zabaglione, whisk in 30ml/2 tbsp unsweetened cocoa powder with the wine or sherry and serve dusted with cocoa powder.

1 Place the egg yolks and sugar in a large heatproof bowl, and whisk with an electric beater until the mixture is pale and thick.

2 Gradually add the Marsala, Madeira or sherry to the egg mixture, 15ml/1 tbsp at a time, whisking well after each addition.

3 Place the bowl over a pan of gently simmering water and continue to whisk for 5–7 minutes, until the mixture becomes thick; when the beaters are lifted they should leave a thick trail on the surface of the mixture. Do not be tempted to underbeat the mixture, as the zabaglione will be too runny and will be likely to separate.

4 Pour into four warmed, stemmed glasses and serve immediately with amaretti for dipping.

COOK'S TIP
Zabaglione is also delicious served as a sauce with cooked fruit desserts. Try serving it with poached pears, grilled (broiled) peaches or baked bananas to create a really special dessert.

FRUIT-FILLED SOUFFLÉ OMELETTE

THIS IMPRESSIVE DISH IS SURPRISINGLY QUICK AND EASY TO MAKE. THE CREAMY OMELETTE FLUFFS UP IN THE PAN, FLOPS OVER TO ENVELOP ITS FILLING OF FRUITS IN LIQUEUR AND THEN SLIDES GRACEFULLY ON TO THE PLATE.

SERVES TWO

INGREDIENTS

- 75g/3oz/¾ cup strawberries, hulled
- 45ml/3 tbsp kirsch, brandy or Cointreau
- 3 eggs, separated
- 30ml/2 tbsp caster (superfine) sugar
- 45ml/3 tbsp double (heavy) cream, whipped
- a few drops of vanilla essence (extract)
- 25g/1oz/2 tbsp butter
- icing (confectioners') sugar, sifted

1 Cut the strawberries in half and place in a bowl. Pour over 30ml/2 tbsp of the liqueur and set aside to marinate.

2 Beat the egg yolks and sugar together until pale and fluffy, then fold in the whipped cream and vanilla essence. Whisk the egg whites in a very large, grease-free bowl until stiff, then carefully fold in the yolks.

COOK'S TIP

You can give your omelette a professional look by marking sizzling grill lines on top. Protecting your hand with an oven glove, hold a long, wooden-handled skewer directly over a gas flame until it becomes very hot and changes colour. Sprinkle the top of the omelette with icing sugar, then place the hot skewer on the sugar, which will caramelize very quickly. Working quickly, before the skewer becomes too cold to caramelize the sugar, make as many lines as you like.

3 Melt the butter in an omelette pan. When sizzling, pour in the egg mixture and cook until set underneath, shaking occasionally. Spoon on the strawberries and liqueur and, tilting the pan, slide the omelette so that it folds over.

4 Carefully slide the omelette on to a warm serving plate, spoon over the remaining liqueur, and serve dredged with icing sugar. Cut the omelette in half, transfer to two warmed plates and eat immediately.

PINEAPPLE BAKED ALASKA

MOST CHILDREN LOVE THE SURPRISE OF THIS CLASSIC DESSERT – HOT MERINGUE WITH ICE-COLD ICE CREAM INSIDE. HERE'S A NEW VARIATION TO TRY OUT ON THEM.

SERVES THREE TO FOUR

INGREDIENTS

- 3 large (US extra large) egg whites
- 150g/5oz/¾ cup sugar
- 25g/1oz desiccated (dry unsweetened shredded) coconut
- 175–225g/6–8oz piece ginger or chocolate cake
- 6 slices ripe, peeled pineapple
- 500ml/17fl oz/2¼ cups vanilla ice cream, in a brick
- a few cherries or figs, to decorate

1 Preheat the oven to 230°C/450°F/ Gas 8. Whisk the egg whites in a grease-free bowl until stiff, then whisk in the sugar until the mixture is stiff and glossy. Fold in the coconut.

2 Slice the cake into two thick layers the same rectangular shape as the ice cream. Cut the pineapple into triangles or quarters, cutting it over the cake to catch any drips. On a baking tray, arrange the fruit on top of one slice of cake. Top with the ice cream and then the second layer of cake.

3 Spread the meringue over the cake and ice cream, and bake in the oven for 5–7 minutes, or until turning golden. Serve immediately, topped with fruit.

COOK'S TIP

Do not use soft-scoop ice cream for this dessert as it will soften too quickly.

Hot Chocolate Soufflés

These rich, individual soufflés have the merest hint of orange in them, and are divine with the white chocolate sauce poured into the middle.

SERVES SIX

INGREDIENTS
- butter, for greasing
- 45ml/3 tbsp caster (superfine) sugar
- 175g/6oz plain (semisweet) chocolate, chopped
- 150g/5oz/⅔ cup unsalted (sweet) butter, cut in small pieces
- 4 large (US extra large) eggs
- 1.5ml/¼ tsp cream of tartar
- icing (confectioners') sugar, for dusting

For the sauce
- 75g/3oz white chocolate, chopped
- 90ml/6 tbsp whipping cream
- 15–30ml/1–2 tbsp orange liqueur
- grated rind of ½ orange

1 Generously butter six 150ml/¼ pint/⅔ cup ramekins. Sprinkle each with a little caster sugar and tap out any excess. Place the ramekins on a baking sheet.

2 Melt the chocolate and butter in a bowl placed over a pan of simmering water, stirring. Remove the bowl from the heat and cool slightly. Separate the eggs and set the whites aside. Beat the yolks into the chocolate mixture. Set aside, stirring occasionally.

3 Preheat the oven to 220°C/425°F/Gas 7. In a large, grease-free bowl, whisk the egg whites slowly until frothy. Add the cream of tartar, increase the speed and whisk until the whites form soft peaks. Gradually sprinkle over the caster sugar, 15ml/1 tbsp at a time, whisking until the whites become stiff and glossy.

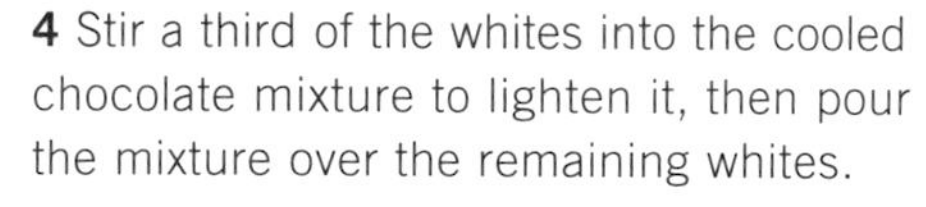

4 Stir a third of the whites into the cooled chocolate mixture to lighten it, then pour the mixture over the remaining whites.

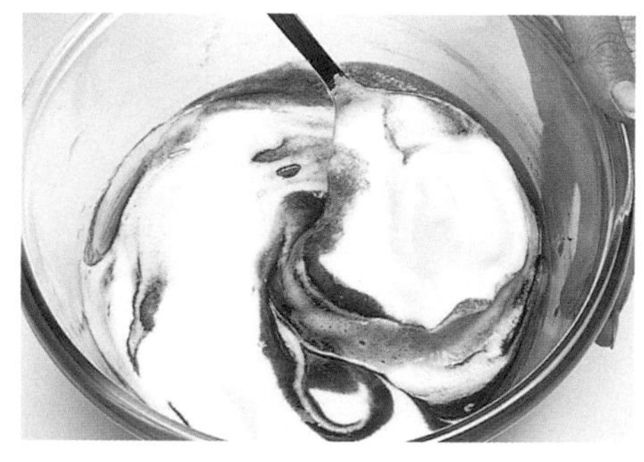

5 Using a rubber spatula or large metal spoon, gently fold the sauce into the whites, cutting down to the bottom, then along the sides and up to the top in a semicircular motion until the chocolate mixture and egg whites are just combined; don't worry about a few white streaks. Spoon the combined mixture into the prepared dishes.

VARIATION

Like orange, coffee complements the flavour of chocolate perfectly. Try using a coffee liqueur, such as Kahlúa or Tia Maria, instead of the orange liqueur in the soufflé mixture and sauce.

6 To make the sauce, put the chopped chocolate and the cream into a small pan. Place over a very low heat and warm, stirring constantly until melted and smooth. Remove the pan from the heat and stir in the liqueur and orange rind, then pour into a serving jug (pitcher) and keep warm.

7 Bake the soufflés in the preheated oven for 10–12 minutes until risen and set, but still slightly wobbly in the centre. Dust with icing sugar and serve immediately with the warm white chocolate sauce.

COOK'S TIP

These soufflés are ideal for serving at a dinner party because they can be prepared in advance, ready for baking at the last minute. Follow steps 1–5 above, then tightly cover the uncooked soufflés with clear film (plastic wrap). Set aside in a cool, but not cold, place until ready to cook. If the soufflés become too cold while waiting to be cooked, allow an extra 2–3 minutes cooking time.

CHOCOLATE PUDDING WITH RUM CUSTARD

WITH MELTING MOMENTS OF CHOCOLATE IN EVERY MOUTHFUL, THESE LITTLE PUDDINGS WON'T LAST LONG. THE RUM CUSTARD TURNS THEM INTO A MORE ADULT PUDDING; FOR A FAMILY DESSERT, FLAVOUR THE CUSTARD WITH VANILLA OR ORANGE RIND INSTEAD.

SERVES SIX

INGREDIENTS
- 115g/4oz/½ cup butter, plus extra
- 115g/4oz/½ cup soft light brown sugar
- 2 eggs, beaten
- a few drops of vanilla essence (extract)
- 45ml/3 tbsp cocoa powder, sieved
- 115g/4oz/1 cup self-raising (self-rising) flour
- 75g/3oz bitter chocolate, chopped
- a little milk, warmed

For the custard
- 250ml/8fl oz/1 cup milk
- 15ml/1 tbsp caster (superfine) sugar
- 2 egg yolks
- 10ml/2 tsp cornflour (cornstarch)
- 30–45ml/2–3 tbsp rum

1 Lightly grease six individual dariole moulds. Cream the butter and sugar until pale and creamy. Gently blend in the eggs and the vanilla essence.

2 Sift together the cocoa and flour, and fold gently into the egg mixture with the chopped chocolate and sufficient milk to give a soft dropping consistency.

COOK'S TIP
To microwave the pudding, spoon the mixture into a microwave-proof bowl (at least 300ml/½ pint/1¼ cups larger than necessary). Cover loosely with clear film (plastic wrap) and microwave on full power for about 5 minutes, depending on the power of your machine. Leave to stand for 5 minutes before serving.

3 Spoon the mixture into the basin or moulds, cover with buttered greaseproof (waxed) paper and tie down. Fill a pan with 2.5–5cm/1–2in water, place the puddings in the pan, cover with a lid and bring to the boil. Steam the large pudding for 1½–2 hours and the individual puddings for 45–50 minutes, topping up with water if necessary. When firm, turn out on to warm plates.

4 To make the rum custard, bring the milk and sugar to the boil. Whisk together the egg yolks and cornflour, then pour on the hot milk, whisking constantly. Return the mixture to the pan and stir while it slowly comes back to the boil. Allow the sauce to simmer gently as it thickens, stirring. Remove from the heat, stir in the rum and pour over the puddings. Serve immediately.

Apricot Panettone Pudding

The combination of the light Italian fruit bread, apricots and pecan nuts produces a wonderfully rich version of traditional bread-and-butter pudding.

SERVES SIX

INGREDIENTS

- unsalted butter, for greasing
- 350g/12oz panettone, sliced into triangles
- 25g/1oz/¼ cup pecan nuts
- 75g/3oz/⅓ cup ready-to-eat dried apricots, chopped
- 500ml/17fl oz/2¼ cups semi-skimmed (low-fat) milk
- 5ml/1 tsp vanilla essence (extract)
- 1 large (US extra large) egg, beaten
- 30ml/2 tbsp maple syrup
- 2.5ml/½ tsp grated nutmeg, plus extra for sprinkling
- demerara (raw) sugar, for sprinkling

1 Grease a 1 litre/1¾ pint/4 cup baking dish. Arrange half the panettone in the base of the dish, scatter over half the pecan nuts and all the dried apricots, then add another layer of panettone on top, spreading it as evenly as you can.

2 Pour the milk into a small pan and add the vanilla essence. Warm the milk over a medium heat until it just barely simmers. In a large bowl, mix together the beaten egg and maple syrup, grate in the nutmeg, then whisk in the hot milk.

3 Preheat the oven to 200°C/400°F/Gas 6. Pour the milk mixture over the panettone, lightly pressing down each slice so that it is totally submerged in the mixture. Set the dish aside and leave the pudding to stand for at least 10 minutes.

4 Scatter the reserved pecan nuts over the top and sprinkle with the demerara sugar and nutmeg. Bake for about 40 minutes until risen and golden.

COOK'S TIP

Panettone is a sweet Italian yeast bread made with raisins, citron, pine nuts and star anise. It is traditionally served at Christmas and is easier to obtain at that time of year. If it is not available, use any sweet yeasted fruit loaf instead.

Rhubarb Meringue Pie

The sharp tang of rhubarb with its sweet meringue topping will really tantalize the taste buds. This dessert is delicious hot or cold with cream or vanilla ice cream.

SERVES SIX

INGREDIENTS

- 200g/7oz/1¾ cups plain (all-purpose) flour, plus extra for flouring
- 25g/1oz/⅓ cup ground walnuts
- 115g/4oz/½ cup butter, diced
- 275g/10oz/generous 1½ cups caster (superfine) sugar
- 4 egg yolks
- 675g/1½ lb rhubarb, cut into small pieces
- finely grated rind and juice of 3 blood or navel oranges
- 75ml/5 tbsp cornflour (cornstarch)
- 3 egg whites
- whipped cream, to serve

1 Sift the flour into a bowl and add the ground walnuts. Rub in the butter until the mixture resembles very fine bread-crumbs. Stir in 30ml/2 tbsp of the sugar with 1 egg yolk beaten with 15ml/1 tbsp water. Mix to a firm dough. Turn out on to a floured surface and knead lightly. Wrap in a plastic bag and chill for at least 30 minutes.

2 Preheat the oven to 190°C/375°F/ Gas 5. Roll out the pastry on a lightly floured surface and use to line a 23cm/ 9in fluted flan tin (quiche pan). Prick the base with a fork. Line the pastry with baking parchment and fill with baking beans. Bake for 15 minutes.

3 Meanwhile, put the rhubarb, 75g/3oz/ 6 tbsp of the remaining sugar and the orange rind in a pan. Cover with a lid and cook over a low heat until the rhubarb is tender.

4 Remove the beans and paper from the pastry case, then brush all over with a little of the remaining egg yolk. Bake for 10–15 minutes, until the pastry is crisp.

5 Blend together the cornflour and the orange juice in a small bowl. Off the heat, stir the cornflour mixture into the cooked rhubarb, then bring to the boil, stirring constantly until thickened. Cook for a further 1–2 minutes. Cool slightly, then beat in the remaining egg yolks. Pour into the flan case.

6 Whisk the egg whites until they form soft peaks, then whisk in the remaining sugar, 15ml/1 tbsp at a time, whisking well after each addition.

7 Swirl the meringue over the filling to cover completely. Bake for 25 minutes until golden. Serve warm, or leave to cool for about 30 minutes and serve, with whipped cream.

Black Cherry Clafoutis

Clafoutis is a batter pudding that originated in the Limousin area of central France. It is often made with cream and traditionally uses slightly tart black cherries, although other soft fruits can also give delicious results.

SERVES SIX

INGREDIENTS
- butter, for greasing
- 450g/1lb/2 cups black cherries, pitted
- 25g/1oz/¼ cup plain (all-purpose) flour
- 50g/2oz/½ cup icing (confectioners') sugar, plus extra for dusting
- 4 eggs, beaten
- 250ml/8fl oz/1 cup full-cream (whole) milk
- 30ml/2 tbsp cherry liqueur

1 Preheat the oven to 180°C/350°F/Gas 4. Generously grease a 1.2 litre/2 pint/5 cup dish and add the cherries.

2 Sift the flour and icing sugar into a large mixing bowl, then gradually whisk in the beaten eggs until the mixture is smooth. Whisk in the milk until well blended, then stir in the liqueur.

3 Pour the batter into the baking dish. Transfer to the oven and bake for about 40 minutes, or until just set and light golden brown. Insert a knife into the centre of the pudding to test if it is cooked in the middle; the blade should come out clean.

4 Allow the pudding to cool for at least 15 minutes. Dust liberally with icing sugar just before serving, either warm or at room temperature.

VARIATIONS

Try other liqueurs in this dessert. Almond-flavoured liqueur is delicious teamed with cherries, while hazelnut, raspberry or orange liqueurs will also work well. Other fruits that can be used in this pudding include blackberries, blueberries, plums and apricots.

PRUNE TART WITH CUSTARD FILLING

PRUNES AND ARMAGNAC MAKE A FANTASTIC COMBINATION BUT, IF YOU PREFER, REPLACE THE LIQUEUR WITH FRESH ORANGE JUICE.

SERVES SIX TO EIGHT

INGREDIENTS
- 225g/8oz/1 cup pitted prunes
- 50ml/2fl oz/¼ cup brandy
- 175g/6oz/1½ cups plain (all-purpose) flour, sifted, plus extra for dusting
- pinch of salt
- 90g/3½oz/scant ½ cup sugar
- 115g/4oz/½ cup unsalted (sweet) butter
- 1 egg, plus 4 egg yolks
- 300ml/½ pint/1¼ cups milk
- a few drops of vanilla essence (extract)
- 15g/½oz/2 tbsp cornflour (cornstarch)
- 25g/1oz/¼ cup flaked (sliced) almonds
- icing (confectioners') sugar, sifted

1 Place the prunes in a mixing bowl and pour over the brandy. Leave in a warm place to soak.

2 Preheat the oven to 200°C/400°F/Gas 6. Place the flour, salt, 50g/2oz/¼ cup sugar, butter and egg, reserving 5ml/1 tsp egg white, in a food processor and process until blended.

3 Turn out on a clean, lightly floured surface and bring the mixture together into a ball. Leave for 10 minutes to rest.

4 Flour a 28 x 18cm/11 x 7in loose-bottomed tin (pan). Roll out the pastry and line the tin; don't worry if you have to push it into shape, as this pastry is easy to mould. Chill for 10–20 minutes.

5 Line the pastry case with baking parchment, fill with baking beans, then bake for 15 minutes. Remove the paper and beans, and bake for 12 minutes. Brush the pastry base with the reserved egg white while it is still hot. Set aside to cool slightly.

6 Bring the milk and vanilla essence to the boil. In a bowl, whisk the egg yolks and 40g/1½oz/3 tbsp sugar until thick, pale and fluffy, then whisk in the cornflour. Strain in the milk and whisk until there are no lumps.

7 Return to the pan and bring to the boil, whisking all the time to remove any lumps. Cook for about 2 minutes until thick and smooth, then set aside to cool. Press clear film (plastic wrap) on to the surface of the custard.

8 Stir any prune liquid into the custard, then spread over the pastry case. Arrange the prunes on top, sprinkle with the flaked almonds and icing sugar, and return to the oven for 10 minutes until golden and glazed. Remove from the oven and leave to cool. Serve hot or at room temperature.

CUSTARD TART WITH PLUMS

When this tart is made with really ripe, sweet plums, it makes a wonderful hot or cold weekend dessert. It is delicious served with thick cream or ice cream.

2 Flour a deep 18cm/7in square or 20cm/8in round loose-bottomed tin (pan). Roll out the pastry and use to line the tin. This pastry is soft at this stage, so don't worry if you have to push it into shape. Chill for 20 minutes.

3 Preheat the oven to 200°C/400°F/ Gas 6. Line the pastry with baking parchment and fill with baking beans, then bake for 15 minutes. Remove the parchment paper and beans, reduce the heat to 180°C/350°F/Gas 4 and bake for about 5 minutes more until the base is dry.

SERVES FOUR TO SIX

INGREDIENTS
- 175g/6oz/1½ cups flour, sifted
- pinch of salt
- 45ml/3 tbsp caster (superfine) sugar
- 115g/4oz/½ cup unsalted butter
- 2 eggs, plus 2 yolks
- 350g/12oz ripe plums
- 300ml/½ pint/1¼ cups milk
- few drops of vanilla essence (extract)
- thick cream or ice cream, to serve
- flaked (sliced) almonds and icing (confectioners') sugar, to decorate

1 Place the flour, salt, 15ml/1 tbsp of the sugar, the butter and one of the eggs in a food processor or blender and process until thoroughly combined. Turn out the mixture on to a clean, lightly floured surface and bring it together into a ball. Cover the pastry and leave for 10 minutes to rest.

VARIATIONS

This tart is equally delicious made with apricots, peaches or nectarines. Make a nutty pastry by replacing 15ml/1 tbsp of the flour with ground almonds.

4 Halve and stone (pit) the plums, and arrange them neatly in the pastry case. Whisk together the remaining egg and egg yolks with the sugar, the milk and vanilla essence and pour over the fruit.

5 Return the tart to the oven and bake for 25–30 minutes. When the custard is just firm to the touch, remove the tart from the oven and allow to cool slightly. Sprinkle with flaked almonds and dredge with icing sugar before serving. Add a generous dollop of cream or ice cream to each portion.

Cookies, Cakes and Breads

Eggs are an essential ingredient for crisp cookies, light and fluffy sponges, moist fruit cakes and rich breads. Eggs produce wonderfully tempting cookies, such as Cinnamon and Orange Tuiles and Oaty Chocolate-chip Cookies, and help the classic whisked sponge used in Fresh Fruit Genoese Sponge to rise beautifully, giving it an incredibly light texture. Frosted Carrot and Parsnip Cake uses not only eggs in the deliciously moist crumb, but also lightly cooked whisked egg whites for the mouthwatering meringue topping. Whole eggs are used to enrich breads, such as Honey and Saffron Bread, while eggs with dyed bright red shells are used to decorate the traditional Greek Easter Egg Bread.

Oaty Chocolate-Chip Cookies

These crunchy cookies are easy enough for children to make by themselves and are sure to disappear as soon as they are put on the table.

MAKES ABOUT TWENTY

INGREDIENTS

- 115g/4oz/½ cup butter or soft margarine, plus extra for greasing
- 115g/4oz/½ cup soft dark brown sugar
- 2 eggs, lightly beaten
- 45–60ml/3–4 tbsp milk
- 5ml/1 tsp vanilla essence (extract)
- 150g/5oz/1¼ cups plain (all-purpose) flour
- 5ml/1 tsp baking powder
- pinch of salt
- 115g/4oz/generous 1 cup rolled oats
- 175g/6oz plain (semisweet) chocolate chips
- 115g/4oz/1 cup pecan nuts, chopped

1 Cream the butter, or margarine, and sugar in a large bowl until pale and fluffy. Add the beaten eggs, milk and vanilla essence, and beat thoroughly.

2 Sift in the flour, baking powder and salt, and stir in until well mixed. Fold in the rolled oats, chocolate chips and chopped pecan nuts.

3 Chill the mixture for at least 1 hour. Preheat the oven to 180°C/350°F/Gas 4. Grease two large baking trays.

4 Using two teaspoons, place mounds well apart on the trays and flatten with a spoon or fork. Bake for 10–12 minutes until the edges are just colouring, then cool on wire racks.

CHOCOLATE TRUFFLES

THESE IRRESISTIBLE AFTER-DINNER TRUFFLES MELT IN THE MOUTH. USE A GOOD-QUALITY CHOCOLATE WITH A HIGH PERCENTAGE OF COCOA SOLIDS TO GIVE A REAL DEPTH OF FLAVOUR.

MAKES TWENTY TO THIRTY

INGREDIENTS

- 175ml/6fl oz/¾ cup double (heavy) cream
- 1 egg yolk, beaten
- 275g/10oz plain (semisweet) Belgian chocolate, chopped
- 25g/1oz/2 tbsp unsalted (sweet) butter, cut into pieces
- 30–45ml/2–3 tbsp brandy (optional)

For the coatings

- cocoa powder
- finely chopped pistachio nuts or hazelnuts
- 400g/14oz plain, milk or white chocolate, or a mixture

1 Bring the cream to the boil, then remove the pan from the heat and beat in the egg yolk. Add the chocolate, then stir until melted and smooth. Stir in the butter and the brandy, if using, then strain into a bowl and leave to cool. Cover and chill for 6–8 hours.

2 Line a baking sheet with greaseproof (waxed) paper. Using two teaspoons, shape the chilled chocolate mixture into 20–30 balls and place on the prepared paper. Rechill the chocolate mixture if it becomes too soft.

3 To coat the truffles with cocoa, sift some powder into a small bowl, drop in the truffles, one at a time, and roll to coat well. To coat them with nuts, roll the truffles in finely chopped pistachio nuts or hazelnuts.

4 To coat with chocolate, freeze the truffles for at least 1 hour. In a small bowl, melt the plain, milk or white chocolate over a pan of barely simmering water, stirring until melted and smooth, then allow to cool slightly.

5 Using a fork, dip the frozen truffles into the cooled chocolate, one at a time, tapping the fork on the edge of the bowl to shake off the excess. Place on a baking sheet lined with non-stick baking parchment and chill. If the chocolate thickens, reheat until smooth. All the truffles can be stored, well wrapped, in the refrigerator for up to 10 days.

GOLDEN GINGER MACAROONS

WITH THEIR WARM, SPICY, GINGER FLAVOUR, THESE SLIGHTLY CHEWY LITTLE BISCUITS ARE GOOD SERVED WITH ICE CREAM AND WILL GO WELL WITH MID-MORNING OR AFTER-DINNER COFFEE.

MAKES EIGHTEEN TO TWENTY

INGREDIENTS
- 1 egg white
- 75g/3oz/scant ½ cup soft light brown sugar
- 115g/4oz/1 cup ground almonds
- 5ml/1 tsp ground ginger

VARIATIONS

You can substitute other ground nuts, such as hazelnuts or walnuts, for the almonds. Ground cinnamon or mixed (apple pie) spice could be added in place of the ginger.

1 Preheat the oven to 180°C/350°F/ Gas 4. In a large, grease-free bowl, whisk the egg white until stiff and standing in peaks, but not crumbly, then whisk in the brown sugar.

2 Sprinkle the ground almonds and ginger over the whisked egg white, and gently fold them together.

3 Using two teaspoons, place spoonfuls of the mixture on baking trays, leaving plenty of space between each. Bake for about 20 minutes until pale golden brown and just turning crisp.

4 Leave to cool slightly on the baking trays before transferring to a wire rack to cool completely.

NUTTY NOUGAT

THIS CHEWY TREAT IS MADE FROM EGG WHITE WHISKED TOGETHER WITH A HOT SUGAR SYRUP. NUTS AND CANDIED FRUITS ARE TRADITIONALLY ADDED BUT OTHER FRUITS, SUCH AS DRIED APRICOTS OR GLACÉ CHERRIES, CAN ALSO BE USED.

MAKES ABOUT 500G/1½LB

INGREDIENTS
- 225g/8oz/generous 1 cup sugar
- 225g/8oz/1 cup clear honey or golden (light corn) syrup
- 1 large (US extra large) egg white
- 115g/4oz/1 cup flaked (sliced) almonds or chopped pistachio nuts, roasted

1 Line a 17.5cm/7in square tin with rice paper and set aside.

COOK'S TIP

If you make this nougat on a very warm day, you will find it takes longer to firm up and you will need to wait a little longer before cutting. It may help to take it out of the tin as soon as it has set.

2 Place the sugar, clear honey or golden syrup and 60ml/4 tbsp water in a large heavy pan and warm over a gentle heat until the sugar has dissolved totally, stirring frequently.

3 Bring the syrup to the boil and boil gently to the soft crack stage, or 151°C/ 304°F on a sugar thermometer.

4 Meanwhile, whisk the egg white until very stiff, but not crumbly, then slowly drizzle the syrup into the egg white while whisking constantly.

5 Quickly stir in the nuts and pour the mixture into the prepared tin. Leave to cool but, before the nougat becomes too hard, cut it into squares.

CINNAMON AND ORANGE TUILES

The aroma of cinnamon and orange evokes a feeling of Christmas and, served with coffee, these chocolate-dipped tuiles are perfect for festive occasions.

SERVES FIFTEEN

INGREDIENTS
- 2 egg whites
- 90g/3½oz/½ cup sugar
- 7.5ml/1½ tsp ground cinnamon
- finely grated rind of 1 orange
- 50g/2oz/½ cup plain (all-purpose) flour
- 75g/3oz/6 tbsp butter, melted

For the dipping chocolate
- 75g/3oz plain (semisweet) chocolate
- 45ml/3 tbsp milk
- 75–90ml/5–6 tbsp whipping cream

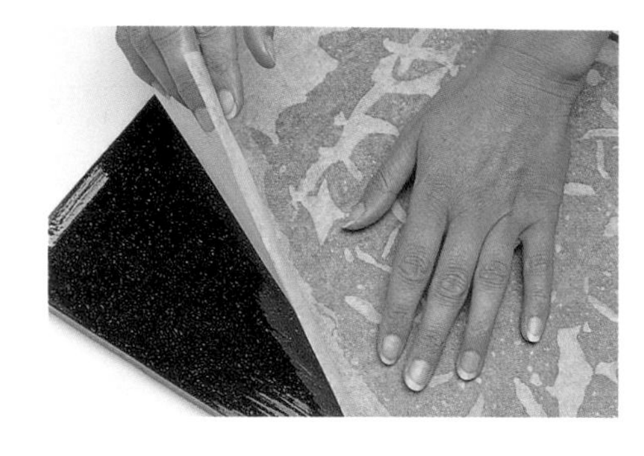

1 Preheat the oven to 200°C/400°F/ Gas 6. Line three large baking trays with non-stick baking paper.

2 Whisk the egg whites until softly peaking, then whisk in the sugar until smooth and glossy. Add the cinnamon and orange rind, sift over the flour and fold in with the melted butter. When well blended, add 15ml/1 tbsp of recently boiled water to thin the mixture.

3 Place 4–5 teaspoons of the mixture on each tray, well apart. Flatten out and bake, one tray at a time, for 7 minutes until just turning golden. Cool for a few seconds then remove from the tray with a metal spatula and immediately roll around the handle of a wooden spoon. Place on a rack to cool.

4 To make the dipping chocolate, melt the chocolate slowly in the milk until smooth, then stir in the cream. Dip one or both ends of the biscuits in the chocolate and leave to cool.

COOK'S TIP

If you haven't made these before, cook only one or two at a time until you get the hang of it. If they harden too quickly to allow you time to roll them, return the baking sheet to the oven for a few seconds, then try rolling them again.

MINT CHOCOLATE MERINGUES

THESE MINI MERINGUES ARE PERFECT FOR A CHILD'S BIRTHDAY PARTY AND COULD BE TINTED PINK OR GREEN. ANY SPARES ARE DELICIOUS CRUNCHED INTO YOUR NEXT BATCH OF VANILLA ICE CREAM.

MAKES ABOUT FIFTY

INGREDIENTS
- 2 egg whites
- 115g/4oz/generous ½ cup caster (superfine) sugar
- 50g/2oz chocolate mint sticks, chopped
- cocoa powder, sifted (optional)

For the filling
- 150ml/¼ pint/⅔ cup double (heavy) or whipping cream
- 5–10ml/1–2 tsp crème de menthe, or mint essence (extract)

COOK'S TIP

You can store these meringues in airtight tins or jars; they will keep for several days.

1 Preheat the oven to 110°C/225°F/ Gas ¼. Whisk the egg whites until stiff, then gradually whisk in the sugar until thick and glossy. Fold in the chopped mint sticks and then place teaspoons of the mixture on baking sheets covered with non-stick baking paper.

2 Bake for 1 hour or until crisp. Remove from the oven and allow to cool, then dust with cocoa, if using.

3 Lightly whip the cream, stir in the crème de menthe, and sandwich the meringues together just before serving.

CURD TARTS

These tasty little tarts, from the north of England, have a light curd cheese filling that sits on a tangy layer of lemon curd.

MAKES TWENTY-FOUR

INGREDIENTS
- 450g/1lb shortcrust (unsweetened) pastry
- 225g/8oz curd (farmer's) cheese
- 2 eggs, beaten
- 75g/3oz/generous ⅓ cup sugar
- 5ml/1 tsp finely grated lemon rind
- 50g/2oz/¼ cup currants
- 60ml/4 tbsp lemon curd
- thick cream or crème fraîche, to serve

COOK'S TIP

Pastry freezes well. Save time by lining the tartlet tins (muffin pans) with pastry in advance, wrapping them in clear film (plastic wrap) and storing them in the freezer. When ready to cook, remove the tins from the freezer and allow to defrost for 1 hour, then fill and bake.

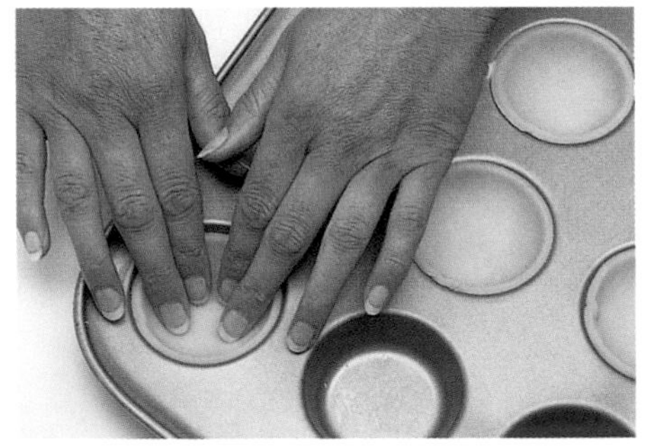

1 Preheat the oven to 180°C/350°F/Gas 4. Roll out the shortcrust pastry thinly, stamp out 24 rounds using a 7.5cm/3in plain cutter and use to line patty or tartlet tins. Chill or set aside in a cool place until required.

VARIATION

For special occasions, add a drop of brandy to the filling.

2 Cream the curd cheese with the eggs, sugar and lemon rind. Stir in the currants. Place 2.5ml/½ tsp of the lemon curd in the base of each tartlet case. Spoon on the filling, flatten the tops and bake for 35–40 minutes, until just turning golden.

3 Serve warm or cold, topped with thick cream or crème fraîche.

ALMOND CREAM PUFFS

IN THESE LITTLE PIES, CRISP, FLAKY LAYERS OF PASTRY SURROUND A SWEET, CREAMY FILLING. THEY ARE BEST SERVED WARM, SO REHEAT ANY THAT BECOME COLD BEFORE EATING.

MAKES TEN

INGREDIENTS
- 275g/10oz puff pastry
- 15ml/1 tbsp plain (all-purpose) flour, plus extra
- 2 egg yolks
- 30ml/2 tbsp ground almonds
- 30ml/2 tbsp caster (superfine) sugar
- a few drops of vanilla or almond essence (extract)
- 150ml/¼ pint/⅔ cup double (heavy) cream, whipped
- a little milk, for glazing
- sifted icing (confectioners') sugar, for sprinkling

1 Roll out the pastry thinly on a lightly floured surface, and cut out ten 7.5cm/3in rounds and ten 6.5cm/2½in fluted rounds. Keeping the smaller rounds for the tops, use the larger rounds to line a patty tin. Chill for about 10 minutes. Preheat the oven to 200°C/400°F/Gas 6.

2 Whisk the egg yolks with the flour, almonds, sugar and essence. Fold in the cream and spoon into the pastry cases. Brush the edges with milk, add the tops and seal the edges. Glaze with milk and bake for 20–25 minutes until golden. Cool slightly. Sprinkle with icing sugar.

FRESH FRUIT GENOESE SPONGE

GENOESE IS THE ORIGINAL FATLESS SPONGE, WHICH CAN BE USED FOR LUXURY GÂTEAUX AND SWISS ROLLS. IT SHOULD BE EATEN QUICKLY, AS IT DOES NOT STORE WELL.

SERVES EIGHT TO TEN

INGREDIENTS
- oil or butter, for greasing
- 175g/6oz/1½ cups plain (all-purpose) flour, sifted
- pinch of salt
- 4 eggs
- 115g/4oz/½ cup caster (superfine) sugar
- 90ml/6 tbsp orange-flavoured liqueur

For the filling and topping
- 600ml/1 pint/2½ cups double (heavy) cream
- 60ml/4 tbsp vanilla sugar
- 450g/1lb/4 cups fresh soft fruit, such as raspberries and strawberries
- 150g/5oz/1¼ cups shelled pistachio nuts, finely chopped
- 60ml/4 tbsp apricot jam (jelly), warmed and strained

1 Preheat the oven to 180°C/350°F/Gas 4. Grease a 21cm/8½in round springform cake tin (pan), line the base with baking parchment and grease the paper with a little oil or butter.

2 Sift the flour and salt together three times, then set aside.

3 Place the eggs and sugar in a mixing bowl and beat with an electric mixer for about 10 minutes or until the mixture is thick and pale.

COOK'S TIP
If you wish to make the Genoese sponge a few days before you need it, it can be frozen. Allow to thaw at room temperature for several hours before filling.

4 Sift the pre-sifted flour and salt into the mixing bowl with the egg and sugar mixture, then fold together very gently. Carefully transfer the cake mixture to the prepared tin.

5 Bake in the centre of the oven for 30–35 minutes or until a skewer inserted into the centre of the cake comes out clean.

6 Leave the cake in the tin for about 5 minutes, then turn out on to a wire rack, peel off the lining paper and leave to cool completely.

7 Carefully cut the cake in half horizontally to create two layers. Place the bottom layer on a serving plate, then sprinkle the orange-flavoured liqueur over the cut side of each cake.

VARIATION
Because a Genoese sponge is made with no added fat, it makes a good choice for those who are watching their weight or following a low-fat diet. Replace the whipped cream filling with low-fat Greek-style yogurt and pile on the fresh fruit.

8 Place the double cream and vanilla sugar in a large mixing bowl and beat together with an electric mixer until the mixture stands up in peaks.

9 Spread two-thirds of the cream mixture over the bottom layer of the cake and top with half of the soft fruit.

10 Carefully place the second half of the cake on top of the layer of cream and fruit and spread the remaining cream over the top.

11 Arrange the remaining fresh fruit on top of the cake and sprinkle with the chopped pistachio nuts. If liked, lightly glaze the top layer of fruit with the warmed apricot jam, then serve.

FROSTED CARROT AND PARSNIP CAKE

THE GRATED CARROTS AND PARSNIPS IN THIS DELICIOUSLY LIGHT AND CRUMBLY CAKE HELP TO KEEP IT MOIST AND ACCOUNT FOR ITS VERY GOOD KEEPING QUALITIES. THE CREAMY SWEETNESS OF THE COOKED MERINGUE TOPPING MAKES A WONDERFUL CONTRAST TO THE CAKE'S LIGHT CRUMB.

SERVES EIGHT TO TEN

INGREDIENTS
- oil, for greasing
- 1 lemon
- 1 orange
- 15ml/1 tbsp sugar
- 225g/8oz/1 cup butter or margarine
- 225g/8oz/1 cup light brown sugar
- 4 eggs
- 225g/8oz/1⅔ cups carrot and parsnip, grated
- 115g/4oz/1¼ cups sultanas (golden raisins)
- 225g/8oz/2 cups self-raising (self-rising) wholemeal (whole-wheat) flour
- 5ml/1 tsp baking powder

For the topping
- 50g/2oz/¼ cup sugar
- 1 egg white
- pinch of salt

1 Preheat the oven to 180°C/350°F/Gas 4. Lightly grease a 20cm/8in loose-bottomed cake tin (pan) and line the base with a circle of baking parchment.

VARIATION
If you do not like parsnips, you can make this cake with just carrots, or replace the parsnips with the same weight of shredded courgettes. Add a pinch of cinnamon and nutmeg to the mixture to give a little extra flavour.

2 Finely grate the lemon and orange. Put about half of the rind, selecting the longest shreds, in a bowl and mix with the caster sugar. Arrange the sugar-coated rind on a sheet of greaseproof paper and leave in a warm place, to dry thoroughly.

3 Cream the butter and sugar until pale and fluffy. Add the eggs gradually, then beat well. Stir in the unsugared rinds, the grated carrots and parsnips, 30ml/2 tbsp orange juice and the sultanas.

4 Gradually fold in the flour and baking powder, and tip into the prepared tin. Bake for 1½ hours until risen, golden and just firm.

5 Leave the cake to cool slightly in the tin, then turn out on to a serving plate.

6 To make the topping, place the caster sugar in a bowl over boiling water with 30ml/2 tbsp of the remaining orange juice. Stir over the heat until the sugar begins to dissolve. Remove from the heat, add the egg white and salt, and whisk for 1 minute with an electric beater.

7 Return to the heat and whisk for about 6 minutes until the mixture becomes stiff and glossy, holding a good shape. Allow to cool slightly, whisking frequently.

8 Swirl the cooked meringue topping over the cake and leave to firm up for about 1 hour. To serve, sprinkle with the sugared lemon and orange rind, which should now be dry and crumbly.

COOK'S TIP
When this cooked meringue frosting cools, it becomes slightly hard on the outside. The cake will keep well for a few days until the crust is cut into.

ND SAFFRON BREAD

A GREAT ALTERNATIVE TO PLAIN TOAST FOR BREAKFAST OR TEA. SPREAD THIS . WHILE IT IS STILL WARM FROM THE OVEN, OR SERVE AS BUTTERED TOAST.

MAKES TWO 450G/1LB LOAVES

INGREDIENTS
- oil, for greasing
- flour, for dusting
- 150ml/¼ pint/⅔ cup, plus 15ml/1 tbsp milk
- several threads of saffron
- 60ml/4 tbsp clear honey
- 450g/1lb/4 cups white (bread) flour
- 5ml/1 tsp salt
- ½ sachet easy-blend (rapid-rise) dried yeast
- 3 eggs
- 60g/2¼oz/4½ tbsp unsalted (sweet) butter, melted and cooled

1 Lightly grease and flour two 450g/1lb loaf tins (pans). Heat half the milk with the saffron in a small pan until the colour seeps out of the saffron threads. Stir in the honey and set aside to cool slightly, then add the rest of the milk.

VARIATION
To make a richer loaf, add raisins or chopped dried apricots. This rich dough also freezes very well. Cook the loaves as above for 20 minutes, then reduce the heat to 180°C/350°F/Gas 4 for a further 15 minutes. Remove from the oven, cool, then remove from their tins, wrap well and freeze. To serve, defrost for about 2 hours, then bake in an oven preheated to 200°C/400°F/Gas 6 for 20 minutes, glazing if necessary.

2 Sift the flour and salt into a large mixing bowl, mix in the dried yeast and make a hollow in the middle.

3 In a separate bowl, beat together two eggs plus one extra yolk and pour into the flour along with the melted butter and cooled milk. Using a fork, work the egg into the flour until the mixture begins to come together.

4 Turn out on to a lightly floured surface and knead gently until you have a silky, soft, smooth, elastic dough.

5 Return the dough to a clean, lightly greased mixing bowl. Lightly grease the surface of the dough and cover the bowl with a clean cloth. Set aside in a warm place and leave for about 2 hours until doubled in bulk and very spongy.

COOK'S TIP
If you find that you have kept the bread for too long and it has become slightly stale, make into breadcrumbs and store in an airtight container in the freezer. They can be used to make a crisp coating for fish.

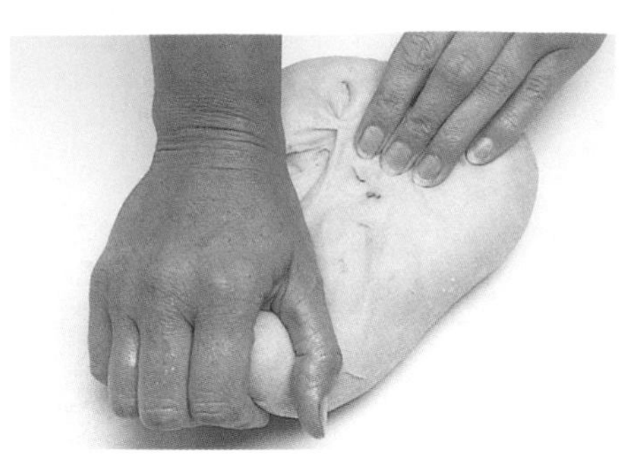

6 Turn the dough out on to a floured surface and knead it well until it is smooth and firm again. Divide into four pieces and shape into smooth round balls. Place them side by side in the prepared tins and set aside in a warm place to double in size again.

7 Preheat the oven to 200°C/400°F/Gas 6. When ready to bake, whisk the remaining egg white and use to glaze the bread. Bake for 35 minutes.

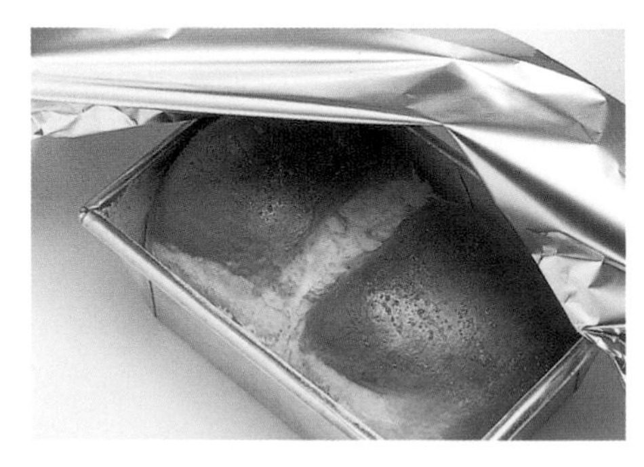

8 Check the bread to make sure it is not browning too quickly, and cover with foil if necessary. Cook for a further 10–15 minutes or until well risen, golden and sounding hollow when tapped underneath. Cool on a wire rack.

GREEK EASTER EGG BREAD

TOPPED WITH BRIGHTLY COLOURED EGGS, THIS ATTRACTIVE PLAITED BREAD IS AN IMPORTANT PART OF GREEK EASTER CELEBRATIONS. THE RED COLOUR USED TO DYE THE EGGS IS THOUGHT TO HAVE MAGICAL PROTECTIVE POWERS.

MAKES ONE LOAF

INGREDIENTS
- oil, for greasing
- 450g/1lb/4 cups unbleached strong white (bread) flour, plus extra
- 2.5ml/½ tsp salt
- 5ml/1 tsp ground allspice
- 2.5ml/½ tsp ground cinnamon
- 2.5ml/½ tsp caraway seeds
- 20g/¾oz fresh yeast
- 175ml/6fl oz/¾ cup lukewarm milk
- 50g/2oz/¼ cup butter
- 40g/1½oz/3 tbsp sugar
- 2 eggs

For the coloured eggs
- 3 eggs
- 1.5ml/¼ tsp bright red food colouring paste
- 15ml/1 tbsp white wine vinegar
- 5ml/1 tsp water
- 5ml/1 tsp olive oil

For the glaze
- 1 egg yolk
- 5ml/1 tsp clear honey
- 5ml/1 tsp water

For the decoration
- 50g/2oz/½ cup split almonds, slivered (sliced)
- edible gold leaf (optional)

1 Lightly grease a baking sheet. First make the coloured eggs. Place the eggs in cold water, bring to the boil and boil gently for 10 minutes. Lift out of the water and place on a wire rack to dry. Mix together the red colouring, vinegar and water in a shallow bowl, then roll the eggs in the mixture. Return to the rack to cool and dry completely.

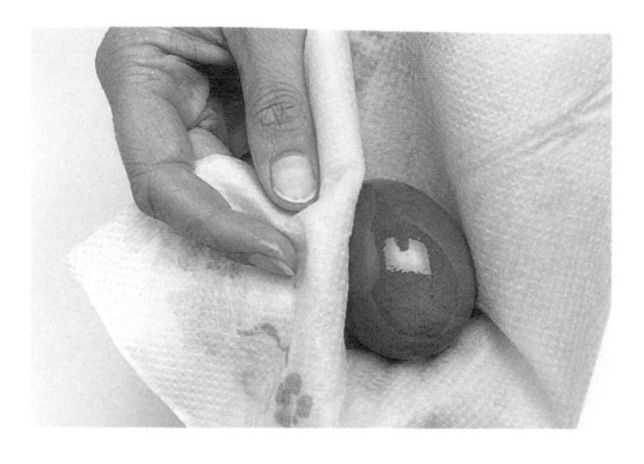

2 When the eggs are cold, drizzle the olive oil on to kitchen paper, lift up each egg in turn and rub all over with the oiled paper.

3 To make the dough, sift the flour, salt, allspice and cinnamon into a large bowl. Stir in the caraway seeds.

4 In a jug (pitcher), mix the yeast with the milk. In a bowl, cream together the butter and sugar, then beat in the eggs. Add the two mixtures to the flour and gradually mix to a dough.

5 Turn out the dough on to a lightly floured surface, and knead until smooth and elastic.

6 Place the dough in a large oiled bowl, cover with oiled clear film (plastic wrap) and leave to rise in a warm place for about 2 hours, or until doubled in bulk.

7 Knock back (punch down) the dough and knead on a lightly floured surface for 2–3 minutes. Return to the bowl, re-cover and leave to rise again for about 1 hour, or until doubled in bulk.

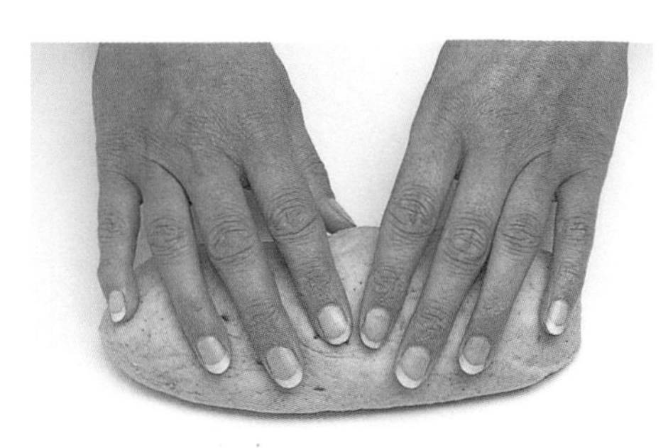

8 Knock back the dough and turn out on to a lightly floured surface. Divide into 3 equal pieces and roll each into a 38–50cm/15–20in long rope. Plait (braid) these together.

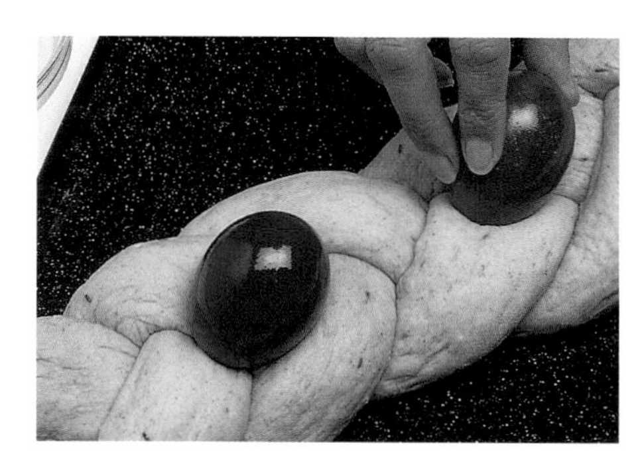

9 Place the dough on the prepared baking sheet and push the dyed eggs into the loaf. Cover and leave to rise in a warm place for about 1 hour.

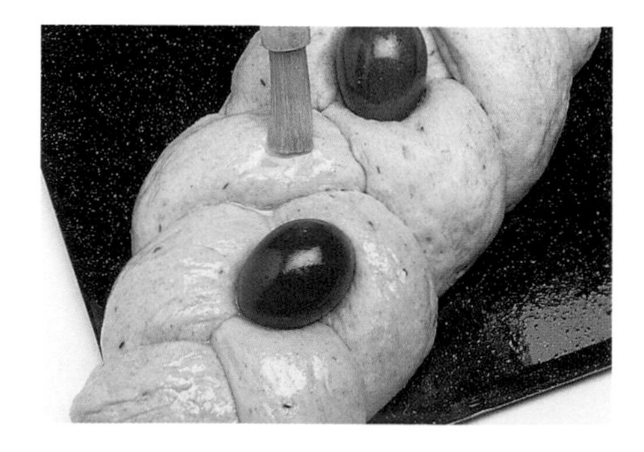

10 Meanwhile, preheat the oven to 190°C/375°F/Gas 5. Combine the egg yolk, honey and water, and brush over the loaf. Sprinkle with almonds and gold leaf, if using. Bake for 40–45 minutes, or until golden and hollow sounding. Transfer to a wire rack to cool.

INDEX